MAX WEBER AND THE SOCIOLOGY
OF CULTURE

Theory, Culture & Society

Theory, Culture & Society caters for the resurgence of interest in culture within contemporary social science and the humanities. Building on the heritage of classical social theory, the book series examines ways in which this tradition has been reshaped by a new generation of theorists. It will also publish theoretically informed analyses of everyday life, popular culture, and new intellectual movements.

EDITOR: Mike Featherstone, *University of Teesside*

Also in this series

Talcott Parsons
Theorist of Modernity
edited by Roland Robertson and Bryan S. Turner

The Symbol Theory
Norbert Elias

Religion and Social Theory
Second edition
Bryan S. Turner

Images of Postmodern Society
Social Theory and Contemporary Cinema
Norman K. Denzin

Promotional Culture
Advertising, Ideology and Symbolic Expression
Andrew Wernick

Cultural Theory and Cultural Change
edited by Mike Featherstone

Changing Cultures
Feminism, Youth and Consumerism
Mica Nava

Globalization
Social Theory and Global Culture
Roland Robertson

Risk Society
Towards a New Modernityy
Ulrich Beck

Max Weber and the Sociology of Culture

Ralph Schroeder

SAGE Publications
London • Newbury Park • New Delhi

SAGE Publications Ltd
6 Bonhill Street
London EC2A 4PU

SAGE Publications Inc
2455 Teller Road
Newbury Park, California 91320

SAGE Publications India Pvt Ltd
32, M-Block Market
Greater Kailash – I
New Delhi 110 048

British Library Cataloguing in Publication data

Schroeder, Ralph
 Max Weber and the Sociology of Culture. –
 (Theory, Culture & Society Series)
 I. Title II. Series
 301.092

 ISBN 0–8039–8549–5
 ISBN 0–8039–8550–9 pbk

Library of Congress catalog card number 92–50380

Typeset by Photoprint, Torquay, Devon
Printed in Great Britain by Billing and Sons Ltd, Worcester

CONTENTS

Acknowledgements   vii

1   *The Thematic Unity of Weber's Writings*   1
    The Interpretation of Weber's Sociology   3
    The Sciences of Culture and the Nature of
        Social Reality   6
    World-historical Stages and Philosophical
        Anthropology   11
    Charisma and Routinization   17
    Spheres of Life   23
    The Inner Logic of World-views   26
    Notes   28

2   *The Uniqueness of the East*   33
    From Magic to Religion   33
    The Ethic of the Confucian Literati and the
        Enchanted Garden   43
    Hinduism and the 'Spirit' of the Caste System   55
    The Islamic 'Warrior' Religion   65
    Notes   71

3   *The Rise of the West*   72
    Ancient Judaism and the Origins of Western
        Rationalism   72
    Early and Medieval Christianity: a Regression in the
        Course of Western Rationalism   84
    The Protestant Ethic and the Spirit of Secularism   96
    Notes   110

4   *The Iron Cage of Modern Rationalism*   112
    Politics in a Disenchanted World   112
    Science and Modern Culture   121
    The Demands of Science and the Ethic of Politics   128
    Science without Foundations   130
    Notes   137

5 *The Sociology of Culture: Weber and Beyond*   141
   Weber's Theory of Cultural Change   141
   Culturalism and Idealism   150
   Weber contra Marx and Durkheim   155
   Weber and Contemporary Social Science:
     the Prospects for Idealism   157
   Notes   163

References   166

Index   173

ACKNOWLEDGEMENTS

I would like to thank friends, colleagues and teachers who helped at various stages of the preparation of this book, especially Martin Albrow, Roland Axtmann, Gerhard Baumann, John Charvet, David Frisby, Ernest Gellner, Martin Greenwood, John Hall, Eric Hirsch, Wolfgang Mommsen, Kenneth Minogue, Jürgen Osterhammel and Sam Whimster. I am also grateful to Stephen Barr, David Chalcraft, David Owen, Tom Osborne and an anonymous reader at Sage who read and made valuable comments on the final draft. I have only myself to thank, however, for the book's errors and shortcomings. To my parents I owe a debt of a different kind and Jennifer and Sven will now finally be able to reclaim our weekends.

1

THE THEMATIC UNITY OF WEBER'S WRITINGS

The writings of Max Weber occupy an uneasy place within the history of sociological thought. Although he is widely regarded as one of the founders of the discipline, there are still fundamental disputes about the overall aim of his works. Only a few of the more well-known parts of his sociology, such as the Protestant ethic thesis and the writings on bureaucracy, have entered the sociological canon with viewpoints that can unambiguously be identified as Weberian. His theoretical position, however, remains difficult to pinpoint. Whereas some have seen Weber as a forerunner of the phenomenological preoccupation with the meanings of social action (Schütz, 1932), others have tried to minimize the differences between his standpoint and Marx's materialism (Parkin, 1982). Again, while some think that he has established a lasting framework for analyzing social structures which has dominated sociology up to the present day (Turner, 1981), there are those who would deny that he is a sociologist at all (Hennis, 1988).

One reason why such conflicting ideas can plausibly be attributed to Weber is that it is difficult to find a uniform theoretical perspective within his writings. There is no one place where he systematically spells out his methodological or theoretical standpoint. This, in turn, has meant that no single interpretation of his thought has achieved the status of orthodoxy. A further reason for this ambiguity is the dispute over which of his works is to be regarded as the central one. Such a question is unavoidable in a body of writings as fragmented as Weber's and it is still unresolved.[1] Some continue to argue that the encyclopaedic *Economy and Society* contains the conceptual apparatus which is the key to a Weberian analysis of society. Others consider his earlier, more narrowly focused studies of particular topics in historical sociology a more reliable guide to his main concerns. This debate is not helped by the incomplete and unprogrammatic nature of Weber's investigations.[2]

The following reconstruction of Weber's thought does not seek to resolve these issues once and for all. What I hope to show, however, is that there is an underlying unity in Weber's social thought. This unity revolves around a central question that is addressed throughout his major works, namely the relation between culture and social life. I will argue that this issue is not only the focus of his famous essay on the Protestant ethic, but that it plays an important role throughout his studies. How, to put it differently, beliefs translate into social reality, or how we can understand the cultural significance of different world-views – these are Weber's central concerns. And if this is so, his project must be understood on the most fundamental level as a contribution to the sociology of culture.[3]

The concept of culture has had a checkered past in the social sciences. The German *Kultur* contained in the *Kulturwissenschaften* (cultural sciences) to which Weber claimed to be contributing at the turn of the century certainly had a different resonance from our understanding of 'culture' today.[4] Perhaps the fact that various conceptions of culture are deeply embedded within different national and historical contexts provides one reason why there has been a lack of steady or cumulative development in this area of the social sciences, although more recently the concept of culture seems once again to have moved to centre stage (for example, Archer, 1988; Featherstone, 1990).

A further reason why no consensus has crystallized in the study of culture is that the boundaries of this area are very ill-defined. For some, the study of society must be completely subordinated to the concept of culture, whereas others would want to abandon this concept altogether inasmuch as it cannot be separated from – or superimposed upon – the rest of society.[5] The question arises in other ways too: where, for example, does the investigation of culture make way for the concept of ideology – and vice versa? Are all beliefs or world-views which affect social life to be subsumed under either or both of these terms, or is there perhaps a third concept (such as that of the social system) which embraces all values and thus makes the concept of culture redundant? We shall see that in a certain sense, Weber's concept of culture was strongly bound to the time and place in which he was writing. Yet at the same time, his understanding of the interplay between culture and social life goes beyond a narrow view of *Kultur* and constitutes a theory of social change which may, as we shall see in our final assessment of his contribution, provide an overall framework for this part of the social sciences.

In order to examine Weber's analysis of cultural change in a systematic way, we must begin by looking at the main assumptions which provide the theoretical underpinning for his studies. These include, for example, his views of the nature of social reality and of human nature. This will also involve determining how, for Weber, social change can be conceptualized as taking place within and emanating from the realm of culture. This task will occupy the rest of the introduction. Once it is completed we will be in a position to test to what extent these theoretical insights can be found in his main writings, especially his studies of the world-religions and his writings on politics and science in the modern world. When we can recognize how these various studies cohere on a basic level, we will be better placed to define his standpoint as a social theorist. This will also allow us to assess the shortcomings and continuing relevance of his approach. Before turning to these tasks, however, we must briefly look at how previous interpreters have tried to locate Weber among the different schools of sociological thought.

The Interpretation of Weber's Sociology

Many sociologists who are sympathetic to Weber think that the most useful way of appropriating his ideas is to apply his concepts to specific problems. This approach has yielded many valuable studies, mainly within the field of historical sociology (Zingerle, 1981). But since for these sociologists, Weber mainly provides a set of tools, they are unlikely to be concerned about our inability to define his standpoint. One representative of this group, Randall Collins, has commented with regard to a ' "true" Weber' that 'perhaps such a thing exists, but we certainly do not know it' (1986a: 3). But while there may not be one 'true' Weber, it is still essential to ask what constitutes a Weberian perspective at a general, theoretical level. And here opinions diverge widely. This will become apparent if the main stages in the reception of his work are briefly retraced.

Whereas Weber's writings were the subject of considerable debate during his lifetime and in the 1920s, his prominence as one of the founders of sociology only emerged in the period after the Second World War when the discipline became institutionalized in the United States (Whimster and Lash, 1987: 1–5). It was mainly through the works of Parsons and Bendix and the increasing availability of Weber's works in English that his ideas became widely disseminated (Parsons, 1937, vol. 2; Bendix, 1960). Parsons and Bendix saw Weber primarily as an empirical sociologist who defended the value-freedom of the social sciences and upheld a liberal political position. It has often been pointed out that this reading of Weber agreed very well with the then prevailing attitudes of liberal pluralism and impartiality within American academic life (see, for example, Factor and Turner, 1984: 180).

The idea that Weber's political analyses were unbiased and liberal was soon challenged by Mommsen who emphasized, among other things, Weber's calling for a strong political leader and his nationalist leanings (1984; 1st German edn, 1959). Similarly Tenbruck, by retrieving the original context in which Weber's methodology emerged, rejected the notion that Weber inaugurated a value-free social science (1959). Instead, he sought to show that Weber's standpoint was a more subtle one in which values were an essential part of a science of culture (*Kulturwissenschaft*) that was, in any case, not only separate from the natural sciences, but also foreign to the whole subsequent development of sociology. These reassessments meant that it became more difficult to identify Weber's place within social and political science.

In order to reestablish Weber's niche within theoretical sociology, it became necessary to reconstruct his sociological project. More recently, in the 1970s and 1980s, the writings of Habermas and Schluchter have gone furthest in this direction (Habermas, 1984; Schluchter, 1981a; 1989). They have put forward an all-encompassing Weberian account of the origins and development of modernity in the manner of building a systematic social theory. Both use the theme of rationalization as the key to a Weberian understanding of social change and to characterize the distinctiveness of modern society. Habermas, in the end, wants to reformulate the Frankfurt School's critical stance towards capitalism within the framework of Weber's theory of how modern society becomes increasingly rationalized, whereas Schluchter seeks to create an all-embracing developmental history of the cognitive and ethical dimensions of modern Western society.[6] Yet while both these reconstructions constitute significant contributions to social theory in their own right, their assimilation of Weber's ideas within the framework of more recent social theory takes the argument several steps beyond Weber himself. Hence their work should be seen as independent contributions to contemporary social theory, rather than representing a new or distinctive interpretation of Weber's own viewpoint.

Such a rediscovery of Weber's original aims has become the most recent focus of the interpretation of his work. The most forceful call for a reassessment has come from Hennis, who argues that his works cannot be understood except by recognizing that they revolve around a theme that has little to do with the way he has been traditionally interpreted (1988). This theme concerns Weber's conception of 'personality' and the social conditions in which the 'personality' can express certain values. Hennis claims that the search for a doctrine about values underlies all of Weber's works which, in his view, are far removed from the present-day concerns of sociology. Instead, he places Weber within an older tradition of political philosophy that is concerned with normative issues and goes back to Aristotle. But although Hennis raises some important questions, such as how we should interpret Weber's conception of the individual, he does not pursue how these could be related to sociological issues in Weber's work, apart from his political ideas.[7]

While Hennis's challenge may be overstated, there are many examples in Weber's writings which suggest that his understanding of the nature of sociology and of value-freedom, among other things, are more complex than Parsons and Bendix initially suggested. Hennis is not alone in recognizing this (see, for example, Factor and Turner, 1984; Scaff, 1989). One problem that Hennis shares with others who address similar concerns is that the aims of Weber's sociology cannot be established by reference to his political or methodological views alone. Habermas and Schluchter are right in stressing that his political standpoint and his conception of the aims of social science are inextricably bound up with his analysis of the emergence of the modern world and that this analysis, in turn, must be understood in the context of his comparative studies of the world-civilizations and his theory of social change. In short, it is impossible to divorce Weber's political and methodological prescriptions from his substantive sociological studies – and vice versa. Furthermore, both rest on certain fundamental assumptions about the nature of social reality and on Weber's outlook on the modern world.

In the interpretation that follows I want to argue that Weber's position as a social theorist only emerges once we recognize the links between the different parts of his work. Establishing the priority among his texts cannot help us to reconstruct Weber's aims since they remain fragmented and do not contain any programmatic statements that would allow us to draw firm conclusions about the nature of his project.[8] This means that we must look to the content of his work itself. Only by seeking out the consistency of his major themes and looking at the actual claims that he puts forward can we arrive at a precise identification of Weber's standpoint.

But again, in terms of the main concern in Weber's writings, one question stands out: namely, to give an account of the cultural significance of the distinctiveness of modern Western culture (1930: 13; 1949: 81). This question, in turn, gives rise to Weber's central preoccupation with the role of ideas in social life. We shall see that Weber thought that this question was dictated both by his material (the unique pattern of Western social development) and by his methodological standpoint (the demand, above all, to understand the 'cultural significance' of our condition).[9] And since in both these areas, his focus is on the relation between culture and social life, all of his studies can be said to revolve around the problem of cultural change. If this problem is at the centre of his position as a social theorist, how did he try solve it? Let us begin by looking at the fundamental presuppositions in his works.

The Sciences of Culture and the Nature of Social Reality

The reason for Weber's focus on the 'cultural significance' (*Kulturbedeutung*) of modern Western rationalism is that he thought that social scientific enquiry is rooted in the fact that human beings are 'cultural beings' or *Kulturmenschen* (1982: 180).[10] The 'sciences of culture' (*Kulturwissenschaften*) are not concerned with the whole of social reality, but in the first instance with those aspects of it which decisively shape the modern social life of cultural beings. And here, as Weber thought he had demonstrated in the *Protestant Ethic* (1930), the most momentous developments had been the disenchantment of the modern world and the creation of the iron cage of capitalism. How could these developments be explained? This woud be the task of a 'science of culture' or what he sometimes also calls a 'science of reality' or *Wirklichkeitswissenschaft* (1949: 72; 1982: 170).

Weber defines culture as follows: ' "Culture" is the endowment of a finite segment of the meaningless infinity of events in the world with meaning and significance from the standpoint of human beings' (1982: 180, my trans.; cf. 1949: 81). This definition applies both to his methodological standpoint and to his view of cultural change. Methodologically, it is because we, as cultural beings, both value knowledge and value certain aspects of social reality rather than others, that the sciences of culture can achieve objectivity (1949: 81 and passim). In terms of cultural change, it is because human beings adhere to certain values or world-views that their way of life may become radically reoriented or remain wedded to everyday existence (1949: 55–7; 1975: 192). This methodological position and the view of how beliefs translate into social reality will be discussed extensively below.

Given this definition of culture, how does Weber conceptualize the pattern whereby culture shapes social life? His most well-known pronouncement on the relation between ideas and social life is contained in the 'switchmen' (or pointsmen, in British railway terminology) metaphor where he formulates as follows: 'Not ideas, but material and ideal interests directly govern men's conduct. Yet very frequently the "world-images" that have been created by "ideas" have, like switchmen, determined the tracks along which action has been pushed by the dynamic of interest' (1948: 280). This statement is intended to suggest that there is a variable relationship between ideas and interests and that, although other factors may often be more important, culture may sometimes play a decisive role. Howsoever we shall come to modify Weber's conception of culture then, one central feature must be that social reality and the social life of human beings become transformed through culture.

Before we examine this relationship more closely, we will need to look briefly at some of the other key concepts that will be used. Weber's own terminology in analyzing cultural change is, again, unsystematic. For example, he uses such terms as 'ideas', 'world-views', 'values' and 'beliefs' without providing definitions. Why then is it more useful to speak of 'the relation between culture and social life' rather than, say, about 'the relation between ideology and society'?

The notion of 'ideology' is inappropriate both because Weber shunned this term and because it has become associated mainly with the Marxist conception of the relation between ideas and society which, as we shall see, is very different from Weber's. Weber thought that the realm of thought or belief has an influence on the conduct of human beings that is, in a certain sense, independent of other social forces. This is why it will be more appropriate to speak of the realm of culture as consisting of 'ideas', although in order to avoid repetitiousness, the terms 'belief' or 'world-view' will also be used (the term 'values', although it is used by Weber, will for the most part be avoided because it is intrinsically problem-ridden).

In a similar vein, it is necessary to speak of 'social life' since Weber has no conception of 'society' as such (on this point, see Frisby and Sayer, 1986: 67–72). The term 'social life' indicates, in keeping with Weber's intentions, that there is no single whole which embraces all social phenomena. Instead, there are only contingently related social forces, and any link between them must be established in the context of particular socio-historical processes. The specificity of the links between ideas and social life can be highlighted by pointing to the fact that there is no larger or more all-encompassing theoretical structure in Weber's writings into which these two terms 'fit', although we shall see that the edifice of Weber's 'science of culture' rests on several underlying assumptions that can be found throughout his works.

One question that is raised by this absence of an overall structure, given that Weber wants to assign an important role to ideas, is the conception of the social world on which such a claim must rest. Here it is important to distinguish between two aspects of his conception of the social world: one is the methodological (or epistemological) issue of how we understand the social world, and the second is what, in Weber's view, the social world consists of. These two must, in the end, be linked. But whereas we can postpone the first question until we come to our examination of his methodological writings, the second, concerning what might be called Weber's ontology of the social world, must be discussed before we can embark on our account of how culture translates into social reality.

What does this conception of the social world consist of? The thrust of Weber's position is that beliefs or values are just as 'real' as material forces (see also Albrow, 1990: 230–4 and passim). This leads only to a further question, namely, in what sense can beliefs be said to constitute a 'real' part of social life? One characteristic that immediately bears on this issue is that on the level of the individual, as we shall see, beliefs cannot be linked directly to their tangible consequences. The beliefs of an individual may result in conduct or in a way of life that is unintended. This means that the beliefs of the individual cannot be 'read off' the reality that they produce. At the same time, on the level of social relations as a whole, Weber is committed to the view that beliefs and, in the case of charismatic leadership, the belief of an individual in so far as it becomes adhered to by others, can transform the nature of social reality. Taking these two points together, we necessarily arrive at the conclusion that in Weber's 'social ontology', beliefs must be separate from and prior to other social forces or facets of social reality.

Weber's conception of social reality must then be one which – whatever else it consists of – also consists of a realm of beliefs which are somehow (in a way which remains to be established) independent of the rest of the social world. A different way of making this point is to consider the possibility that Weber considers the *whole* of social reality, rather than just part of it, to be governed by values or beliefs. But this cannot be the case, since Weber often refers to material or other constraints to which ideas are subject (for example, 1968: 341). The only possibility, then, is that social reality consists both of the values or beliefs of persons (which are irreducible to other social forces) and of material or other social forces which are separate from these – and that somehow the non-ideational world can become transformed by the ideational one and vice versa.[11] Weber is, in short, a 'social-ontological dualist'.

If this position seems to be merely an obvious or common-sense one, it needs to be remembered that it is irreconcilable with positivism, which stipulates that there is only one – so to speak continuous – social reality. For a similar reason Weber's approach is also incompatible at this fundamental level with the positions of Marx and Durkheim. This, again, is a point that we shall need to return to in our final assessment of Weber's approach.

How then are world-views and social life interrelated? Before we can answer this positively, we must briefly discuss one approach to this issue that must rejected. One way of sidestepping the issue of how ideas translate into social life is to focus on Weber's conception of rationality, and hence on individual social actors and on the different types of social action. But although it has been suggested that Weber should be seen as a theorist of social action (Kalberg, 1985a: 895), Weber rarely uses these concepts or an action-oriented approach in his substantive writings.[12]

It is somewhat different with Weber's conception of rationalization, since this term occurs throughout his substantive studies. The problem is that Weber attaches several different meanings to this term, as he himself admits (1930: 26).[13] And while it will on some occasions be necessary to refer to the actual processes to which he applies this term, we shall follow Weber here in subsuming 'rationalization' in the most general sense under his conception of Occidental rationalism (1981b: 20; cf. 1930: 25–6).

After this digression, we can now return to the question of the relation between culture and social life. In order to do this, we must distinguish between three aspects of the way in which beliefs play a role in social life for Weber: the dynamic of charisma and routinization, the differentiation between the spheres of life, and the inner logic of world-views. Each of these aspects of his conception of the role of ideas will now be introduced briefly and described in more detail later. It may be useful, however, to indicate the significance that will be attached to these three. These, it will be argued, are the *only* essential constituents of Weber's conception of cultural change. They provide Weber with a way both of analyzing social change and of answering his central question concerning the distinctiveness of the modern world. This claim, once again, is one to which we shall need to return in our concluding assessment of his theory.

Let us take each of these aspects in turn. The first of these, the pattern of charisma and routinization, occurs in different forms throughout Weber's writings. The concept of charisma is used essentially to explain the origin of new systems of ideas. But while Weber wants to attach great significance to the way in which these new world-views can have a potentially revolutionary impact on social life (and how, in this sense, they can be a 'dynamic' cultural force), he also recognizes that this impact is bound to diminish with time. That is to say, a typical pattern is that formerly powerful belief-systems become well-established among a group of followers and become integrated within everyday life. This is what Weber means when he speaks of the routinization or rationalization of charisma.

The routinization of charisma takes place in two ways. First, there is typically a systematization of the belief-system. This means that a stratum of interpreters elaborates the belief-system so that it constitutes a coherent whole and its tenets are extended to apply to various aspects of everyday life. Secondly, there is an accommodation of the belief-system to the interests of various strata of believers. As a result, its content corresponds more and more closely with what these strata, on the basis of their social position, had already been predisposed to believe or with their everyday conduct. The fact that the opposition between charisma and routinization is such a basic feature of Weber's sociology has led one of his interpreters to say that these two forces are 'the essential origins of all social change as such' (Mommsen, 1983: 395). This comment rings true inasmuch as these two concepts together account for the creation of new ideas and their inevitable systematization and accommodation.

The second aspect of Weber's conception of cultural change is his notion of the differentiation between the spheres of life. Weber distinguishes between several spheres of social life – the most important being the political, economic, religious and intellectual spheres. The religious and intellectual spheres are, as we shall see, the predominant sites of cultural change. The point of Weber's distinction is that these spheres can either overlap, in which case beliefs in one sphere tend to reinforce those in another, or they may become differentiated and come into conflict with each other. Wherever the spheres of life become more differentiated, there is a greater potential for the impact of ideas. Conversely, an overlap between them typically means that ideas remain enmeshed within the social fabric. The differentiation between the spheres of life is thus an important indication of how much or how little scope there is for cultural change.

The third aspect of cultural change consists of the autonomous logic of world-views, their development in so far as it takes place separately from other social forces. Here Weber's view is that there can be shifts in the meaning of a world-view or belief-system because its central tenets dictate a certain logic of development. Weber typically sees such a development as the result of tensions between the all-embracing explanation of the world which is usually offered by a belief-system – and an empirical reality which is bound to elude such an explanation. This 'inner logic of world-views', as Weber calls it, is an important aspect of cultural change since the meaning and coherence of a belief-system is bound to influence the impact it has on those who are under its sway (1948: 328, 340; see also Tenbruck, 1980).

In the chapters that follow I shall try to show that these are the only parts of Weber's conception of cultural change which are important in his substantive analyses. In other words, although his sociology yields a wealth of empirical information about how ideas and social life are interrelated, Weber's main argument as to how this interrelation takes place can be reduced to the three aspects that have been enumerated above.

After this brief overview of the various ways in which Weber conceives of cultural change, they must now be described in more detail. Before this can be done, two points must be made about Weber's social thought in general in order to set the scene for our discussion: one is the developmental framework – his outline of the stages of history – in which his conception of cultural change is embedded, and the second is the view of human nature which underlies this conception.

World-historical Stages and Philosophical Anthropology

Weber's writings contain a developmental framework by means of which the role of belief-systems in social life can be distinguished in three stages: magic, religion and science.[14] This does not mean that he is putting forward a philosophy of history with three evolutionary steps. It is not necessarily the case that social relations pass through each of these stages since, for example, magical elements can still be found in the modern scientific world. But it is clear from Weber's substantive analyses that the stages of magic, religion and science are successive to the extent that the earliest social units were dominated by magic, that this was followed (after the transitional period which Eisenstadt (1982) – following Jaspers – has labelled 'the axial age') by the age of the world-religions, and that science increasingly dominates modern social life. To say that there is a developmental pattern in Weber's analyses therefore simply means that there is a division into three partially overlapping and yet on the whole successive stages.

The distinction between these stages is particularly evident in terms of the different roles that beliefs play in social life. Take, for example, magic and religion. What sets magic apart from religion is the fact that in magic, extraordinary powers are believed to reside within tangible embodiments. These tangible embodiments include symbols, cult objects as well as the person of the magician. Further features of magical forces are that they exist only on a local level and that the various magical powers are not unified within a single, all-embracing realm of the divine. But because magical forces reside within concrete embodiments and do not belong to a separate domain of the sacred, they must also be integrated within the other spheres of social life. The impact of magical forces on social life is therefore one of promoting stability, or of reinforcing existing social relations by endowing them with sacred authority.

The same can be said of the impact of magic on the individual: Weber thinks that magical forces can be manipulated directly and this is typically done for the sake of obtaining worldly goals. But since, from the viewpoint of modern science, those who believe in magic are mistakenly attributing causal efficacy to magical forces, their efforts at achieving these goals must be in vain. If we jump ahead for a moment to the stage of science, we can see that for Weber, the application of scientific knowledge, finally, *is* able to transform the world because, unlike magical belief, it is based on the *true* relation between causes and effects.

The world-religions, by contrast with magic, reorient the believer's inner life in accordance with other-worldly or transcendent goals. This inward reorientation may, in turn, change the person's outward conduct. Religion may therefore be able to reshape social relations. This capacity of religion is evident from the various attributes which Weber assigns to belief-systems which are included in this category: religion, by which he basically means the five major world-religions listed below, is marked by the belief in the existence of an other-worldly deity or realm. All legitimation for religious powers or beliefs must ultimately be derived from a transcendent source. Some of these sources are personal deities (in Islam and Judaeo-Christianity) whereas others are impersonal realms (in Hinduism, Buddhism and Confucianism). And whereas the former are systematized around the notion of a single, transcendent, and all-powerful deity, the latter posit an eternal and unchanging realm on which their world-view is based. Despite this difference, they all share the characteristic that their appeal is universal. In addition, all of them are independent of concrete embodiments and therefore subject to reinterpretation on an abstract level. Hence they represent ideals which are to varying degrees independent of social reality. That is, they are not completely enmeshed within the social fabric.

With these characteristics, the role of the world-religions is quite different from that of magic. It ranges from the promotion of social stability (directly or through the mediation of worldly representatives and institutions) to the radical reorientation of the believer towards an other-worldly goal of salvation, a reorientation that may also lead to important changes in economic or political conduct.

The modern stage of science, finally, is one in which this transcendent realm of all-encompassing meaning is forced to give way before the growth of scientific knowledge and the technique of means–ends calculability. World-views which hitherto claimed a monopoly on truth are increasingly forced to retreat into the sphere of private conviction since the growth of objective knowledge about the natural and social worlds increasingly displaces our magical and religious understandings of the world. This partly accounts for Weber's pessimistic outlook on the modern world. The 'disenchantment' of the modern world, as he calls it, means that belief-systems which formerly constituted a revolutionizing force within social life are bound to play a diminishing role. At the same time, Weber acknowledges the benefits derived from the increasing knowledge about – and mastery over – the natural environment. This domination of the natural world ultimately rests on the central underlying assumption which governs scientific enquiry, namely, that the whole of reality is ultimately knowable or calculable.

Science, like religion, aims at being an all-encompassing system of thought. Yet unlike religion, it is directed towards explaining the world in terms of causes rather than other-worldly meanings. And although scientific enquiry is independent of social reality (where, as we shall see later, some qualifications are needed in relation to the sciences of culture), the impact of its application throughout the various spheres of social life is far-ranging. Science, in Weber's view, extends the technique of establishing the most efficient way to achieve a given end throughout the spheres of intellectual life, of politics and economics. This leads to the elimination of irrational forces in the sphere of intellectual life and to the creation of more efficient forms of administration and organization in the spheres of politics and economics. On the level of the individual, conduct oriented by reference to transcendent values is increasingly displaced in the modern world. Instead, individuals tend to become more and more dominated by the pursuit of immediate everyday needs. Weber remarks that, within the modern world, 'we are all individualists *against* the stream of material forces' (Weber, 1980a: 64). There is, to put it differently, a levelling of far-reaching values.

Magic, religion and science can thus be seen to dominate Weber's analysis of cultural life. As we shall see, this tripartite schema puts its stamp on the whole of his conception of the role of ideas. Another central assumption that can be found in Weber's writings, however, is a certain conception of the individual. This, what may be called his philosophical anthropology, suggests that there are different stages in which social relations allow for individuality to be expressed in different ways. These stages, again, closely follow those outlined above.

Before this pattern can be spelled out, it is useful to outline some of the main features of Weber's conception of the individual. Weber thinks that in everyday life, each person is confronted by a multitude of norms and beliefs. In this unfettered everyday condition (that is, before the systematic ethical teachings and unified belief-systems are encountered), the individual adheres simultaneously to a plurality of norms and adopts a variety of beliefs in an unsystematic and unenduring manner. A transformation of the individual can only take place because the multitude of norms which govern conduct can be approached in two ways. On the one hand, the individual can continue to submit to the conflicting norms and beliefs which are imposed by everyday life. In this case, life is shaped by circumstances that are given in the sense that the individual's conduct does not rise above a routine existence. On the other hand, the individual can adopt certain basic norms as constant guidelines for conduct, not compromising in situations in which conflicting values demand a deviation from these norms. This gives life a shape of the person's own making, even in the face of adverse circumstances.

This conception of the individual is encapsulated in Weber's notions of 'personality' and 'inner distance' (Schroeder, 1991). As Weber puts it in his methodological writings, ' "personality" . . . entails a constant and intrinsic relation to certain ultimate "values" and "meanings" of life' and it is this attitude which lifts the individual above the 'dull, undifferentiated and vegetative underground of personal life' (1975: 192). In other words, the steadfast adherence to certain norms creates an inner distance with which the everyday world may be overcome. The ways in which belief influences the individual, for Weber, fall within the range of permutations that lie between the extremes of adapting to the world or overcoming it.

We are now in a position to outline Weber's philosophical anthropology. It follows from our previous discussion of the three stages that the stage of magic is characterized by the adaptation of the individual to existing norms and powers. Human beings are surrounded by a plurality of powers which are believed to embody an extraordinary force. Yet the norms which issue from these powers have not been systematized. Thus magic takes the form of a manipulation of these extraordinary powers in order to achieve specific practical ends. Typical examples of these include the pursuit of material welfare and protection against evil spirits. Magic is therefore a stage at which the discrete and practical orientations which guide human beings are left undisturbed. Norms are not internalized, but instead they remain external to the individual in the form of an unsystematic plurality.

The stage of religion provides a range of different orientations on the part of the individual, from being confronted by a multitude of external norms, to a point where norms have been internalized and systematized. Each of the major world-religions is somewhere along this scale. The contrast between the two extremes can be illustrated by comparing the ascetic Protestant with the Confucian literati. Among the features of Protestant dogma that Weber emphasizes in the *Protestant Ethic* is that it radically devalues the world. The Protestant's attitude to worldly matters is one of restraint from any activity that might endanger the chances of salvation. This includes economic activity, which potentially involves the believer in a realm of uncertain ethical character and may encourage selfish or materialistic interests. So that although Protestant dogma does not actively discourage economic activity, it nevertheless focuses the believer's attention on a purely other-worldly goal.[15] The Confucian, on the other hand, has no constraints on the pursuit of material gain. Indeed, Weber thinks that, in general, the pursuit of commerce is positively encouraged among the Chinese (1949: 237). If, however, the ascetic Protestant is discouraged from undertaking economic activity and the Confucian is encouraged in this regard, why is it that the manifest consequences of these two contrasting attitudes are almost the opposite of the religious attitudes which they promote?

An answer can only be given by reference to the conception of the individual that was outlined above. Although there are no specific beliefs or ethical injunctions which prevent the Confucian literati from actively engaging in economic affairs, there is nevertheless a web of external norms which is prescribed by the elaborate code of conduct that governs the life-style of the literati as a stratum. This web of external norms places severe restrictions on the rational and methodical pursuit of economic gain. The Protestant believer, on the other hand, turned towards the pursuit of economic ends in practice, despite the fact that there were obstacles to it in theory. Once the Protestant's purely other-worldly religious orientation had been systematically internalized and had produced an attitude of strict asceticism, the methodical pursuit of other-worldly goals could then be turned towards worldly concerns. Or, to put it differently, only when the purely religious goal of Protestantism was aimed in a non-religious, practical direction – did the believer exhibit the type of conduct that contributed to economic activity suited to capitalist social relations. At the level of religion then, there is a range of orientations from the point at which the individual is faced by a plurality of external norms, to one where these norms have become internalized in a systematic fashion.[16]

This development during the stage of religion also leaves its mark on modern life. In the modern world, which is dominated by science, a levelling of far-reaching ideals takes place because of an increasing concern with the satisfaction of immediate, everyday needs. In the light of this pessimistic outlook on the modern social order, Weber advocates an ethical ideal which seeks to counteract it. This ideal is based on his account of the stage of religion: the individual must maintain an inner distance by means of a steadfast adherence to inward norms which guide his or her personality.[17] This type of personality will avoid adapting itself to the practical necessities that are imposed by modern social life. In other words, a person who upholds certain fundamental principles or norms may be able to resist accommodation to the demands that are made by a routinized world. Such a standpoint bears resemblance to Protestant asceticism in so far as it advocates a steadfast conscience and conduct oriented to unyielding principles. Yet it also differs from Protestantism in so far as it is a secular ideal which does not represent the adoption of a *given* faith. Instead, within the modern world, Weber's ethical ideal is one of the individual as an autonomous chooser of values.

The notion of the declining significance of all-embracing religious faiths in the modern world gives rise to Weber's comparison of modernity with the pre-religious world of magic, in which there was a similar rivalry between a multitude of contending gods or demons (1948: 156). In the modern age of science, the individual must once again make a choice as to which of these demons should guide his or her life. With the advancement of science, all-embracing faiths are banished from public life and formerly shared world-views are forced to retreat into the realm of personal conviction. The stage of science is therefore one in which the ideal of human beings lies in upholding certain norms in the face of a world in which it is increasingly difficult to do so. Or, to put it within the terms of Weber's philosophical anthropology, the norms which have been internalized during the stage of religion are threatened at the stage of science by the advancement of scientific mastery over the external world.

Charisma and Routinization

Our discussion of the conception of the individual provides us with the most irreducible unit of analysis in Weber's writings, whereas the three stages constitute the broadest framework in which his account of cultural change is set. At this point, having examined the main presuppositions which underlie his thought, we can return to the level of his analysis of concrete social change, namely to the relationship between culture and social life. The first aspect of this relationship, as we have seen, is how cultural change takes place over the course of time. And the pattern which, in Weber's view, recurs throughout history is the struggle between charisma and the routinization.[18] The paradigm for this struggle can be found in Weber's study of *Ancient Judaism* (1952), where the revolutionizing fervour of the prophets is eventually transformed into rabbinical legalism.

Here we are immediately faced with a problem and must distinguish between two quite separate levels on which Weber analyzes the struggle between charisma and routinization. The first is concerned with the bearers of authority. On this level Weber takes the concepts of charisma and routinization from his sociology of domination and applies them to his sociology of religion. Thus the concept of charisma is used to locate the origin of authority within a charismatic figure to whom certain special or extraordinary qualities are attributed (1968: 241–54, 1111–56). Along the same lines, the routinization of this authority occurs when this special endowment is either directly transmitted to others through heredity or devolves upon a group of followers (1968: 241–54, 1111–56). In other words, on this level Weber is concerned with religious authority (or also authority attaching to non-religious belief-systems) and its carriers.

The second level is the one on which Weber's general ideas about cultural change find their expression. On this level the struggle between charisma and routinization describes the flux between the initially revolutionizing impact of beliefs and their eventual accommodation to everyday life.[19] Not the origin of world-views, but their subsequent force in shaping conduct and social relations is important on this second level. Weber thinks that this pattern, whereby the initial impact of a belief-system becomes more and more entrenched within routine social life, is one which recurs throughout history.[20] This, as he puts it on one occasion, is 'essentially the "tragedy" of all attempts to realize ideas within reality' (Weber, 1924b: 445). The term 'charisma' on this level refers to the novel impact of a belief-system on social life. Routin-

ization, on the other hand, takes place either through the systematization of a belief-system by a stratum of religious virtuosi, or
through the accommodation of this belief-system to the predispositions of certain strata of believers. The result of both processes is a
weakening or routinization of the impact of the belief-system.

These two levels can briefly be illustrated by reference to Weber's
study of *Ancient Judaism*. On the first level, the conception of a
single, transcendent, and all-powerful god owed its origin to the
charismatic authority of the early Judaic prophets. The routinization of Judaism took place as this authority was transferred from the
early prophets to a stratum of priests. On the second level, on the
other hand, this new belief-system was able to challenge traditional
norms and demanded a new social order on the basis of god's all-
encompassing plan. Routinization set in with the creation of a
legalistic form of religiosity by a stratum of rabbinical scholars in
late Judaism, and through the accommodation of the belief-system
to the interests of lower-ranking strata. Both developments meant
that religion eventually became integrated into routine, everyday
life and thus lent stability to traditional social relations.

In his analysis of cultural change, Weber fails to distinguish
adequately between these two levels – the specific level of the
transformation of authority and the more general level of the
changing impact of belief-systems. The problems that arise from this
confusion of levels are particularly evident in Weber's study of
Protestantism. The revolutionizing influence of early Protestantism
cannot be ascribed to the charismatic authority of Luther or Calvin,
since Weber nowhere describes them as charismatic leaders. Their
significance lay only in the reinterpretation of Christian doctrine
which they offered. Also, no mention is made of the routinization of
charismatic authority in this case. There is, however, clearly a
pattern whereby the Protestant idea of predestination and of a
'calling' initially exercised a revolutionary impact which only
became routinized gradually through the systematization of Protestant doctrine and through its accommodation to the needs of
various strata of believers.[21]

There are three possible explanations for this divergence between
the two levels of the struggle between charisma and routinization.
The first is that Weber wants to account for the ultimate origin of a
belief-system by locating it concretely within the authority of an
individual prophet, rather than presenting a religious world-view as
though it were created simply within the realm of ideas. This
solution to the problem of the ultimate origin of beliefs is then made
to play the dual role of explaining the source as well as the impact of
a belief-system.

Secondly, this divergence may arise because Weber has over-looked a fundamental difference between how the concept of charisma is used at the stages of magic and of religion. At the stage of magic, charisma does indeed reside directly *within* the religious adept, and its transformation and impact remains linked to this tangible source. At the stage of religion, however, not only does the authority both of the prophet and of his followers derive from a transcendent or intangible source, but the impact on believers and on social life is often the result of the belief-system *itself*, and not directly dependent on the authority of its proponents. The transferral of charismatic authority and the impact of belief-systems are therefore quite different at the stages of magic and religion.

The third reason for the divergence between the two levels has already been mentioned in passing. Weber seems to take the terms charisma and routinization from his sociology of domination and applies them in his sociology of religion without noticing the shift in meaning that has taken place. In this manner he blurs the distinction between the authority of religious adepts and the changing impact of the belief-system.

This divergence between the two levels on which charisma and routinization operate cannot easily be resolved. The ambiguity that he creates here will have to be kept in mind throughout our examination of Weber's writings and we will have to return to it at the end of our discussion. In the meantime it may be pointed out that more emphasis will be given to the second, more general level of charisma and routinization, especially in the stages of religion and science. The reasons for this will become clear when we look at Weber's main writings.

But even if we keep this divergence clearly in mind, the pattern of charisma and routinization still presents difficulties. A further problem is that the relation between charisma and routinization is always a dynamic one. At the level of religious authority, as we have seen, these two concepts serve to give an account of a process or pattern of development which includes the origin, maintenance, and institutionalization of belief-systems.[22] But Weber does not specify the mechanisms by which the transition between these two opposing poles takes place, nor does he indicate the sequence of steps which must be part of this process. The same problem arises at the level of the impact of belief-systems and their accommodation to everyday life. The dimension of how this impact on social life changes over the course of time is not systematically spelled out by Weber. The only way to resolve this problem is to look at how the struggle between charisma and routinization actually takes place in each of Weber's substantive studies. Again, once this has been done in the chapters that follow, we will be in a better position to make some general comments about his analysis.

It has already been mentioned briefly that routinization consists of two elements: the systematization of the belief-system by the leading religious (or indeed any intellectual) stratum, and the accommodation of the belief-system to the predispositions of certain strata of believers. The systematization of the belief-system can take place in different ways, and we shall need to trace different paths of systematization in the context of looking at Weber's substantive studies in the chapters that follow. With the accommodation of beliefs to the predispositions of various strata, however, there is one feature which is constant throughout Weber's writings – namely, the actual predispositions of these strata themselves. These predispositions can therefore be briefly summarized.

All belief-systems or world-views must, according to Weber, in some way accommodate the needs of the groups that adopt them. He sometimes gives formal expression to this idea with his notion of 'elective affinities' (1948: 284; see also Thomas, 1985). Although Weber nowhere defines this basic idea, a sense of what he means can nevertheless be culled from the various places where it is applied. The idea is that once beliefs have come into existence through the assertion of charisma, their reception among certain strata depends on the predispositons of these strata. Or, to put it the other way around, the way in which the attributes of social groups give shape to their beliefs can only be understood by means of identifying their inherent predispositons. These predispositions, in turn, depend on the social circumstances of the various strata, on their position in relation to other strata and on their common way of life (Kalberg, 1985b: especially 48–54).

Three contrasts with Marx's theory of ideology can illustrate the nature of these predispositons. The first is that in Marx's theory, the adoption of an ideology is dependent on material interests (for example, Marx, 1977: 164). Certain classes are the carriers of belief-systems on the basis of their economic circumstances. For Weber, on the other hand, the adoption of a world-view never depends on economic circumstances alone, but always also on the prestige of the location of a status group and on its position of esteem relative to other strata. In the light of these criteria, non-material factors, such as the prestige accorded to a stratum of intellectuals on the basis of its specialized knowledge, are often decisive for a stratum's interests – or, in Weberian terms, its predispositions (again, these two terms will be used interchangeably).[23]

The second contrast arises from the fact that the origins of the ideologies of classes in Marx's theory are embedded within an all-encompassing theory of historical change. The ideological interests of a class vary and are dependent upon the mode of production, and hence on the historical stage in which they occur. For Weber, by contrast, the predispositions of similarly located social strata are the same in all places and at all times. In the light of this inherent or almost innate nature of the attributes of social strata, Weber allows himself very broad generalizations about the types of belief towards which certain strata are disposed.[24]

Finally, there is a difference between Marx and Weber in terms of the content of belief-systems. Marx's account of ideology suggests that its content must be shaped entirely by the economic circumstances of the class which adopts it. Or, to put it differently, the economic attributes of a class determine the content of its belief-system. The predispositions in Weber's theory, however, only partly account for the content of a belief-system. In the first instance, its content is a product of the prophet's revelation or the charismatic leader's world-view. The predispositions of social strata merely serve to reinterpret or reshape the content of the belief-system according to its own needs and to select those among its tenets which fit in with these needs. Or, as Parkin puts it: 'Different social strata tend to respond mainly to those features of doctrine that seem to resonate most closely with their own specific life-situations and experiences' (1982: 53).

What then are the inherent predispositions of social strata in Weber's schema?[25] In the first place, peasants almost invariably embrace a magical world-view: 'Only rarely does the peasantry serve as the carrier of any sort of religion other than their original magic' (Weber, 1968: 470). Of the few exceptions to this rule (1968: 469–72), the only example of historical significance is the adoption of a religion of salvation by the ancient Judaic peasantry, and this, according to Weber, was a result of exceptional circumstances. Apart from this, the peasantry remained predisposed towards magic, a type of religiosity whose main effect is traditionalism.

The petty bourgeoisie, on the other hand, may be able to step outside the confines of magic since 'by virtue of its distinctive pattern of economic life, [it] inclines in the direction of a rational ethical religion, wherever conditions are present for the emergence of such a religion'(1968: 482). This predisposition is made possible by the fact that the 'economic foundation of the urban man's life has a far more rational character, viz., calculability and capacity for purposive manipulation' (1968: 482–3). The rational ethical religions of this stratum are thus likely to incorporate either a personal saviour who dispenses salvation, or an ethic of compensation in the beyond.

As regards elites, the predispositions of this stratum depend on whether this group holds economic, political, or intellectual power. Economic elites tend to adopt purely pragmatic attitudes towards religious world-views and to ignore their content: 'The more privileged the position of the commercial class, the less it has evinced any inclination to develop an other-worldly religion' (1968: 478). Or again: 'Everywhere, scepticism or indifference to religion are and have been the widely diffused attitudes of large-scale traders and financiers' (1968: 479).

Among political elites, bureaucratic strata tend not to embrace religious conceptions of salvation or ethics, but are instead prone to opt for 'an opportunistic and utilitarian . . . doctrine of conventions' (1968: 476). Only under certain conditions (Weber seems to have Islam in mind here) do leading political strata take an active part in promoting religion.

Intellectual elites (Weber also calls them 'culture carriers' with their distinctive and all-important 'way of life'(1981b: 23, my trans.; cf. 1930: 30)) must develop a rationally coherent world-view both in order to satisfy their inherent need for an overall meaning of the world and to preserve their status (1968: 506). Their world-views must give a meaningful account of the world as a whole, and although there are many such world-views, they all have in common that they provide a place for the individual believer within this meaningful schema. Weber writes: 'Thus, the demand has been implied: that the world order in its totality is, could, and should somehow be a meaningful "cosmos". This quest . . . has been borne precisely by strata of intellectuals' (1948: 281).[26]

As an aside, it is interesting to note that Weber himself, presumably a member of the intellectual stratum, does not seem to share this predisposition. He explicitly rejects the view that nature or the world as such have an overall meaning (1958: 340).[27] Instead, following Mill, he postulates that if one proceeds from empirical reality, one can only arrive at a plurality of values and hence, by implication, at a plurality of conflicting and irreconcilable viewpoints about the overall meaning of the world (1948: 149). Nevertheless, Weber *did* think that many contemporary intellectuals still possessed such an innate predisposition towards believing in an overall meaning of the world, something which he attacks in his essay 'Science as a Vocation' (1948: 129–56).[28]

Finally, bourgeois religiosity exhibits propensities towards a variety of beliefs (Weber, 1968: 477). Nevertheless, with the exception of several small sects (1968: 479) and the leading economic strata mentioned above, the only bourgeois stratum which was an active carrier of religious belief were the Protestants, combining an ethical religion of salvation with economic rationalism. This means that the unique emergence of a large urban middle class coincided with the rise of a unique type of belief-system which consists of an ethic of asceticism and the active pursuit of worldly goals.

These predispositions towards certain types of belief will always and everywhere be found among the strata listed here.[29] The notion of 'elective affinities' can therefore be seen as an attempt to explain why certain religious and other doctrines – and not others – tend to be adopted by various social strata, and how their content is accommodated to the needs and interests of these strata.

Spheres of Life

The second aspect of Weber's conception of cultural change revolves around the different parts of social life. Weber distinguishes between several spheres of life – the economic, political, religious, and intellectual spheres.[30] And again, it is particularly the last two of these in which cultural change takes place. The distinction between spheres of life operates both on the level of social relations as a whole and on the level of the individual. On the level of social relations, the different spheres are distinguished in order to show how beliefs in one sphere of life may reinforce or come into conflict with those in another. On the level of the individual, each sphere of life makes certain demands on the individual's practical and ethical conduct which may reinforce or conflict with the demands of another sphere.

The point of this separation is to allow Weber to highlight the significance of the realm of beliefs and to distinguish between the ethical demands in different spheres in terms of how they overlap with – or become differentiated from – those of other spheres. An increasing differentiation between two spheres of life typically promotes the development of new beliefs and modes of conduct in each sphere. In other words, differentiation promotes social change. Conversely, the lack of differentiation between two spheres prevents the further development of beliefs and modes of conduct in these spheres, and therefore constitutes a blockage to social change.

To take some prominent examples of these processes from Weber's writings: in modern times, a conflict develops between the intellectual sphere – dominated by science – and the sphere of politics. In Weber's view, these two spheres are becoming increasingly differentiated. In his lectures on 'Politics as a Vocation' and 'Science as a Vocation', he draws out certain practical conclusions from this process of differentiation (1948: 77–128, 129–56). The intellectual or scientific sphere will increasingly demand that the scientist should refrain from imposing personal values on his or her work. In keeping with this demand, Weber warns against the promotion of political values in the guise of scientific truth. The scientist must be dedicated to objective knowledge and forgo the advocacy of values. The political leader, on the other hand, must struggle for the realization of a personal world-view in the market-place of conflicting ideals, rather than claiming validity for these ideals on the basis of their alleged truth. Or, to put it differently, the politician's struggle takes place precisely against the background that no objective foundations for political values is possible. These two demands will, in Weber's view, increasingly come into conflict with each other.

Another example of conflict is the one which develops between the brotherly ethic of the Christian religions and the unbrotherliness of modern economics. The religious demand to share material goods with fellow-believers can no longer be accommodated in the economic sphere of modern capitalism with its characteristic imper-sonality, its 'culture' of a 'vocational workaday life' and orientation towards profit-seeking (Weber, 1948: 357, see also 331). This conflict can only be avoided by a relativization of the religious ethic or within pockets of modern capitalism that are unaffected by the competitiveness of the economic sphere.

An example of harmony or of reinforcement between two spheres of life can be found in the overlap between the intellectual and religious spheres which existed during certain periods. Although the standpoint of intellectuals has often been one of scepticism towards religion and has, especially in the modern world, created a tension with this sphere, Weber points out that during many periods the priestly role in education and in conserving learned traditions often resulted in a mutual reinforcement between these two spheres (1948: 351). Priestly status and power could be enhanced by control over the dissemination of learning, while intellectualism was bol-stered by the authority and organization of the church and its propagandists.

Another example of mutual reinforcement is furnished by the dual status of the Confucian mandarins, who were at once the carriers of a world-religion *and* a stratum of political administrators. The fact that they combined the roles of Confucian ethical teachers and of bureaucrats meant that the powers of this stratum in the religious and political spheres of life reinforced each other (Weber, 1949: 142–3; 1968: 593–4).

Apart from the particular instances of conflict or overlap between the spheres of life, there is also an overall pattern in Weber's writings. This pattern follows the developmental stages of magic, religion, and science, and consists in the fact that in each stage, the spheres of life stand in a different relation to each other.

At the stage of magic, there is little differentiation between these spheres, so that for the most part, political, economic and religious factors are closely linked. The status and role of the charismatic magician, for example, will often encompass all three of these spheres. Thus the magician may at once be a law-giver, economic adviser and ritual expert. Similarly, the cohesion of small social units such as kin groups is often preserved because its ties extend simultaneously across all three spheres of life. At the stage of magic then, there is a large degree of overlap between the functioning of the political, economic and religious spheres which reinforces existing social relations.

At the stage of religion, although the functions of the spheres of life initially overlap, they become increasingly differentiated. The beginnings of the world-religions still saw a large degree of overlap between the different spheres of life, and Weber's studies focus particularly on the close links between the religious sphere and the economic and political spheres. In the Occident, however, the sphere of religion became increasingly separated from economics and politics by making its own, purely religious demands on believers. This development culminates in Protestantism, where the religious sphere finally became completely divorced from the political and economic spheres.[31] At the stage of religion then, we see the gradual emergence of the religious sphere as an independent force in social life.

In the modern world finally, this functional differentiation becomes so pronounced that the different spheres not only make separate, but often also irreconcilable demands. Under pressure from the political, economic, and especially the intellectual spheres, the sphere of religious life is increasingly forced to retreat into the purely personal or 'irrational realm' (Weber, 1948: 351). Furthermore, as we have just seen, the conflict between the intellectual and political spheres is sharpened to such an extent that radically different demands are made by each sphere. The demands of the economic sphere, combining instrumental efficiency with the competitiveness of the market, in turn, produce tensions with the political and intellectual spheres.

Such reinforcement and conflict between the different spheres of life represent an increasing differentiation and closely follow the stages of magic, religion and science. As we shall see, this development of the relation among the various spheres plays an important part in Weber's account of cultural change.

The Inner Logic of World-views

The third aspect of cultural change can be found on the level of ideas themselves. Weber frequently refers to an 'inner logic' in the development of world-views.[32] This inner logic is the result of a tension between world-views – which typically postulate that there is an overall meaning of the world – and the way in which reality encroaches upon this meaning.

It follows immediately from the way this tension is construed that one baseline assumption in Weber's thinking must be that reality is something which does not have a single, overall meaning. One of the ways in which this assumption manifests itself has already been noted above in Weber's distancing himself from what he sees as the typical standpoint of intellectual strata. But since the idea that the world has no one single meaning relies, among other things, on his methodological position, it will be pursued in the discussion of science below. Suffice it to say at this point that Weber thinks that conflicting world-views and what he calls the 'experience of the irrationality of the world' are an inescapable fact about social reality (1948: 123). It follows from this standpoint that any attempt to construe an all-encompassing world-view – which makes claims, for example, for the absolute validity of certain values or for the triumph of good over evil – is bound to come into conflict with reality.[33] The tension that arises from this conflict between world-view and reality will determine the direction in which a world-view develops. Weber sets out then to reconstruct the inner logic of this tension and to trace its subsequent development. But since the content or meaning of a world-view can, for Weber, constitute the most important aspect of how beliefs translate into social life, the reconstruction of this inner logic must be an essential element of his conception of cultural change.

The inner logic of world-views is well illustrated by the emergence of Occidental monotheism. The early Judaic prophecy proclaimed that a completely transcendent and all-powerful god guided the religious and political fate of his people. This religious world-view was bound to come into conflict with the world in so far as one part of the doctrine demanded that god should on occasion enter the course of world-history in order to alter the fate of believers. When reality failed to meet this expectation, this shortcoming had to be explained. A monotheistic world-view could therefore only find its consistent conclusion in the Protestant god of predestination, a 'logical' development in the sense that this god had already predetermined all future worldly events, while his divine plan was at the same time completely unknowable. The Protestant world-view thus provided a coherent solution to the problem of how the will of a transcendent deity could be reconciled with changing realities.

Similar patterns occur in the other world-religions. With the idea of an inner logic of world-views, Weber is able to reconstruct the development of certain doctrines in terms of the tensions between world-view – or, at the stage of religion, the sacred – and reality. In this way he can account for the changes that world-views undergo in a systematic manner. He can show how these world-views were constantly reinterpreted to meet the exigencies of reality. It needs to be added that this part of Weber's account of cultural change is not confined to his analyses of the world-religions since a similar logic can be found at the stages of magic and science.

The point of this chapter has been to outline the main elements of Weber's conception of cultural change. Yet this is only a skeleton outline of his conception. At this stage we need to examine how these elements operate throughout his substantive studies. Only then will it be possible to see what kinds of claim Weber makes for the role of ideas in social life. Such an examination of his studies will be the task of the following chapters.

For the time being, let us note that we have identified three important elements of Weber's conception of cultural change: the struggle between charisma and routinization, the differentiation between the spheres of life and the inner logic of world-views. Furthermore, it has been seen that a certain view of human nature and a schema of three developmental stages underlies this conception. These elements of Weber's thought will allow us to reconstruct the analysis of cultural change as the central theme of Weber's sociology, a theme which is consistent both in that it can be found throughout his writings and inasmuch as it offers a coherent approach to understanding social change.

We will need to assess then, how the concept of culture provides a key to understanding Weber's comparative historical sociology – as well as his methodology and his outlook on the modern world. It should be emphasized that no attempt will be made to assess the accuracy of Weber's analyses in terms of contemporary scholarship. Instead, this study merely intends to examine the coherence of the account of cultural change in his writings. A brief indication will nevertheless be given of some of the major debates which have arisen in response to his arguments concerning the role of culture in social life, especially in the case of the world-religions.[34]

Apart from enabling us to reconstruct a distinctive Weberian theoretical perspective, this will also provide answers to two questions. One is whether Weber's studies offer a convincing account of cultural change within the framework of his own writings, and the other is how well his theory fares by comparison with more recent approaches in the social sciences to culture and its role in social life. Let us turn first, however, to examining how the various elements of Weber's conception can be found in his major substantive studies.

Notes

1. For a recent summary of this debate, see Schluchter (1989: 433–63 and appendices I, II).
2. The currently ongoing publication of a new edition of Weber's work in German may, however, shed some light on this issue.
3. Francis's essay (1966) was the first to draw attention to Weber's usage of the concept of culture. More recently, Scaff has commented on this aspect of Weber's work (1989: esp. ch. 3).
4. Overviews of approaches to 'culture' in the social sciences can be found in Merquior (1979: ch. 2) and Thompson (1990: 122–35).
5. The latter is Radcliffe-Brown's view. See Kuper (1983: 55).
6. Schluchter's attempt to establish an exhaustive categorization of the cognitive and ethical orientations of individual actors is shared by Kalberg (1990). Both multiply the dimensions along which world-views, types of rationality, different modes of conduct and the like can be distinguished in a series of diagrams and typologies. Against this, the approach taken here suggests that an approach aiming at abstract classification of individual orientations is unlikely to be able to take the place of Weber's account of concrete historical processes.
7. Furthermore, Hennis's interpretation misleads in so far as he wants to ascribe to Weber a normative position which Weber himself would reject and which is derived from the American political philosopher Leo Strauss. Strauss's philosophy is best described as a mystical version of Platonism. He postulates a realm of truth that is completely divorced from the world and to which only a few great thinkers – and those who understand their texts according to Strauss's reading – have access. Hennis similarly wants to set a realm of norms against the realm of practical politics. His Straussian interpretation of Weber is idiosyncratic, however, since Strauss himself, and more recently his follower Bloom, have attacked Weber's alleged relativism (Strauss, 1953; Bloom, 1987). This idiosyncracy also marks Robert Eden's Straussian interpretation of the relation between Nietzsche and Weber (1983). Strauss's standpoint is, of course, completely incompatible with Weber's search for an objective social science inasmuch as it is closed off from empirical investigation and sets itself against a non-normative social science.
8. No attempt will be made here to enter the debate about which of his texts should be accorded priority or whether the sequence of his writings allows us to identify shifts in his position. The interpretation offered here, I would argue, is consistent with all of his writings. If there is nevertheless more reliance on the studies of the world-religions (Weber, 1930; 1948: 267–301, 323–59; 1951; 1952; 1958) and less on other works, it should be remembered that these constituted a project which he himself conceived and which occupied the greater part of his working life, whereas *Economy and Society* (1968) is a set of (often fragmentary) contribu-

tions to a massive encyclopaedia of the social sciences and the *General Economic History* (1927) consists of lecture notes of one of his university courses transcribed by students.

9. As we shall see, Weber thought that his methodology was at once given by the nature of social reality and at the same time constrained by how we must understand our place within this social reality. In this sense, Weber's position was a Kantian one, a point which will emerge more clearly below.

10. The term culture occurs frequently in Weber's writings (see especially 1981b: 9–26; 1982: 146–290), but this is not always evident in the English translations (1930: 13–31; 1949: 49–188). Interestingly, Weber at one point planned a ' "sociology of cultural *contents* (art, literature, world–views")' (Winckelmann, 1986: 36) which would have considerably extended the range of his enquiries.

One contemporary of Weber's who sought to develop a sociology of culture was his brother Alfred. The limitations of the latter's approach by contrast with the one to be presented here can easily be recognized in Alfred Weber's programmatic introduction to the sociology of culture (1920/21: 1–49), where the 'inner drives' of a 'personality' are likened to the 'lower' and 'higher' stages of culture. The implication that one form of culture is superior to another is one that Max Weber explicitly rejects (1930: 29). Alfred Weber's ideas about culture have, however, subsequently strongly influenced the sociology of culture and civilizations of Norbert Elias (see Kuzmics, 1984).

11. Whether these beliefs attach to individuals, groups or institutions is something that will emerge in our discussion of Weber's studies, but does not detract from their constituting a part of social reality that is separate from the world of non-ideational social relations.

12. In the theoretical introduction to his main sociological treatise, *Economy and Society*, Weber distinguishes between four types of social action: instrumentally rational, value-rational, affectual and traditional (1968: 24–6). *Economy and Society* is therefore sometimes seen as a new departure for Weber (see, for example, Collins, 1986b: 127–9). Yet even in this work, the concepts of social action are almost never applied and Weber departs little in its substantive parts from the themes and methods he had pursued throughout his career. The only type of social action that he frequently refers to is instrumentally rational action. This type of social action is characteristic of modern political administrations and of the economics of the modern capitalist market. Weber defines it as the use of the most efficient means to achieve a given end (1968: 24, 26). But as a description of modern institutions, the concept of instrumental rationality can not stand on its own. It could only be useful if it could be contrasted with the workings of the other types of rationality. But such applications are very scarce. Moreover, as we shall see, the nature of modern bureaucracies and markets and their unique efficiency emerges more clearly through Weber's historical account of the emergence of these institutions, rather than through a concept that applies to individual social action. A final point against this approach to Weber is that the theory of social action, which has since become an established school within sociological theory, simply did not exist in Weber's time. Trying to impose such a framework on Weber's writings would therefore mystify his own, quite different, understanding of social conduct.

If rationality and social action do not provide us with a schema for interpreting Weber's social theory, neither do various related concepts, such as his distinction between substantive and formal rationality. The only place where he uses this set of terms extensively is in his sociology of law. He describes modern law as formally rational since the individual is treated equally and without regard to personal qualities. Yet in fact, he says, the modern legal system is substantively irrational since it favours those who wield economic power and who are able to take advantage of the formal freedoms which are guaranteed by law (see also Brubaker, 1984: 16–20, 35–43). But again, such an explicit description is more useful than the concepts of formal and substantive rationality themselves, especially since the application of these two concepts is almost entirely limited to the sociology of law and difficult to relate to other areas of social life.

13. Among those interpretations that have specifically focused on the concept of rationalization are those of Abramowski (1966), Kalberg (1978), Küenzlen (1980), Caldwell (1983) and Andreski (1984). The differences between their approaches and the present one are pointed out in the appropriate places. None of these works, however, address the unity of this theme throughout the major areas of Weber's sociology. Abramowski, although he gives a wide-ranging descriptive account of rationalization in Weber's sociology, does not systematically analyze the mechanisms by which the various processes take place. Kalberg's analysis is exhaustive in the sense that it deals with most of the areas which Weber investigated. Yet he limits the discussion of the concept of rationalization mainly to two perspectives: on the one hand, he focuses on the view of Weber's typology of the different kinds of social action; and on the other, following Tenbruck (1980), he analyzes rationalization in terms of the development of world-views. His chapter on rationalization in the religious sphere is restricted to these two perspectives and therefore only establishes the contrasts between asceticism and mysticism and between magic and religion. Hence he does not provide a systematic account of the different types of rationalization in Weber's studies of the world-religions. Küenzlen examines the contemporary sources for Weber's sociology of religion. In terms of rationalization, he only examines the essays on 'The Social Psychology of the World-Religions' and the 'Religious Rejections of the World and their Directions' (Weber, 1948: 267–301, 323–59) and tries to apply the insights from these two essays to Weber's sociology as a whole. Andreski and Caldwell both justly criticize Weber for the confusing and inconsistent use of the concept of rationalization, although it could be argued that there is nevertheless a systematic coherence underlying Weber's usage of this concept. A particularly clear attempt to give an account of Weber's conception of rationality, at least in terms of his view of modern society, can be found in Brubaker (1984).

14. The division into three stages is mainly applied here to Weber's writings on religion and on the modern world. Yet the same tripartite division could similarly be applied to his writings on economics, law, politics and music. The term 'developmental history' has been used in relation to Weber's world-historical perspective by Schluchter (1981a), although his usage differs from the present one. On the intellectual background of Weber's developmental framework, see Roth (1987).

15. Weber says of the 'works of Calvin, of Calvinism, and the other Puritan sects' that 'we cannot well maintain that the pursuit of worldly goods, conceived as an end in itself, was to any of them of positive ethical value' (1930: 89).

16. Compare the comment in Campbell's *The Romantic Ethic and the Spirit of Modern Consumerism* that 'only in modern times have emotions come to be located "within" individuals as opposed to "in" the world' (1987: 72).

17. This belief of Weber's surfaces frequently in his writings. Interestingly, it can also be found in writings that have nothing to do with his sociology. For example, in the report that he prepared in his role as administrator of the hospitals in Heidelberg during the First World War, he notes greater professionalism among the nurses whose personalities exhibit an inner distance (1984: 40–1).

18. This theme is explored in terms of Weber's writings on politics by Mommsen (for example, 1974a: 112).

19. There are interesting similarities here between Weber's view of the development of religions and those of David Hume (1976) with his idea of the oscillation between polytheism and theism.

20. Although the terms charisma and routinization should be reserved for socio-historical *processes*, there are obvious parallels here with the contrast between extraordinary and everyday conduct of the *individual* believer.

21. One way of avoiding this inconsistency is to reply that it was the charisma of the ancient Judaic prophets which created Western monotheism, and hence it was *their* charismatic authority which was ultimately responsible for the power of Protestant ideals. Yet this reply only poses a further problem: surely the *personal* authority of the Judaic prophets themselves can do little by way of explaining the powerful new impact of the Protestant system of beliefs. To explain this impact, an explanation needs to be provided at the level of the belief-system, rather than one which is limited to the level of religious authority.

22. A clear example of the fact that Weber sees this opposition as a process or development is given when he describes the creation of bureaucracies or factories as 'lifeless machines which are coagulated spirit' (1980a: 332, my trans.; cf. 1968: 1402).

23. Weber himself tends to use 'interests' when he is contrasting material and ideal interests and 'predispositions' to refer more specifically to the attributes of strata.

24. This does not mean that these predispositions are, so to speak, transhistorical essences. The position of economic, political or cultural power of a stratum, as well as its position to other strata must be taken into account. Within this framework, strata in a similar position and with a similar way of life will share the same predispositions.

25. Apart from Weber's scattered comments on these predispositions, a brief summary of them can be found on pp. 282–4 in *From Max Weber: Essays in Sociology* (1948).

26. Compare the remark of Berger and Luckmann that 'only a very limited group of people in any society engage in theorizing, in the business of "ideas", and the construction of *Weltanschauungen*' (1967: 27). Weber provides an overview of the predispositions in *Economy and Society* (1968: 512).

27. In this sense, he clearly stands on the non-believing side of the question posed in the title of MacIntyre's essay 'Is Understanding Religion Compatible with Believing?' (1970).

28. In exempting himself from predispositions or interests, he can be seen as a forerunner of Mannheim's idea that intellectual strata were interest-free or 'free-floating' (Mannheim, 1936).

29. This list is not exhaustive since predispositions may be shaped by a combination of factors.

30. 'We are placed into various life-spheres, each of which is governed by different laws' (1948: 123). In the German original, Weber interchangeably uses both the

term '*Lebensordnungen*' – or life-orders – and '*Wertsphären*' – or value-spheres. See, for example, Weber (1920–1, vol. 1: 537; cf. 1948: 323). Here we will use 'spheres of life' to capture the meaning of both German terms. The idea of the spheres of life is most explicitly discussed in Weber's essay on 'The Religious Rejections of the World and their Directions' (1948: 323–59), but it also plays a role in his other writings. In this essay, Weber also discusses the aesthetic and the erotic spheres of life, but since these are marginal in Weber's writings and of limited interest to the issues discussed here, they will be omitted. The idea of the spheres of life has been discussed by Brubaker (1984) and Hennis (1988) but both authors limit themselves to discussing the significance of the spheres of life for Weber's conception of the modern world.

It may be useful to clarify that for Weber (confusingly), both religion and science belong within the intellectual sphere, although religion dominates this sphere in the pre-modern world, whereas science dominates (and in this sense replaces religion) in the modern world (1948: 354–5). Again, the term culture, which Weber does not refer to as a 'sphere', is more all-encompassing than the idea of an intellectual sphere, but is dominated by religion in the pre-modern world and science in the modern world.

31. It should be noted that this applies to the impact of religious belief on the individual believer. This is the aspect that Weber focuses on in *The Protestant Ethic and the Spirit of Capitalism* (1930), while he ignores the theocratic elements of Protestantism.

32. This idea is developed by Tenbruck (1980), who limits the discussion to Western rationalism, however.

33. World-views are bound to be, as he puts it, 'strongly exposed to the imperative of consistency' (1948: 324).

34. Schluchter has edited several collections of essays which attempt such an assessment (1981b; 1983; 1984; 1985; 1987; 1988), where there are also useful references to material in English.

2

THE UNIQUENESS OF THE EAST

From Magic to Religion

The most general framework for Weber's analysis of cultural change is the question: what accounts for the cultural distinctiveness of modern social life? To identify these distinguishing features, he recognized that it was necessary not only to trace the genesis of the modern Western world-view, but also to establish how other, non-modern and non-Western world-views differed from it. Magic, for Weber, is both the precursor to the world-views of the great religions (*Kulturreligionen*, Weber, 1980b: 367; cf. 1968: 611) and at the same time, religion and the modern scientific world-view are defined by contrast with magic. Our analysis of cultural change and of the logic of different world-views must therefore begin with Weber's comments on magic.

The section on magic which occupies the introductory sections of Weber's chapter on the sociology of religion in *Economy and Society* (1968: 399–451) is rarely referred to in the secondary literature. This omission seems justified inasmuch as Weber's idea of magic would find little support within subsequent thought about 'primitive religions'. Evans-Pritchard, for example, put Weber's ideas about magic into the camp of 'intellectualist' theories of primitive religon. 'Intellectualist' theories, Evans-Pritchard argues, typically assume that the meaning that magical practices have when they are reconstructed in the minds of anthropologists within a modern, scientific culture must be the same as that which it has for the adherents of magic themselves (1965: esp. ch. 2). As we shall see, Weber's view of magic is indeed prone to this error. But for the purposes of the argument advanced here, the importance of Weber's ideas about magic go beyond whether he can help us to understand this phenomenon per se.

Much like one of his fellow 'intellectualists', Malinowski (1974), Weber thought that there is a similarity between magic and science. They share, for example, a purposive, practical orientation which sets them apart from the other-worldly aims of religion. Unlike some 'intellectualists' such as Frazer (Evans-Pritchard, 1965: 28), however, he did not think of magic as a hopelessly ineffective form of pseudo-science which doomed 'primitive' peoples to an inability to cope with their environment. In the course of his discussion of science, for example, he suggests that it is in fact human beings in the modern world who may in some ways have a more limited understanding of their bewilderingly complex environment than 'primitive' peoples within a less complex one (1948: 139). One reason for examining Weber's view of magic then is that he not only distinguishes between magic and religion, but also compares magic with modern science.

There are two further reasons why Weber's view of magic should not be ignored despite his 'intellectualist' approach. The first is that Weber asserts that as a rule, the orientation of the mass of believers, even in the world-religions, is always and everywhere magical (1968: 468, 470). There are two important exceptions to this rule: Ancient Judaism and Protestantism. Magical elements still remained during the reign of these two religious systems, yet they were nevertheless on the whole free from magic. As we shall see, Weber devotes a great deal of argument to explaining this exceptionalism. Still, his view of magic is important so that a strong contrast can be made between the magical belief of the masses and the various types of religious belief of the elites. This also means that it will be necessary to focus on whether the attitude of the elites reinforces, tries to alter, or remains indifferent to the magical beliefs of the masses.

Secondly, magic is an essential part of the dynamic of world-views. What Weber calls the 'routinization' of a belief-system is often at the same time a move towards belief taking on the features of magic. While the initial doctrine of a world-religion may, for example, be completely devoid of magic, both its modification by priestly strata and its accommodation to the predispositions of believers tend to force a religion to incorporate magical elements. In this way Weber's conception of magic sheds light on the typical transformations within the world-religions.

This brings us to his account of magic itself. Weber devotes a mere two sections in his sociology of religion to magic and these, apart from occasional comments elsewhere, constitute the whole of his systematic treatment of this topic. Here he sketches a strong contrast between magic and religion which emerges most forcefully in the diametrically opposite types of rationality which characterize these two stages. In Weber's view, magic has a rational aim which is pursued by irrational means, whereas religion is characterized by an increasingly irrational aim and increasingly rational means to salvation (1968: 400, 428). There is in fact, he says, a continuum between these two orientations, but these two poles can be clearly identified.

What lies behind this puzzling use of the ideas of rationality and irrationality? To get behind this, let us look first at the *aims* of magic and religion. Why is magic characterized by rational aims? Of all the forms of magic described by Weber (and to which we shall turn in a moment), one feature that clearly sets them apart from the world-religions is their practical or 'this-worldly' orientation. That is, the sacred is always conceived of as securing external advantages, such as protection from evil. 'Extraordinary' forces are called upon, or in Weber's terminology 'coerced', for their effectiveness in providing the believer with worldly goods, happiness and security. These goals are 'rational' then, in a sense in which Weber often uses this term and which indicates the presence of instrumental or means–ends oriented behaviour.

Inasmuch as it is practical or instrumental, this type of rationality is continuous with everyday conduct: 'Magical behaviour or thinking must not be set apart from the range of everyday purposive conduct, particularly since even the ends of religious or magical actions are predominantly economic' (1968: 400). This immediately leads to another feature of this type of rationality, namely that its efficacy is thought to rest on practical experience. Belief in the magician's charismatic or extraordinary powers rests on the repeated demonstration of success. For these reasons, Weber can speak in this context of a 'practical and calculating rationalism' (1968: 424).

The 'irrationality' of the aims of the world-religions, on the other hand, refers to their increasingly exclusive religious motivation. Sacredness is considered more and more as an end-in-itself as it moves further away from the consideration of concrete worldly aims. Happiness and welfare in this world are of little concern compared with the ultimate goal of salvation.

Such an aim is irrational (at least by contrast with a rational or instrumental aim) in so far as it is completely 'other-worldly' and non-instrumental. It cannot be legitimated by reference to tradition or worldly success because it is oriented towards an ideal future – such as salvation in the beyond – nor can it be understood in relation to practical considerations because there are no tangible ends. In other words, in its pure form, this type of religious orientation consists of striving for a goal defined only by the religious doctrine of salvation, rather than by practical concerns. It is therefore the more irrational, the more its motivation is shaped by purely non-everyday or transcendent ends.

The opposite applies in each case to the *means* applied by magic and religion to pursue their respective aims. The belief in magical means is 'irrational' from 'the standpoint of our modern views of nature' because of its 'fallacious attributions of causality' (1968: 400). To put it more bluntly, from the viewpoint of modern science, magic does not work.[1] This failure is best understood in terms of Weber's account of the origins of magic in charisma. In its most pure form, magic for Weber stems from an extraordinary power that is thought to be embodied *directly* within certain objects or persons. This power, whether inherent as a natural endowment, or 'produced artificially . . . through some extraordinary means', must nevertheless reside ultimately within the objects or persons themselves (1968: 400). Even if magical charisma assumes abstract or symbolic forms, it never originates from a transcendent source and therefore cannot be legitimated from such a source.

Now this is irrational for Weber because this belief is not grounded in any theoretical or underlying coherence. It is a straightforward ascription of extraordinary power which is justified only by the fact that there is a following which believes in its effectiveness, something which, by the standards of explanation in religion and science, must be seen as irrational.

The means of achieving salvation in the world-religions, on the other hand, are 'rational' in the sense that this quest consists of everyday efforts which are not supra-human. Whatever the believer's attitude towards the ultimate mystery of salvation, it is nevertheless possible to proceed by certain steps towards a given end. Salvation does not rely on extraordinary powers, but only on believers themselves. This type of belief and conduct is rational then in that only worldly or everyday means can bring about the desired religious effect.

The distinction between magic and religion on the basis of 'rationality' and 'irrationality' provides one of the main pillars on which Weber's analysis of culture and cultural change rests. Yet an abstract typology of 'rationality' in his writings is impossible since he attaches different meanings to this term in different contexts. Only when this context is clearly spelled out can we pinpoint its meaning. Here, what is important about the distinction between 'rationality' and 'irrationality' is that two world-views, defined by contrast with each other, have very different consequences for social conduct. And Weber wants to differentiate between the consequences of magic and religion as separate cultural forms.

Bearing this in mind, we can now trace the development of various types of magic and their impact on social life. For Weber, magic always involves an attempt to gain control over the external environment. Its forms must therefore inevitably tend towards proliferation and differentiation. Unlike the world-views of the world-religions, which can be unified at an abstract level, magic lacks a transcendent basis on which extraordinary powers and practices could be unified and systematized. This means that there can only be a proliferation of various means by which particular effects are achieved. Weber devotes the major part of his section on magic to categorizing the permutations among various types of objects, persons, and deities in which magical power is believed to reside. What they all have in common as forms of magic, however, is that an extraordinary power must always be thought to have a concrete embodiment.

The most undifferentiated form of magic, in Weber's view, is where magical power is thought to be embodied in a person who can bring about supernatural events by virtue of an innate capacity. This belief is the original source of charisma.[2] 'The oldest of all "callings" ' or professions, Weber points out, 'is that of the magician' (1981a: 8). From this point, charisma develops by a process of abstraction towards the notion that certain forces are 'behind' this extraordinary power – although they remain within the world (1968: 401). Weber defines animism, for example, as the belief that spirits, souls or demons inhere within certain tangible objects and thereby give them their efficacy. At a further stage of abstraction, there are 'invisible essences' which are indirectly accessible and can be manipulated symbolically, as opposed to 'naturalism' where they are controlled directly (1968: 403–5). With an increasing differentiation between various functions of magical power, special domains are created for separate powers. There are gods of the kin group, of political or local associations, or those that are assigned specific tasks or jurisdictions (1968: 407). The systematization of these symbolic powers leads to myth, and with priestly systematization of various forms of worship, what Weber calls cultic, ritual, and taboo norms are developed.

The development of these different types of magic brings about changes in the embodiments of the sacred and the way they are believed to be efficacious. What is important, however, is that magical powers remain tangible and accessible to direct or indirect manipulation. They are tied to specific meanings that operate within the limited context of seeking to achieve worldly ends. As Weber points out, the significant feature of these deities and practices is not whether they are natural, symbolic, or inherent in the person, but simply 'that new experiences now play a role in life' (1968: 403). In other words, there is no shift in the cognitive basis on which these permutations rest. But this also means that there can be no qualitative shift in the impact of magic on the life of its adherents.

Magic can multiply the objects to which sacred meaning is attached, but it cannot revolutionize social life.

There are other reasons for the limited impact of magic. One is the sharp division between the carriers of magic and ordinary believers. Where charisma consists in the personal qualities of the magician, for example, the efficacy of magic is restricted to the deeds of a particular person and can only occasionally affect lay belief. A similar point has been made by the anthropologist Jack Goody in the context of describing the impact of literacy: 'The magic of the spell is dependent, at least in part, upon the virtual identity of the speaker and the spoken' (Goody, 1977: 150). This limitation, Goody suggests, is characteristic of belief in pre-literate societies in general.

Furthermore, Weber thinks that non-written norms can only be promoted by those who have proven their success in the coercion of spirits. Their status must, in other words, have been established in a direct way. But this means that once magicians have become differentiated as a separate stratum, they develop an interest in preserving their ritual or cultic monopolies. These monopolies can only be maintained by means of continually producing tangible effects and in this way meeting the needs of the mass of followers. Yet this, in turn, results in a widening gap between the interests of a group of specially qualified magicians and ordinary believers, with the latter only occasionally involved in the practice of magic. This occasional involvement is bound to be fragmentary and merely provide an external experience among the mass of believers who, in any case, lack control over the manipulation of the sacred.

With magic then, its bearers must directly accommodate the needs of believers, while believers demand tangible results. This combination means that no tension can arise between the sacred and an existing way of life. But without this tension, magic can only have a limited effect on everyday conduct. Weber therefore concludes that, at this stage, the combination of the interests of the priesthood and the needs of the laity rule out the rise of monotheism (1968: 419).

At this point it is clear why magic has a stabilizing or traditionalist effect on social life. This effect can now be summarized as follows. The inflexibility of the means employed with magic creates a static system of norms and ritual prescriptions which reinforces traditional conduct. Charisma, inasmuch it is tied to concrete embodiments and tangible successes, easily becomes routinized. Moreover, the unchallengeable position of the magicians constitutes an obstacle to cultural change because by attaching sacred norms to economic, political, and other functions, the magician sanctions their traditional role as well. Ancestor cults and caste taboos, for example, reinforce the existing social cohesion among – or barriers between – kin and status groups. And the fact that local deities may extend their jurisdiction over certain (non-religious) functions and impose their ritual orthodoxy upon them produces a stereotyping in these other spheres – especially the economic and political spheres. Again, an example is provided by the worship of a local god which may reinforce the authority and cohesion of a particular political association – if the god's function is to determine the political fate of this group.

Apart then from the cognitive basis of magic and the immediacy of the interests of magicians and believers, it is the interpenetration of the sphere of belief with the other spheres of life that creates an obstacle to cultural change. This interpenetration, in turn, is a result both of the fact that magic pursues a multiplicity of goals, as well as of the absence of the possibility of unifying the sacred. All in all, magic represents a 'complex of heterogeneous prescriptions and prohibitions derived from the most diverse motives and occasions' while at the same time, there is 'little differentiation between important and unimportant requirements' within this form of belief (1968: 437–8). Precisely because of its predominantly instrumental nature, magic is bound to produce an increasingly extensive web of irrational powers and obligations which lend stability to social life.

The importance of the role of magic only emerges, however, by way of contrast with the world-religions. As we have seen, the world-religions are characterized by a different type of rationality, and hence produce an altogether different cultural dynamic. Nevertheless, it should be remembered that, despite this clear-cut distinction, magic and its characteristic features and consequences can still be found throughout the reign of the world-religions. For Weber, magic in this case typically represents a more routinized 'popular culture', which exists side-by-side with the 'great tradition' or 'high culture', to use a different terminology. In this respect, magic has been the dominant world-view throughout most of human history.

Yet this should not blur Weber's theoretical distinction. In addition to the different forms of rationality exhibited in each, he lists three features of the world-religions which set them apart from magic: world-religions rely on the existence of a prophecy, a rational metaphysic and religious ethic, and a body of lay believers (1968: 427). How do these three features contribute to the increasing irrationalization of religious goals and to the creation of a rational path to salvation?

Weber thinks it is the hallmark of the founders of religious world-views that they offer a view of the 'world as a meaningful totality' (1968: 451). That is, the world as a whole must have a meaning outside of what is empirically given. It should be emphasized that this is a feature of all the great religions – again, Weber refers to them as *Kulturreligionen* (1980b: 367). This is notable because here we have what is, from the viewpoint of a sociology of culture, an answer to Weber's lack of a concept of 'society': the unity that this concept affords elsewhere is here taken on by the unity of 'culture' in the form of the *Kulturreligion*. With this unity, a tension is produced between the meaning that an all-encompassing world-view gives to life and one's everyday and practical conduct within the world. Irrespective of whether a prophecy postulates an impersonal divine order or a transcendent and omnipotent ruler – in both cases the religious goal or reality is seen as a divine revelation which goes beyond everyday life and has validity outside of it.

The prophets create this transcendent reality in the religious sphere either by leading an exemplary life which becomes the single path to achieving salvation, or they see themselves as tools of god and try to disseminate his ethical code on earth. The point again is that in both cases, the prophets endow the world with a new and all-embracing meaning. Unlike magicians, they are not merely transmitters of existing knowledge or manipulators of sacred forces. The religious meaning created by the prophecy provides a standard against which practical norms and social arrangements can be judged. This sacred framework is thus irrational in so far as it goes beyond empirical reality and is untainted by practical considerations. The increasing irrationalization that Weber speaks of signifies that religious orientations become more and more divorced from the other spheres of life and from the concerns of everyday life.

The second characteristic of the world-religions is their reliance on a rational metaphysic and religious ethic. These provide a new cognitive baseline against which the everyday perception of reality and norms can be set. The rational metaphysic of a religion establishes the relation between the sacred and the world. This can take the form of an impersonal and eternal order which accounts for the transience of the world or, alternatively, it will consist of an active and omnipotent deity which is responsible for the historical fate or the eventual salvation of believers. In either case, the world-religions share an all-embracing and unified world-view as a way of fundamentally and coherently (and in this sense 'rationally') understanding the world in terms of a sacred order.

Whereas a rational metaphysic provides the theoretical foundation for the relation between the sacred and the world, the rational religious ethic establishes the link between salvation and religious conduct. A state of salvation can be reached by fulfilling certain norms or by achieving a union with the divine through certain techniques. The means for achieving salvation are thus 'rational' then in the sense that they are worldly and are attainable by following methodical procedures. Again, it should be recalled, however, that from the point of view of *non-religious* everyday and practical pursuits, this goal must seem increasingly 'irrational'.

Finally, Weber thinks that a laity is an essential feature of the world-religions since there must be a group that can be identified as sharing the belief in this all-embracing and transcendent reality. Given the variety of religious beliefs, the great religions cannot be defined by reference to the objects of worship alone, but must include those who, apart from the representatives of the prophet's world-view (typically priestly strata), share an orientation to this cultural entity.

The effects of the world-religions on social life take many forms. Two characteristics, however, make for a radical departure from magic. First, a tension remains between empirical reality and the sacred order, whatever form it may take. This can have various consequences, ranging from the preservation of exclusive access to this order by a priestly stratum – to the direct efforts of believers to penetrate this design by their religious strivings. Yet in all cases, this tension must be accommodated, and this means that either the believer's orientation or the social order must undergo change. Secondly, unlike the practical aims of magic, the orientation of the followers of the world-religions is towards an other-worldly goal. Despite the fact that magic and the world-religions may be hard to separate in practice, this analytical distinction remains.

The conception of magic is central to Weber's writings in so far as it contains the foundations for his conception of cultural change and at the same time provides a contrast to the cultural dynamic initiated by the world-religions. At the stage of magic, the various spheres of life remain intertwined and there is little separation between the sphere of beliefs and the spheres of political and economic life. Moreover, the inner logic of world-views is constrained because there can be no systematic unification of a magical world-view. Instead of being subsumed within a view of the world as a 'meaningful totality', magical forces tend to proliferate and become more specialized (1968: 451).[3] Charisma at this stage cannot radically transform social life since it is tied to direct embodiments. Or, as it has been put elsewhere, 'charisma is *born* routinized, so to speak, and does not *decline* into such a condition' (Gellner, 1981: 14). Such an immediate routinization occurs because charismatic authority can only devolve upon followers in a direct fashion, such as through hereditary transmission, rather than being able to constitute an entity apart from its embodiments, as in Weber's view of the world-religions. Finally, routine social life is not transformed since the worldly goals of magic overlap with their everyday conduct and the most diffuse needs can be accommodated.

All this can be summed up by recalling the sense in which Weber thinks magic is 'rational': it is instrumental in that practical and worldly goals are pursued by direct means. Yet the 'rationality' of magic is ineffective because, unlike the instrumental rationality that characterizes modern social life, it is based on the false belief that persons or inanimate objects have effective supernatural powers. Hence Weber can say that 'the dominance of magic . . . is one of the most serious obstructions to the rationalization of economic life . . . magic involves a stereotyping of technology and economic relations' (1927: 361). For Weber, magic remains an 'enchanted garden' which, as we shall see, will only be systematically eliminated with the rise of Western rationalism. Nevertheless, even in his comments on magic, Weber already displays a characteristic concern with the origin and transformation of culture and its relation to the other spheres of social life.

Weber's conception of magic may not be very useful for the study of those cultural systems which he considers to be prior to and separate from the world-religions. Anthropologists have developed far more complex ideas about the nature of 'primitive' religions. It may be noted in passing, however, that although a variety of approaches to the function of 'primitive' religions has been developed, the problem of the ultimate origins of magic or of belief still troubles anthropologists. When Bloch recently suggests, for example, that 'our answer . . . to the question "where does ideology [or here, culture] come from?" is: it comes from the past', he is not offering a solution so much as restating a central theoretical problem in anthropology (1989: 133). The importance of Weber's conception of magic, however, does not lie in solving this debate, but rather in providing a contrast with his view of religion and science and in accounting for the continuing prevalence of traditionalism after the advent of the world-religions. The contrast with religion will become more pronounced in later chapters since the first world-religion which we will examine, Confucianism, still has a strong affinity to magic.

The Ethic of the Confucian Literati and the Enchanted Garden

In the *Religion of China*, Weber offers the strongest contrast to the 'Protestant Ethic' within his comparative schema. His conclusion is that the Confucian ' "mentality" ' with its 'autonomous laws' had 'effects strongly counteractive to capitalist development' (1951: 249) and to the ' "capitalist spirit" ' (1951: 247), despite the fact that political and economic conditions were often favourable to it (1951: 249).[4] But if Protestantism was a necessary condition for the rise of capitalism in the West, and Chinese religion was an insurmountable obstacle to its emergence, then we must ask what features of Chinese cultural life can account for this difference? The answer can be provided by examining five aspects of Chinese religion: the Confucian world-view, its ethic, the link with the sphere of politics, the effect on economic behaviour, and the nature of the heterodox religions. After examining each of these factors it will be possible to present a comparison with Protestantism.

For Weber, the world-view of a religion is the single most important factor by means of which culture shapes social life. A world-view is decisive for the religion's goal of salvation and its ethic. The world-view of Confucianism is based on an impersonal and eternal divine order, an order which preserves the harmony of spirits within the world. The impersonal nature of the sacred here can be attributed to the absence of a prophecy which radically separated the demands of a transcendent ruler from an imperfect world. In the West, a personal god came into being partly because it was thought that he was responsible for the changing political fortunes of his chosen people (1951: 26). China, on the other hand, remained peaceful throughout long periods of its history by comparison with other civilizations, and this stable social order could be attributed to the tranquil and harmonious order of the divine (1951: 26).

Within Weber's schema, the Confucian world-view, unlike those of the other world-religions, is anchored in magic. This means that the classification of Confucianism in terms of the dichotomy between magic and religion which has just been established is problematic. Is Confucianism a religion at all for Weber? We shall leave this problem aside for the moment and return to it later. Let us merely note here that the magical anchoring of the Confucian world-view can be attributed to the fact that there is no notion of a fate in the beyond, nor any metaphysical basis for an ethic of salvation. Instead, an impersonal and unchanging divine order remains external to the fate of the Confucian in so far as there is no orientation towards salvation in the beyond.

The objects of Confucian worship, Weber suggests, are rather the magical forces which protect the harmony between heaven and earth: these 'superhuman beings were stronger than man but were far below the impersonal supreme power of Heaven' (1951: 29). Assuming an intermediate position between the divine order and human beings, these superhuman beings must be considered magical. Whereas it is characteristic of the other world-religions that they have deities that are not embodied in worldly forms, and believers therefore strive for other-worldly ends, within a magical world-view there are directly manipulable spirits which are worshipped in order to achieve worldly ends. For the Confucian, influence over these spirits is all-important and tied to the preservation of harmony between heaven and earth. This harmony, in turn, will lead to material welfare and security.

The first point to note about the Confucian world-view then is that, like all forms of magical religiosity, it fosters traditionalism. Here as elsewhere, the manipulation of spirits must be achieved by proven methods. While a personal creator-god demands that the world be constantly reshaped according to his will, the belief in magical spirits leads to 'the inviolability of tradition as the proven magical means and ultimately all bequeathed forms of life conduct were unchangeable if the wrath of the spirits were to be avoided' (1951: 240).

This traditionalism also manifests itself in the ethic of literati, who were the bearers of a uniform Confucian culture. The ethical ideal of the literati was closely bound up with the underlying Confucian world-view, their aim being to achieve a harmony within themselves which inwardly reflected the external harmony of the divine heaven. Such an achievement of inward harmony would provide magical power over good and evil spirits and could only be gained by rigid self-control. The literati gained self-control by subjecting their emotions and their way of life to a strict code which was attached to their position. Their ideal was therefore one of self-perfection.

For Weber, the ideal of cultivation of the Confucian literati constituted a lay or status ethic rather than a religious ethic in the narrow sense. In so far as a religious ethic is one of the requirements of a world-religion, as we have seen above, here is another reason why Confucianism cannot unambiguously be classified as such. In this case, there is a status ethic of the leading stratum of political office-holders, whereas in the other world-religions, intellectuals typically promote a separate religious doctrine of salvation because they are in competition with other – and especially political – strata. The Confucian literati, however, possessed a monopoly of power, and again, since China was a stable patrimonial bureaucracy with relatively tranquil political relations, the ethic of this stratum could become firmly entrenched (1951: 151).

The literati were not priests, but rather a group whose status and cohesion were based on a certain way of life. Their prestige rested on writing, a skill which the masses associated with magic, and on knowledge of the Confucian literary texts. And although this training was a 'purely lay education', it was also 'partly of a ritualist and ceremonial character and partly of a traditionalist and ethical character' (1951: 126). Above all, the educational qualifications of this stratum were a requirement for holding administrative office. A position within the Chinese bureaucracy was solely dependent on the results achieved in state examinations.

The ethic of the literati thus consisted not only of a unified world-view, but was also shaped by a uniform education and a certain conception of the duties of office. Yet in spite of the centrality of this ethic, Weber did not think that it was an ethic that produced an inner reorientation, as did the Protestant ethic. The literati were bound to a rational and methodical life-style like the Puritans, yet the Confucian emphasis was on external conformity to a way of life.

Hence the Confucian ethic reinforced existing social relations, rather than changing them. The Confucian way of life was one of adaptation to a plurality of discrete norms and practices. The Confucian 'gentleman', as Weber calls him, did not systematically reorient his whole life towards a transcendent goal, as did the Puritan, but rather upheld the ideal of propriety which was expected of his stratum. Adjustment to the world, rather than mastery over it, characterized the ethic of the literati (1951: 248). Or, put differently, the ideal of self-perfection and cultivation of the Confucian 'gentleman' made him into an end-in-himself, rather than a tool of god's will (1951: 228).

In view of their monopolies of political office and literary training, the literati had every reason not to upset traditional social relations. If, for example, popular belief had been systematized into an ethic of salvation, it would have gone beyond mere traditional piety and thus potentially undermined their authority. The literati neglected the religious life of the masses and there remained a large gap between high and popular religion. Whereas the ethic of the literati sought honour after death, the religion of the masses had more mundane aims. Popular religion was concerned with material well-being and the aversion of evil spirits. To this end, the religiosity of the masses consisted of piety towards the patrimonial ruler and towards the literati who were endowed with charisma and with the ability to manipulate magical spirits, and of cult and ritual aimed at an unsystematic plurality of animist spirits and functional gods. From the viewpoint of the literati, popular religion was a good tool for domesticating the masses, while for the masses, the provision of material welfare, longevity, and good fortune met their everyday needs.

The ethic of the literati and the piety of the masses was therefore bound to result in traditionalism. Yet these, for Weber, were not the only obstacles to social change in this case. He also stressed the close links between Confucian religion and other aspects of Chinese social life. Religion and the other spheres of social life remained undifferentiated here, particularly since religious belief and political authority reinforced each other. In this respect, the Confucian world-view again played a central role. The fixed and harmonious order of the cosmos was thought to encompass the whole of social life, which meant that the believer had to fit into an unchangeable social order. Apart from this, the interplay between religion and social life can be found on three levels: the religious authority of the literati, the ancestor cult of the Chinese village, and patrimonial rulership at the level of the state.

The first level has already been touched on: the literati combined religious and political authority by being at once endowed with charismatic religious authority and at the same time office-holders within the state bureaucracy. This made for their interest in maintaining the stability of the official state religion.

At the local level, the ancestor cult was the predominant form of religiosity. It endowed relations within the kin group (Weber uses the term *Sippe*, sometimes translated as sib) with an aura of inviolability. Authority was derived in this case, according to Weber, from an original attribution of charismatic powers to the elders of the kin group. From this point, it developed into a more extensive system of inviolable rules governing relationships within the family. The result was that, on this level, 'family piety, resting on the belief in spirits, was by far the strongest influence on man's conduct' (1951: 236). For the reasons given above, the religion of the literati left this form of religion completely untouched.

An important consequence is that since the ancestor cult sanctioned the duty of piety within the family, there could never be a voluntary or impersonal association which could supplant this unit. The cohesion of the kin group was paramount in the Chinese village. And as in all forms of magic in Weber's view, worship of the ancestors did not go beyond the instrumental aim of material welfare. In practice then, since family piety was the highest virtue at this level, the individual's social relations, particularly legal and economic ones, were completely constrained by family ties.

The cohesion of the kin group could retain its traditional form at the village level because it lay beyond the reach of the bureaucracy of the patrimonial state. Confucianism was linked to the state by virtue of the charismatic powers which were ascribed to the patrimonial ruler. The Chinese monarch was thought to control the spiritual forces which ruled nature and society: 'He was the old rainmaker of magical religion translated into ethics. Since the ethically rationalized "Heaven" guarded eternal order, the charisma of the monarch depended on his virtues' (Weber, 1951: 31). If ill fortune occurred – in the form of a bad harvest, for example – the emperor's charisma was to blame, perhaps because of an act of ethical impropriety. The Chinese monarch was thus at once a religious figurehead and the guardian of the social order, responsible for the welfare and security of his subjects. Again, we can see the unity of the religious and political spheres, with the authority of the state legitimized by the religiosity of the monarch and the literati officials. Obedience towards rulers on the level of the state thus existed side by side with the ancestor cult and a plurality of spirits on the local level. And again, the fact that the roles of patrimonial ruler and supreme Confucian pontifex were united in the person of the Chinese monarch meant that the state's institutional aims could not be divorced from religion: 'Patrimonialism, being ethically oriented, always sought substantive justice rather than formal law' (1951: 102). That is, the patrimonial ruler was responsible for the welfare of his subjects according to the demands of ethical fairness while the subjects, in turn, adopted a pious attitude towards the state.

The three levels linking religion and social life – the village, the literati and the patrimonial ruler – only conflicted to a limited extent. It proved impossible to break down the cohesion of the kinship group at the local level, although this prevented the central government and its officials from extending their rule into the sphere of village life. Again, the literati had only limited control over the ritual propriety of the monarch, while the monarch needed the officials to domesticate the masses. This careful balance and the close link between religion and the social life helped to maintain traditional piety in the family, prevented social turmoil arising from popular belief, and preserved the status position of the literati officials and the legitimacy of the monarch's rule.

In the light of these characteristics of Confucian religion, Weber's view of why it constituted an obstacle to Western rationalism readily emerges. The entrenchment of religion within other spheres of social life and the purely traditionalist religious ethic in this case combined to prevent social change. The ethic of the literati on its own was bound to promote economic traditionalism. Since the Confucian gentlemanly ideal was one of self-perfection and attaining universality through a literary education, this elite had to reject the idea of professionalization. The Puritan conception of specialized work in a calling was alien to this way of life.

Nevertheless, it is important to note that the Confucian ethic did not reject the accumulation of wealth as such. On the contrary, Weber points out that 'in no other civilized country has material welfare ever been so exalted as the supreme good' (1951: 237). Moreover, in their role as state officials, the literati adopted a utilitarian cast of mind, carrying out their administrative duties along practical and rational lines – as was the manner of all bureaucratic strata according to Weber (1951: 136). The ethic of the literati must, however, be seen as traditionalist since there was no inner compulsion which could lead in the direction of a rational and methodical way of life. For the literati, material welfare had to remain a traditional concern.

In practice, the religious premium was placed on adjustment to the world, including its present economic conditions. Despite their sober and utilitarian attitude to their office, this attitude could not become the impersonal and business-like manner of the Puritan who 'dissolved everything into the pure business relation' (1951: 241). Instead, this stratum was bound in the first place to maintaining the harmony of the divine and to an ideal of self-perfection which precluded the mere means–ends calculation of utilitarian advantage – and only thereafter to his bureaucratic duties (Weber, 1968: 1050).

Economic traditionalism was also reinforced by kinship relations and by the state. The cohesion of the kin group prevented the formation of impersonal contractual relations that are required by the modern capitalist enterprise. The bureaucratic apparatus of the state, although organized along functional lines and imbued with a utilitarian spirit, was a patrimonial rather than a modern bureaucracy since it did 'not strictly separate between office and person, between administrative and legal procedure, and between formal law and substantive justice' (Schluchter, 1983: 40). The traditionalism of this bureaucracy is also in evidence in the rigid hierarchy of tax administrators, setting a limit to the degree of administrative centralization since each tier sought to maintain its sphere of authority.

It should be noted that although patrimonial bureaucracy in

China (as elsewhere) can be seen as a *political* hindrance to social change, it must at least equally be considered as a *cultural* factor in so far as it rested on the religious authority of the ruler. For Weber, obedience to patrimonial rule relied in this case on religious authority since the principle of 'filial piety' also extended to the ruler. In the end, however, Weber still claims that the most important hindrance to the emergence of capitalism was not patrimonialism but rather 'the lack of a particular mentality' (1951: 104).

Before we turn to this obstacle, we must briefly consider the two heterodox Chinese religions, Taoism and Buddhism. Although their religious aims were quite different, their impact on economic life was similar. These two religious movements became widespread, particularly in the form of popular religiosity, because they were tolerated by Confucianism. Taoism offered a world-view that was different from Confucianism in so far as it was based on the notion that spirits operate both at the level of the universe and in the smallest events in the natural world – or, as Weber put it, that 'macrocosm and microcosm [are] correspondent' (1951: 199–200). Such a belief led to a mystical path to salvation among the Taoist virtuosi, their goal being a union with the divine. The followers of Lao-Tzu rejected the scripturalism and the ideal of cultivation of the Confucian literati. Instead, they sought to minimize their mundane attachments through a withdrawal from the world and through a retreat into a state of mystical possession. Buddhist virtuosi shared this goal of a mystical union through a withdrawal from mundane affairs. Weber's view is that both heterodoxies, by prescribing a contemplative path to salvation, resulted in accommodation to existing worldly powers.

At the level of the religion of the masses, Taoism and Buddhism took the form of magic. Both had extensive theories of how spiritual forces were at work in the natural world. The belief in the pervasiveness of extraordinary powers throughout the universe and nature led Weber to call the Chinese religious world an enchanted 'magic garden' (1951: 200), a magical world-view which did not lead to an ethic of indifference to the world, as it did with the virtuosi, but led to the popular belief that magical events were responsible for the fate of human beings in this world, especially their material welfare. To influence these magical forces, only ritual and cult worship, in addition to obedience to the monarch who had control over these spirits, could be effective. Magical forces, however, represented a fixed and closely-knit order which was unchangeable so that, while Taoism played a large role in the everyday life of the masses, none the less because 'of its a-literate and irrational character [it] was even more traditionalist than Confucianism' (1951: 200).

How then does the *Religion of China* illuminate Weber's view of cultural change? An important contrast, which was mentioned in the introduction, can be made between the Protestant ethic and the ethic of the Confucian literati. At first sight, the two ethics seem to produce the same type of conduct: ' "Rationalism" – was embodied in the spirit of both ethics' (1951: 247). The conduct of both was methodical and utilitarian. Yet the result of the Confucian ethic was to support the traditional economic order, whereas the Protestant ethic revolutionized it. The difference is that the Protestant believer's rational and methodical life-style entailed an inner re-orientation. Proof of one's worth in a calling led eventually to the single-minded pursuit of economic success. Clearly, what is important here for Weber is the psychological pressure resulting from Protestant belief.

The reverse is true of the Confucian ethic. The gentlemanly way of life demanded by the Confucian ideal of self-perfection was imposed from the outside. The main goal of the literati was to conform to this life-style. Rather than being motivated by a central inward conviction, the psychological premium was on internalizing a plurality of norms and formal attitudes that had been established by tradition. Or, as it has been put elsewhere, 'there is no room for great individualism, nor for passion in this doctrine; what is called for instead is respect for social conventions' (Hall, 1986: 39).

The contrast between these two ethics is highlighted in Weber's distinction between 'rational mastery of the world' and 'rational adjustment to the world' (1951: 248). Both modes of conduct are rational in the sense of being systematic or methodical. But mastery over the world leads to the Protestant's reshaping of social life in accordance with god's will. This attitude is 'rational' in the additional sense that it tries to overcome worldly imperfections by achieving control over them. The adjustment of the Confucian literati, by contrast, means that conduct has to fit into pre-established forms: 'The watchful self-control of the Confucian was to maintain the dignity of external gesture and manner, to keep "face" ' (1951: 244). The aim in this case is to restrain the emotions by submitting them to external controls. This way of life, however, could only perpetuate existing social norms and institutions. The crucial difference between the Confucian and Protestant ethics then is the difference between norms imposed from the outside as against an inward compulsion.

Drawing out this difference allows us to clarify Weber's viewpoint as a whole, particularly the relation between the Protestant ethic thesis and the other studies of religion. For it shows that the emphasis in interpreting the Protestant ethic must be in understanding the psychological motivation of its adherents, rather than on the characteristics of dogma as such, or on the type of economic pursuit derived from it. The core of Weber's study of Protestantism (as we shall see more clearly later) is how this world-view issued in a certain way of life, the all-important middle term being the inward state of the believer. In the case of Confucianism, similarly, we find that a world-view produces a certain mentality which, in turn, shapes the way of life of a stratum. But in this case, the mentality leads to an accommodation of the way of life to external constraints – and this accounts for the impact of this religion on economic life. It is therefore impossible to relate cultural change to tangible or empirically verifiable phenomena in both cases. Instead, Weber's mode of explanation relies on the mentality of individuals and the way of life which derives from it.

Another aspect of the study of Confucianism that merits attention in the light of Weber's view of cultural change is the lack of differentiation between the religious sphere of life and the political and economic spheres. In Weber's other studies of religion, and especially in the *Protestant Ethic* (1930), it is precisely the distance of religious goals and practices from other goals which makes religion an effective agent of social change. For example, the fact that the Protestant believer's motivation is purely religious, and does not contain an admixture of political and economic aims, is precisely what makes it so single-minded and revolutionizing of conduct. Furthermore, there is a clear-cut separation in that the Protestant is to a large extent free from institutional ties, ties that would also impose obligations in the political and economic spheres.

The reverse is true in the case of Confucianism. Chinese religion is tied to political and economic factors at every level: its world-view is based on the harmony between the impersonal heaven and worldly events; the ethic of the literati is at once religious and bureaucratic; the magic of the masses posited the existence of spirits throughout the social world; the monarch exercised control over these spirits as well as providing social welfare; and finally, kinship relations were religiously sanctioned. All in all, the lack of differentiation played a major part in the traditionalism of the Confucian religion.

Another central aspect of cultural change in this case is the logic of the Confucian world-view. In this respect, as we shall see, Protestantism represents a 'last phase' according to Weber because the relationship between god and the world has been 'systematically unified' (1951: 226). Here, the tension between god and the world had arrived at a consistent conclusion with the transcendent and the worldly realms completely separated. Again, Confucianism represents the opposite extreme because it produced no such tension: 'The world was the best of all possible worlds; human nature was disposed to the ethically good' (1951: 227). The harmony of the divine order and the world, by contrast with the tension between a perfect divine realm and one of human imperfection, construed one as a reflection of the other. This direct correspondence, in turn, was the basis for the Confucian ideal of adjustment to a traditional social order.

Finally, the struggle between charisma and routinization took place in a way here that sets it apart from Weber's interpretations of the other world-religions. We may recall that Weber's theory typically interprets religious belief as following a pattern in which an extraordinary and transcendent divine power is transformed into a practical form of religiosity that is integrated within everyday life. In Confucianism, however, this struggle was muted because no transcendent ideal was established that could conflict with everyday reality. The ideal of Confucianism was concretely embodied within the life-style of the literati. This way of life then, with its rigidity and formalism, could not become more of a routine form of religiosity than it was already. By contrast with ancient Judaism (which, as we have seen, is Weber's model in this respect), Confucianism illustrates that if charisma is attached to a certain way of life, rather than to a transcendent ideal, then religion must play the role of reinforcing traditionalism.

Of all the studies of the world-religions, the *Religion of China* provides the clearest counterexample to Weber's Protestant ethic thesis. Yet the characteristics of cultural life which constitute an obstacle to social change are similar to those which can be found throughout Weber's sociology. In this case, they provide a strong contrast to Protestantism. The differentiation between spheres of life is noticeably absent, there is no development of the Confucianism world-view towards a tension between the divine and the world, and finally, the struggle between charisma and routinization fails to materialize because charisma is embodied in the routine way of life of the literati. It is this combination of elements, the mentality and the way of life of the literati, together with the 'enchanted garden' of popular religion, to which Weber attaches greatest weight in contrasting the cultural dynamic of Confucianism to that of the West.

At this stage, we can return to a question that was raised earlier: namely, in what sense can Confucianism be classified as a world-religion at all, given that it has several features that are unlike those of the other world-religions? Is Confucianism not closer to magic according to Weber's own distinction between magic and religion, despite the fact that he classifies it among the five major world-religions – perhaps only by virtue of its large number of adherents (1948: 267)? There are at least two points which speak strongly against the classification as a world-religion: the Confucian world-view is rooted in magic, and the priestly stratum is not a purely religious one.

One way around this problem has been suggested by Wolfgang Schluchter, who distinguishes between the world-rejecting or salvation religions on the one hand, and world-affirming or 'political' religions on the other (1989: 144). For him, Confucianism, Taoism, and possibly Islam belong to the latter category. But although the absence of a conception of salvation is important, the magical basis of the Confucian world-view, as we have seen, is even more so. Moreover, the conduct of the Confucian is an 'adjustment' to the world rather than, as in Schluchter's terminology, an 'affirmation' of it.

A more useful way of classifying Confucianism would be to say that although it is a world-religion, it is nevertheless unique in terms of the degree to which it incorporates elements from the stage of magic. It should be seen as a world-religion because here, as in the other world-religions, there is an elite stratum with a uniform ethic (which is at least partly of a religious nature) and which succeeds in achieving cultural hegemony. In the light of the mainly magical nature of its world-view and the political role of its leading stratum of carriers, however, the impact of Confucianism is closer to Weber's idea of magic than any of the other world-religions. As long as these aspects which distinguish Confucianism from the other world-religions are kept in mind, we may therefore follow Weber in treating it as one of the world-religions.

The cultural dynamic that Weber attributes to Chinese religion can now be summarized as follows: Chinese religion effectively blocks social change because of the strong affinity to magic. The differentiation between the various spheres of life is limited because no doctrine of salvation – and hence no purely religious aim – emerged in Confucianism. The inner logic of the Confucian world-view was impeded by the harmony between the divine order and the world. What did take place was a 'rational systematization' of magic (1920–1, vol. I: 458; and note above). Yet the limits of this systematization are those that we have already encountered in dealing with magic: only a proliferation and differentiation of magical symbols and spirits could occur within this enchanted garden. Similarly, the struggle between charisma and routinization was frozen since the charismatic authority of the literati and of the emperor were tied to a rigid way of life. Thus the everyday conduct of the masses and their routine beliefs also remained unchallenged.

Severe obstacles therefore prevented the kind of cultural dynamic that emerged in the West. This is true despite the fact that the ethic of the literati included a practical and calculating rationalism which carried over into their creation of an unrivalled bureaucratic apparatus. Nevertheless, their way of life reinforced traditionalism since it was imposed from the outside. We shall see, incidentally, that this account of the constraints imposed on the individual and an accommodation to the everyday world is echoed in Weber's account of modern bureaucratization.

Unlike his writings on magic, which are mostly ignored, Weber's study of Chinese religiosity continues to be the subject of debate. Of the criticisms that have been levelled against his analysis, two examples may be singled out here because they represent the sides from which his arguments are typically attacked. The first is that he overrates the importance of 'ideal' factors in his explanation, and the second that his description of this 'ideal' factor, the ethic of the literati, is off the mark.

Mark Elvin claims that an 'economic and ecological explanation of China's failure to create her own industrial capitalism' represents a more adequate analysis of Chinese development (1984: 379). Elvin does not, however, discount the ideal factor as such (1984: 380). Instead, he tries to argue against Weber's view of the role of ideas. For instance, he gives brief examples from Chinese economic thought which are intended to demonstrate that there were also ideas that facilitated rather than prevented the rise of capitalism. But these are only mentioned in passing (Elvin, 1984: 385), whereas the thrust of his refutation of Weber's thesis lies in pointing to the lack of clarity of his approach: 'If [Weber's] argument turns on the distinction between "adjustment" and "mastery", careful definitions are required and criteria for the discrimination in practice of one from another. Weber gives neither' (1984: 382).

Against this, and in the light of the account given here, it may be said that although Weber was not always as clear in giving definitions as he might have been, the central point that is criticized by Elvin has emerged forcefully in our discussion: namely, that his argument must be understood as an attempt to describe the different types of psychological impetus which result from the ethics of the world-religions. In these terms, as we have seen, Weber provides an elaborate distinction between an ethic which produces inward compulsion as against one in which formal demands are made from the outside.

A more forceful criticism that has been made is that Weber is mistaken in his description of the Confucian ethic. Thomas Metzger claims that instead of an adjustment to the world, there was in fact a tension in the ethic of the literati such that neo-Confucian thought 'had a clear-cut, transformative tendency towards transcendence of the status quo' (1977: 203). This criticism is more damaging to Weber's thesis since Metzger, too, wants to accord significance to the Confucian ethic in explaining social change in China. Yet he differs from Weber not only in his description of this ethic, but also in his assessment of its role: 'While Weber had to explain China's failure, we have to explain its success', success in the sense that he thinks the Confucian ethic in Weber's sense plays an essential part in explaining 'why . . . some societies [are] more effective than others in coping with their problems and rising to the challenges of modernization' (1977: 235). Perhaps a dialogue with this assessment of the Confucian ethic offers the best opportunity for establishing the merits and shortcomings of Weber's study of China.

Hinduism and the 'Spirit' of the Caste System

The circumstances which prevented the emergence of Western rationalism in India are very different from those which Weber analyzed in the case of China. In order to make this and other comparisons possible, we must focus on three aspects of his study of Indian religion: the presuppositions and content of the Hindu world-view, the nature of the religious ethic that results from it, and the effects of both world-view and ethic on social life.

The Hindu world-view is all-important for the cultural dynamic of this religion, and we may begin with a brief account of its main features. Hinduism is cosmocentric, based on the belief that the universe is a rational and well-ordered whole. The contrast here is with a theocentric view in which god is seen as the creator of the world who provides its order. Theocentrism demands that a rational order must be actively imposed on the world, whereas cosmo-centrism produces a search for insight into the rational and harmonious order which exists throughout the universe. This type of belief is based on the idea that all of reality, including the natural world, has a coherent and unalterable meaning. Even the gods have no special place within the Hindu world-view, since they themselves are but transient beings within an immutable cosmic order.

For Weber, this presupposition of a rational, eternal, and harmonious order is the keystone of Indian religion. It serves metaphysically to anchor the ethical and social conceptions of Hinduism, and in particular the belief in the transmigration of souls (*samsara*) and the doctrine of ethical compensation (*karma*). As he points out, these are the only two basic principles that are shared by all Hindus (1958: 118). Belief in the transmigration of souls means that the soul is seen as immortal and that an individual soul cannot cease to exist, but continues living in a series of reincarnations. The doctrine of ethical compensation stipulates that the merits or demerits of all ethical actions attach permanently to the soul of the doer and determine the soul's fate. All ethically significant acts are added up and the total determines the individual's fate upon rebirth.

These two core beliefs are closely tied to the presupposition of an eternal and cosmocentric order. The notion of a meaningful and unchanging essence which underlies all things metaphysically supports the belief that there is a never-ending cycle of rebirths of the soul and an all-embracing tally of good and bad deeds. Together, Weber thinks, these ideas constitute 'the most consistent theodicy ever produced by history' (1958: 121). Inasmuch as all religions have to account for suffering and evil in the world, the Hindu worldview offers a solution which is completely coherent: the individual must suffer in this world, but this merely represents a transitory phase and there will be full compensation for this suffering in future lives. The consistency rests, of course, on the presupposition of an eternal and rationally ordered cosmos which underlies the whole of reality.

The theodicy of ethical compensation, in turn, provides the justification for the most important creation of Hindu religion, the idea of the caste-order. Weber points out that the idea of a caste-order, a 'combination of caste legitimacy with *karma* doctrine', existed as a 'finished idea' even before it became widespread. It was developed purely as the result of Brahmanic thought, rather than being 'the product of any economic "conditions" ' (1958: 131). With the idea of a caste order, the Brahmans, a priestly stratum, sought to impose the doctrine of ethical compensation onto a heterogeneous population. They developed the idea that the ethical merit of life determines one's fate in the next world into the doctrine that ethical behaviour consists of different rituals and duties which are appropriate to different stations in life. According to the doctrine of *dharma*, ethical obligations are tailored to the particular occupation of the believer. But the occupation of the believer had been determined by birth, which was, in turn, a consequence of previous ethical merits. In this way, the caste system could attach social significance to religious behaviour and conversely attach religious significance to social distinctions.

How did this world-view and its consequences come to dominate

Indian society? The origins of the caste system lie, in Weber's view, in the Brahmanic elaboration of this order on the level of ideas. A typical pattern whereby the caste system initially spread was that the higher-ranking strata of a non-Hindu group neighbouring on a Hindu area would start to imitate the Brahmans which inhabited the Hindu area. Eventually, they would claim a status equal to the Brahmans and start enforcing ritual duties among the various occupational strata. But why would any occupational stratum submit to such burdensome ethical and ritual obligations? Weber's answer is that religious legitimation was important for any stratum, even the lowest-ranking ones, because it defined their position relative to other strata and hence secured a monopoly in certain occupations in which only caste members could engage. This positioning also secured the social status of one group *vis-à-vis* other strata.

As for the demands established by the caste system, they were to obey the ritual and ethical prescriptions attached to a particular caste. The highest religious premium was placed on fulfilment of caste obligations. Ethical injunctions were combined here with the social duty imposed by the caste system to stay within the rank-order of the various occupations, an order which had been permanently fixed. Hence Weber describes the religious ethic established by the caste system as 'organic social ethics', since the ethical duties of believers were embedded within an immutable order of hierarchical social relations (1948: 359).

Not only did the Hindu world-view lead to this distinctive ethic, but it also underpinned the social mechanisms whereby the different occupational strata were kept apart. Internally, in terms of the awareness of members, the religious criteria which separated castes were those of status privilege and of the status of their economic activity. Externally, castes were separated through regulations about sharing food (commensalism) and marriage (connubium). In this way, religion governed not only the ascription of social and economic prestige, but also social interaction. Hence Weber's description of caste as a 'closed status group': 'status group' because it is based on a ranking of social honour, and 'closed' because of the external barriers which surround it (1958: 39–40).

It can be seen then that the Hindu world-view encompassed all aspects of religious life, from its abstract metaphysical presuppositions to a plurality of concrete ritual and social prescriptions. Against this background, it becomes clear why Weber regarded the Hindu world-view as the cornerstone of this religion. A world-view, in his analyses of cultural change, allows him to derive an ethic and a corresponding way of life. In the case of Hinduism, however, there was no single or universal ethic. The Hindu world-view dictated that every caste had its own ethical and ritual obligations. This also meant that different ethical prescriptions could be valid in different spheres of life, such as those of political or economic activity. The importance of the relativity of these ethical demands to particular castes and to particular spheres of life was that no tension could arise between a universal ideal of conduct and the way of life of believers. Instead, ethical ideals were integrated into a rigidly stereotyped system of social relations.

As elsewhere, the most important religious ethic within Hinduism was that of the religious elite. The ethic of the Brahmans shaped the nature of Hindu religiosity as a whole since, in Weber's terminology, Hinduism was an 'exemplary' rather than an 'ethical' prophecy (1968: 447–8). Unlike Occidental religion, Hinduism did not create universal ethical norms, but rather demanded that believers should follow the exemplary path to salvation of the Brahmans.

But although the mass of believers were enjoined to observe Brahmanic ritual propriety, there was at the same time a large gulf between the Brahmanic religious ideal and that of non-Brahmanic believers: the Brahmans strove for complete release from the cycle of eternal rebirth, rather than merely seeking to optimize their chances for a better rebirth. Their ultimate goal was a union with the divine, a state of mystical enlightenment, and an escape from the cycle of eternal rebirth altogether. This entailed going beyond the merely worldly obligations of fulfilling ritual duties and constitutes, in Weber's classification, an attitude of world-rejection.[5]

Salvation for the Brahman could be attained only through world-rejection, achieving a state of mystical knowledge in which union with the divine caused the release from earthly existence. For Weber, the difference between a mystical goal of illumination as against carrying out of religious duties within the world merely for the sake of a better rebirth is all-important. It is a difference which could only be neutralized against the background of the Hindu organic social ethic, which justified the coexistence of different religious aims among different social strata through the conception of an organic social hierarchy (1958: 172).

How did a separate Brahmanic ethic come about? First, because the Brahmans developed from a guild of magicians into a caste of priests. This transformation took place with the consolidation of Brahmanic power. The position and prestige of the Brahmans increasingly rested on their mystical knowledge rather than on magic. The development towards a unified world-view and ethic accords with Weber's idea that all intellectual strata whose prestige rests on knowledge are predisposed to seek an overall meaning of the world, in this case one which is removed from all political and economic engagement.

Most important for Weber are, of course, the consequences of the Brahmanic ethic for the way of life of this stratum. The Brahmanic quest for salvation resulted in flight from the world and in a devaluation of worldliness in favour of a transcendent mystical realm. Considering the Brahman's goal of union with the divine, a preoccupation with worldly matters could only distract him. Weber puts a lot of emphasis on this contrast between the search for an extraordinary experience or a state of knowledge as against everyday or practical concerns because while he thinks that the Brahmans developed a very sophisticated and ascetic technique for attaining their religious goal, the fact that this technique was oriented towards withdrawing from the world – instead of a rational mastery over it – negated the influence of asceticism on practical behaviour.

In short, the effect of the Brahmanic ethic was an indifference to practical and worldly affairs. The Brahmans remained an apolitical stratum. The ultimate aim of the man of wisdom was to act 'as if he acted not' when fulfilling his religious duties (1958: 184). He would seek to minimize the significance of worldly attachments in order to concentrate solely on his mystical goal. The Brahman's striving is rational then, in the sense that he is able to give a coherent meaning to the world through his idea of a union with the divine; yet the means to achieve this goal are irrational in so far as they lead him to seek an incommunicable and fleeting experience, rather than organizing everyday conduct in a methodical way.

This indifference to everyday concerns meant that this stratum could not reshape the social world. They did, however, occupy a central position in Indian social life on the basis of their superior religious knowledge. Only the Brahmans could interpret holy texts and determine how ritual and ethical duties should be carried out. Their path to salvation set them apart from the mass of believers. From the viewpoint of the hierarchy of social status then, the Brahmans ranked highest because of their religious qualifactions.

Being located at the apex of the social hierarchy, the Brahmanic caste provided a reference point by which the religious and social standing of the other strata was measured. The Brahmans determined the caste ranking of the other strata and also their religious and social obligations. This also explains why they failed to undertake a rational systematization of popular belief. As long as they enjoyed a monopoly of religious authority, their interest as a stratum did not lie in developing Hindu belief into a uniform and accessible doctrine but rather in maintaining the traditional multitude of religious beliefs and ritual practices.

As a result, Weber thinks that the mass of Hindu believers remained tied to a belief in magic. The majority of Hindus knew little of the details of Hindu doctrine, yet they worshipped the Brahmans as bearers of magical powers. The Brahmans were essential mediators between the average Hindu believers and their religious goal. Only the Brahmans could assign ritual duties to each caste and oversee ritual propriety. And again, it was ritual rather than the adherence to doctrine which constituted the religiosity of the mass of Hindu believers. Weber suggests that, in effect, the religious belief of the masses amounted to little more than the worship of the magical powers of the Brahmans, since Hinduism as a world-view was unable to supplant the popular hold of magic.

The combined effect of magic and subordination to the religious elite was to bind the mass of believers more closely to their traditional way of life. A web of magical powers served to sanction existing social arrangements. Moreover, the worship of the Brahmans by the mass of believers could only ensure their continued submission to an immutable system of caste regulations. As a religion of the masses then, Hinduism strengthened existing social ties by endowing them with a fixed religious significance.

Apart from the masses, Weber also briefly mentions the effect of Hinduism on what he calls the 'aliterary middle classes' (1958: 335). Their religiosity was coloured by reliance on a living saviour, the typical attitude of a stratum predisposed to a conception of personal salvation. In this case, their living saviours were 'gurus', teachers of the Vedas and administrators of personal pastoral care. The gurus were believed to be redeemers with the power to dispense grace to the believer. Weber calls this 'a form of emotional redemption religion' (1958: 309), a type of religiosity that produces occasional states of intense emotion, but does not lead to rational and methodical conduct.

Weber's conclusion about Hinduism is that it could not transform social life. Although the Brahmans methodically strove for salvation, their efforts were directed towards being a vessel – rather than a tool – of the divine. The traditional conduct of the mass of believers was reinforced by a web of magic and ritual, obligations imposed on them by the Brahmans. The emotional religiosity of the middle class likewise had little value for an active reshaping of the world. In sum, the effect of religion alone was a strong obstacle to social change.

Nevertheless, Weber argues that an important reason for the socially conservative force of the caste system lay elsewhere: namely, in the link between caste and a central institution within

Indian social life – the kinship system. The origins of this system whereby relations between family members are endowed with religious significance lies, for Weber, in the attachment of extraordinary or magical qualities to members of the kinship group, rather than to individuals. He calls this the 'principle of clan charisma' (1958: 49) since it endows kinship organization both within and between clans with different degrees of status and authority. The attachment of charisma to kinship organization reinforced existing social relations by preventing clan members from entering into social relations as unfettered individuals. Inasmuch as legal and economic ties too were governed by this system, they were at the same time fixed by tradition.

Weber's argument then, is that the combination of caste and clan principles produced an unbreakable traditionalism: 'It is clear that the magical charisma of the clans contributed greatly to the establishment of the firm structure of caste estrangement, actually containing it *in nuce*. On the other hand, the caste order served greatly to stabilize the sib' (1958: 54). Caste and the organization of kinship overlapped in the sense that both systems determined the individual's social relations on the basis of birth, into a family as well as into an occupational group. Heredity as the principle which determined social status was thus given a twofold legitimation. But this meant that the combined effect of these systems in underpinning traditionalism possessed twofold strength.

Overall, the effect of Hinduism, including its relation to the kinship system, was to reinforce traditionalism in Indian social life, particularly the political and economic spheres. As regards politics, the Brahmans as a caste did not develop a hierarchical organization and hence could not wield political power as a group and had difficulty holding their own against secular rulers. Forced to acknowledge kingly power, they could be taken advantage of to further the political ends of the Indian rulers. Not only were they organized ineffectively, but their striving for mystical salvation also led them away from practical involvement in everyday political matters.

The economic sphere was also beset by traditional religious barriers. Again, the Brahmans were prevented from methodical economic pursuits by their search for a mystical experience of the divine. The ideal was that of the world-rejecting mendicant monk. More generally, the caste system prevented the development of free wage labour and created barriers that economically isolated caste groups from each other: 'This situation is as if none but different guest peoples, like the Jews, ritually exclusive toward one another and toward third parties, were to follow their trade in one economic area' (Weber, 1958: 112). Equally important in reinforcing economic traditionalism was the widespread belief in magic. Weber comments that the 'most highly anti-rational world of universal magic . . . affected everyday economics' (1958: 336). Here as elsewhere, the idea that material benefits could be gained with the aid of magical forces constituted a severe obstacle to economic change.

Weber reaches similar conclusions about the two heterodox religions in India, Jainism and Buddhism, despite their different world-views. For Weber, there are in fact striking similarities between Jainism and Protestantism. An ethic of asceticism, for example, was widespread among the laity. In addition, unlike Hindus, the Jains rejected the authority of the Brahmans and eschewed ritualism and magical practices. As for the Jain ethic, it resembled the ethic of Protestantism in that it produced an attitude that actively encouraged commercial activity (1958: 200). As a result, the Jains as a sect became known as successful traders in India. Nevertheless, Jainism remained a small sect and had to integrate itself into the wider organic social order dictated by Hinduism.

Buddhism similarly remained within the confines of the existing Hindu dominated social order. While remaining within the Hindu cosmology, a different path to salvation was derived from the Buddhist world-view: since the soul was bound to a wheel of permanent rebirth, the only way to achieve salvation was to eliminate the will altogether, thereby extinguishing the illusory thirst for life. Among Buddhist monks, this was to be achieved through methodical contemplation. For the layman, Buddhism offered a lesser path to salvation, in this way accommodating the religious needs of the masses. During the period in which Buddhism was pre-eminent, one indication of its popularization was the fact that the king became the bearer of spiritual power and was seen as a benign provider. Buddhism could be used then as a tool for the patrimonial domestication of the masses. Moreover, in competing with Hinduism, Buddhism embraced a multitude of magical elements to cater to the needs of believers.

Weber concludes that although Buddhism became a major world-religion outside of India, its effect within India itself was limited. Its leading stratum was devoted to contemplation and religious demands upon the laity were left unsystematized. Furthermore, as has been pointed out elsewhere, because of its exclusive focus on salvation and inability to organize social life, Buddhism was, in the end, unable to challenge the dominance of Hinduism (Hall, 1986: 70). Hinduism, on the other hand, was able to integrate Buddhism because instead of trying to eliminate heterodoxy, it remained open to alternative paths to gaining salvation (Weber, 1958: 329; see also Hall, 1986: 72).

To highlight the effect of Indian religion on social life, a brief contrast with Weber's analyses of Occidental religions may be useful. One way of making this comparison is by looking at the struggle between charisma and routinization. In Judaism and Protestantism, the notion of a completely transcendent and all-powerful deity imposed unyielding demands on believers, transforming their inner lives and requiring an active reshaping of the world. The Hindu conception of the sacred, by contrast, imposed an absolute order on social relations and in this way reinforced a stable social order and a routine way of life. Rather than producing a tension with the social world, the notion of the sacred conferred legitimacy upon it. Only the Brahmans could transcend this fixed social order by escaping it altogether. Weber's conclusion in this regard is echoed in Dumont's study of Indian religion. The Hindu conception of the sacred demanded 'that the society must submit and entirely conform to the absolute order, that consequently the temporal, and hence the human, will be subordinate, and that, while there is no room here for the individual, whoever wants to become one may leave society proper' (Dumont, 1970: 286).

A second comparison that can be made between Occidental and Indian religion is that, unlike the Judaeo-Christian world-view, the path of Hindu dogma along an 'inner logic' was not subject to tension. Once the idea of caste had been developed in Brahmanic thought, it was, for Weber, the 'most consistent theodicy ever produced by history' (1958: 121). The Hindu version of the transcendent was not only consistent with the existing worldly order, but also sanctioned its immutability. It allowed for a plurality of gods and spirits which could remain unsystematized and coexist harmoniously with the world as it is against the background of an eternal order. So that whereas the Occidental religions produced a tension with the world, Hinduism imposed a sacred order upon it.

A third comparison presents itself in relation to the different spheres of life. In Judaism and even more consistently in Protestantism, the conception of the sacred was completely separate from the world. With this differentiation between the spheres of life, political and economic relations could develop unhampered by religious obstacles. The Indian caste system, on the other hand, lacked such differentiation. The caste system endowed economic and political distinctions with religious significance and the overlap between spheres of life meant that Hindu social relations were enmeshed within a tightly woven fabric.

Again, whereas Judaism and Protestantism held out the promise of salvation and produced a religious ethic for the mass of believers, Hinduism only offered salvation for the few. The gap between the Brahmans and the masses was unbridgeable. Yet even for the Brahman, striving for salvation did not result in a methodical way of life since he was a 'vessel', rather than a 'tool' of god. For Weber, the only attitude consistent with being a vessel of the divine is to reject involvement in worldly affairs since any such involvement poses a threat to inner peace. The Brahmanic ethic could therefore only result in indifference to the world. Apart from this, Indian religion was unable to revolutionize the social order because the magic of the masses was left intact.

In the end, the *Religion of India* (1958) leads Weber to the same conclusion as his other studies of the non-Western religions: namely, that ideas were a necessary (though not sufficient) factor in preventing social change. Put differently, the sphere of culture played a decisive role in social life. Or, in Weber's words, 'the core of the obstruction was . . . embedded in the "spirit" of the whole system' (1958: 112). This 'spirit' of the caste system, consisting of the link between *karma* and caste, was the product of Brahmanical thought – a point that Weber deliberately makes in such a way as to suggest that this origin cannot be 'reduced' to material conditions (1958: 131). The priestly systematization of the Hindu world-view established 'natural social and ritual orders' (1958: 153) and thus inextricably linked religious thought with social life. Similarly, the Brahmanic attitude of world-flight, which decisively shaped the conduct of this stratum, was created at the level of ideas whereby their 'personal holy status' and their 'sacred knowledge' were given a fixed social basis (1958: 152).

It should also be pointed out that we can get a clearer picture of Weber's account of the conduct of the Brahmans and of Buddhist monks by referring to his conception of the individual.[6] Both religious ideals constitute a flight from the world in so far as their aim is to seek a state of contemplation or mystical enlightenment. The goal of the virtuosi is 'possession' of the divine or of being its 'vessel'. In other words, the beliefs and ethic of this stratum led to turning inward and away from the world, instead of an active mastery over it.

From the viewpoint of his comparative approach then, Weber succeeds in showing that the emergence of Western rationalism was prevented in this case by the lack of differentiation between the religious and economic spheres of life and the world-rejecting ethic of its leading stratum. Not only were economic relations between the various castes ruled out, but several barriers reinforced traditional economic conduct.

The present-day status of Weber's study of India is as much in dispute as his other studies of the world-religions, and again a great deal of his analysis has been superseded by more detailed studies of Indian religion. A recent evaluation of his study, however, suggests that his conclusions are still reliable, at least with regard to his central concerns; namely, the effects of Brahmanism, Buddhism, and of the religion of the masses on economic life. The main points of this assessment are worth quoting at length. In terms of the Brahmans, 'Weber's remarks . . . were extremely perceptive. Even if today they would have to be supplemented, his conclusions as to the social implications of the most orthodox part of Hinduism remain valid' (Gellner, 1982: 537). With regard to Buddhism, 'as with Brahmanism, Weber is not a good guide to the practice of Buddhists. Nevertheless he has some very perceptive remarks to make about the doctrine which are surely correct in their assessment of its effect on the action of its adherents' (Gellner, 1982: 538). And finally, concerning the religiosity of the masses: ' "This most highly anti-rational world of universal magic also affected everyday economics. There is no way from it to rational, inner-worldly life conduct." From the viewpoint of Weber's interests, these judgements are fair' (Gellner, 1982: 540). Apart from this, the *Religion of India* adds an important dimension to his conception of cultural change: ideas play a decisive role in social life not only in so far as they determine the conduct of its leading strata, but also, as Weber argues, because of the way in which a whole way of life is pervaded by a certain 'spirit'.

The Islamic 'Warrior' Religion

Unlike his studies of the other world-religions, Weber devotes only a few scattered comments to Islam. His intention was to present an overview of all the world-religions, but he did not live to complete this task. Nevertheless, it is important to piece together his remarks about Islam because it is possible that he departs here from his typical mode of analysis.

As in the other studies of the world-religions, the Islamic world-view plays a crucial role, particularly its content and initial reception among the leading strata of carriers. The prophet Muhammad and the Qur'an created a new religious orientation which included a comprehensive system of theological and ethical precepts. Initially, this new doctrine was addressed to urban strata (1968: 473–4), strata which, in Weber's view, are usually predisposed towards doctrines of ethical salvation (1968: 482–3). Soon, however, a warring feudal aristocracy became the main carrier of Islam. Turner, in his reconstruction of Weber's view of Islam, suggests that 'Weber seemed to imply that the prophet more and more clearly realized that his position depended on the successful mobilization of the warriors' (1974: 34). This shift in the stratum to which the new doctrine was addressed meant that Islam became a 'warrior religion' (Weber, 1968: 624, 626). This way of identifying Islam highlights that Allah's role is to determine the fate of believers in *this* world, rather than promising salvation in the next: 'The ruling conception was that predestination determined, not the fate of the individual in the world beyond, but rather the uncommon events in this world, and above all such questions as whether or not the warrior for the faith would fall in battle' (1968: 574). It is not surprising then that the religious premiums of this religion were tailored to the needs of a warring feudal aristocracy which became its main carrier: 'Military booty is important in the ordinances, in the promises, and above all in the expectations characterizing particularly the most ancient period of the [Islamic] religion' (1968: 624).

Such a conception of the individual's relation to the divine is very different from that of the other world-religions. Unlike Hinduism, Buddhism and Judaeo-Christianity, Islam offers no conception of individual salvation in the beyond. It is also different from Confucianism, despite the fact that both religions share the lack of a radical devaluation of this world. The life-style of the Confucian literati was governed by an extensive system of ethical regulations, whereas in the case of Islam Weber speaks of the 'great simplicity of religious requirements and the even greater simplicity of the modest ethical requirements' (1968: 626). These differences from the other world-religions serve to underline the unique and central feature of Islam: namely, that 'an essentially political character marked all the chief ordinances of Islam' (1968: 625).

It is this political character which constitutes the uniqueness of Islam.[7] No other world-religion displays such close links between religion and politics. That is not to say, of course, that the connections between religion and politics in the other world-religions are unimportant. We have already seen, for example, that the Confucian elite was able to combine religious and political power. What is distinctive about Islam is that politics is decisive for religious life at two levels where it does not play a decisive role in the other world-religions: at the level of the world-view and in terms of the impact of Islam on social life.

How is the Islamic world-view linked with the political sphere? It has already been pointed out that the divine is seen as responsible for the warrior's military fate in this world, as opposed to promising salvation in the beyond. Hence, Weber thinks, the 'ideal personality type in the religion of Islam was not the scholarly scribe (*Literat*), but the warrior' (1968: 626). This ideal gives rise to an economic ethic that contrasts strongly with the Protestant ethic. It is an ethic that gives positive significance to attaining wealth by political or military means and displaying this wealth as a sign of status and worldly blessing (1968: 624). In the light of this emphasis on wealth, status and luxury, Weber thinks that this economic ethic is 'purely feudal' (1968: 624). It is 'diametrically opposed to' the Protestant devaluation of worldly wealth and luxury in favour of religious salvation in the beyond (1968: 624).

Weber admits that periodically, an asceticism in the sense of military discipline was prevalent among Islamic warriors (1968: 626–7). Yet Islamic asceticism only imposed 'largely external and ritual demands' (1968: 575). Nowhere in Islam does Weber find attempts to extend methodical control over life of the type that could be conducive to reshaping the world. As was briefly indicated above, however, not only is the development of this ethic attributable to the content of the Islamic world-view, but it also fits in with the predispositions that Weber ascribes to warrior strata in general: 'The life-pattern of a warrior has very little affinity . . . with the systematic ethical demands of a transcendental god. Concepts like sin, salvation, and religious humility have not only seemed remote from all ruling strata, particularly the warrior nobles, but have indeed appeared reprehensible to its sense of honour' (1968: 472). This absence of an ethic that was favourable to worldly economic activity also applies to Sufism. Sufism was, in Weber's view, directed towards a 'mystical quest for salvation' – a religious orientation that entails a passive state of inwardness, rather than one of actively reshaping the world (1968: 555).[8]

In terms of popular religion, Islam was even further removed from an ethic of actively reshaping the world. First, because the religion of the masses had to rely on intermediaries to interpret the relation between the individual and the divine. As Turner points out, no 'centralized ecclesiastical machinery exists in Islam' (1974: 61). Thus, within popular religion, the service of personal intermediaries was essential for the interpretation of Islamic dogma and the supervision of ritual. The resulting division between religious personnel and the masses of the faithful weakened the impact of religion since it widened the gap between the religious requirements of the bookish virtuosi and a popular form of religion which fit in with everyday life.

Weber also points out that 'Islam and Catholicism were compelled to accept local, functional, and occupational gods as saints, the veneration of which constituted the real religion of the masses in everyday life' (1968: 488). This development took place partly in response to the difficulty of adapting the warrior's belief that god controlled his fate to the everyday needs of the mass of believers (1968: 575). An acceptance of local and concrete embodiments of the sacred, Weber notes, also 'became influential in Islam's missionary enterprise because of its great simplicity' (1968: 626). Here, as elsewhere, the religion of the masses was not rid of its popular magical elements (1968: 575). At the level of popular religion then, Islam created a 'thoroughly traditionalistic ethic of everyday life' (1968: 626).

Weber's conclusion about Islam is that the ethic of the virtuosi failed to produce an ethic of methodical conduct and that the religion of the masses remained tied to traditionalism. In the light of this assessment, Weber might be expected to say that the reason why Western rationalism did not emerge under Islam was that, by contrast with Protestantism, it did not create a suitable world-view and way of life to encourage this development. Curiously, Weber's argument about the obstruction to this development takes a different form.

We have already seen that Weber's view of Islam is unique among his studies of the world-religions in so far as there is a close link between the Islamic world-view and the political sphere. Yet Weber's explanation of *how* this impact obstructed social change is different in kind from those which he gives in his other analyses of the world-religions. In the case of Confucianism, we have seen that a particular 'mentality' was responsible for the failure of this development. In India, the 'spirit' of the caste system as a whole constituted the main religious obstacle. And in the case of Protestantism, as we shall see later, its 'ethic' is responsible for transforming social life. The case of Islam seems to be different: 'Industrialization was not impeded by Islam as the religion of individuals . . . but by the religiously determined structure of the Islamic *states*, their officialdom and their jurisprudence' (1968: 1095, emphasis in original). If this statement can be taken as the key to Weber's view of the relation between Islam and social change, then it marks a fundamental departure from his overall approach. Notably, this comment does not seem to spring from the fact that he ignored the impact of the Islamic 'warrior ethic' on economic life: many of his remarks contrast the individual Muslim's attitude to the world with that of the Protestant ethic. Nevertheless, in this case Weber's explanation emphasizes the state and he seems to regard the political realm as *the* major obstacle to social change. Turner brings this out in a different way when he says that 'Weber's outline of the Islamic ethic of world-accommodation was quite secondary to his concern for social structures' (1974: 75).[9]

In what sense does the 'religiously determined structure of the Islamic *states*' (Weber, 1968: 1095) constitute an obstacle to social change? First, because the state under Islam is an example of Weber's ideal type of the patrimonial state. Although Islam also contained feudal elements, Turner points out that 'the employment of slaves and mercenaries in the army, the promotion of favourites to the vizierate and other court positions, the absence of a cohesive landowning aristocracy, independent legal system and autonomous cities were . . . regarded as primarily patrimonial' (1974: 81). But the patrimonial state, in Weber's view, 'lacks the political and procedural *predictability*' which is 'indispensable to capitalist development' (1968: 1095, emphasis in the original). The arbitrariness of patrimonial rule was nowhere more in evidence than in the all-encompassing nature of Islamic law: 'In Islam there was, at least in theory, not a single sphere of life in which secular law could have developed independently of the claims of sacred norms' (1968: 818). The close links between Islamic religion and the state are thus all-important for social relations.

Assuming that Weber's key pronouncement on the relation between Islam and social change can be taken at face value, the most important obstacle here is how religion was tied to politics – rather than the religious world-view and its ethic. Or, put differently, not cultural but political change – or, in this case, stability – was the primary obstacle.

With this consideration in mind, we can now try to summarize Weber's ideas about Islam in the light of his analysis of cultural change. Islam is different from Weber's studies of the other world-religions because the spheres of religion and politics are interconnected at a level which does not tally with his other studies. In each of Weber's other analyses of the world-religions, despite the fact that the religious and political spheres often overlap, he still thinks that it is appropriate to speak of a religious world-view and its impact of religion on social life, an impact that can be singled out from among the other spheres of life. This seems not to be the case with Islam. The Islamic world-view, with its conception of the worldly fate of the warrior, displays a political orientation even at the level of the relation between the individual and the sacred. This political world-view, in turn, decisively shaped the nature of Islamic religiosity as a whole. Most important in this respect were the

Islamic ethic and particularly the relation between Islam and the state.

Despite his conclusions about Islam, the various elements of Weber's conception of cultural change can nevertheless also be found here: the routinization of charismatic authority took place in a way that is by now familiar. A consolidation of priestly power took place, as did the accommodation of the religious doctrine to the predispositions of the warriors and the masses. An inner development of the world-view is evident inasmuch as the notion of Allah's responsibility for the warrior's fate changed in accordance with political events: It 'manifested its power especially during the wars of the faith and the wars of the Mahdi' but 'tended to lose its importance whenever Islam became more civilianized' (1968: 574). In other words, the distinctive features of this world-view came into the foreground whenever it could be construed as being in accordance with reality, but receded when this accordance with reality was less recognizable.

Weber's ideas about Islam and the question of whether his remark about the relation between Islam and the state should be regarded as definitive are inconclusive. Perhaps the elaboration of his remarks on this topic would have forced him to reconsider the basis of his comparative account of the rise of the West. A different possibility is that he would have brought his ideas about Islam into line with his other writings. Whatever the case may be, it can be noted in passing that Weber's emphasis on political institutions has subsequently received support (Turner, 1974; Gellner, 1981), whereas the 'cultural' side of his argument, and especially the notion of a warrior ethic, has been subject to the criticism that it presents too simplistic a view of the carriers of Islamic religion (see the contributions of Levtzion and Lapidus in Schluchter, 1987).

Weber's emphasis on the link between religion and the state in his explanation of why Islam impeded social change might have changed the whole nature of his comparative argument. In his other studies, Weber examines the impact of religion as an independent variable while in the other spheres of social life (politics and economics) he stresses the similarity of the different civilizations' levels of development. But in the light of his analysis of Islam, he would have had to analyze the connection between religion and the state in his other studies, too, in order to remain within this comparative framework. Islam therefore raises some important problems concerning Weber's overall approach, although they cannot be resolved by reference to his few remarks on this topic alone.

Notes

1. Weber's 'intellectualist' standpoint is clearly evident here. For more recent discussions of the 'rationality' of science, see Elkana (1981: 27–42) and Gellner (1988: esp. ch. 3).
2. It may be useful to recall here the importance that is being attached to charisma in Weber's thought. As Merquior puts it, 'the concept of charisma . . . is the core of [Weber's] world-view and appraisal of the historical process' (1980: 188). Perhaps here we can see the ultimate origin of cultural change as such.
3. Confusingly, Weber sometimes says that a 'rational systematization' of magical forces takes place at this level (see 1951: 196, where it is wrongly translated as 'systematic rationalization'; cf. 1920–1, vol. I: 458). Yet by this he means that *within* the limits of the proliferation and specialization of magical forces, their powers may be extended to cover a broader range of events which are susceptible to magical influence. The difference between 'systematic rationalization' and 'rational systematization' is important, as we shall see below.
4. The fact that Weber's argument is not just about the obstacles to modern capitalism or to the capitalist spirit, but more generally about the obstacles to Western rationalism is evident not only from the 'Introduction' to his studies of the world-religions (1930: 13–31), but also from his contrast between Confucian and Protestant rationalism (1949: esp. 226–49) and between 'Asian intellectual culture' as against the 'pure factual rationalism of the West' (1958: 342; see also 329–43).
5. On this point, see also Schluchter (1989: 140–6).
6. Weber explicitly makes this contrast in terms of his conception of 'personality'. He distinguishes between meeting the ' "demands of the day" ' (1958: 342) and ' "matter-of-factness" ' (1920–1, vol. II: 378, my trans.; cf. 1958: 388) which constitute the 'specifically occidental significance of "personality" ' and which is 'alien to Asia' (1958: 342) as against 'Asia's partly purely mystical, partly purely innerworldly aesthetic goal of self-discipline [which] could take no other form than an emptying of experience of the real forces' of life (1958: 342) and in which 'life conduct was oriented to striving for the extraordinary' (1958: 343).
7. Schluchter is uncertain as to whether to classify Islam as a 'political religion' or to place it in the camp of 'world-rejecting cultural religion or salvation religion' (1989: 144). But since Weber explicitly states that 'Islam was never really a religion of salvation' (1968: 625), the political character of Islam should be seen as decisive in setting it apart from all the other world-religions.
8. Apart from this brief remark, Weber's comments on Sufism are very sparse.
9. The argument that the 'institutional' dimension of Islam was more important than the 'ideological' one in terms of the impact of Islamic religiosity on economic development has been made in a different form by Gellner (1981: 5–6).

3

THE RISE OF THE WEST

Ancient Judaism and the Origins of Western Rationalism

Weber's study of *Ancient Judaism* has a special place among his analyses of the world-religions, firstly, in the light of its unique role in the emergence of Western culture and secondly, because it provides the clearest illustration of the struggle between charisma and routinization. This is clear from the outset of the study. Judaism, according to Weber, 'was free of magic and all forms of irrational quest for salvation' (1952: 4).[1] Moreover, 'world-historical interest in Jewry rests upon this fact' (1952: 4). Ancient Judaism was the starting-point for the process of 'disenchantment' (the literal translation of the German term *Entzauberung* is 'de-magicification'), which distinguishes Occidental civilization from all others (Weber, 1930: 105). And as the elimination of magic and the emergence of a rational path to salvation play a decisive part in the rise of Western rationalism, it may be useful to describe the contrast between magic and Judaism in detail before going on to examine the development of Judaism itself.

The elimination of magic can mainly be ascribed to the world-view of Judaic religiosity. Several elements of this world-view are completely antithetical to magic: the first is universalism. Yahweh was not a local or a functional god.[2] Although he was originally seen as being at the helm of a political confederation, his powers were subsequently conceived of as reigning over all spheres of life and the promise of other-worldly salvation was open to all. Also Yahweh did not merely provide external advantages and protection from evil, but was regarded as a source of both harm and benefit. In marked contrast with magic, his prestige increased even as he brought about the suffering and enslavement of his peoples (Weber, 1952: 364).

Most important, however, were the features of Yahweh himself. As in magic, so too in Judaism there was 'the conviction that only a divine miracle, not human power, could bring about salvation' (1952: 246). But the two are nevertheless completely different: although Yahweh was seen by believers as being responsible for specific miraculous events, the decisive characteristic for Weber was the underlying basis of these powers, the fact that he controlled the whole course of history. The same applies to the divine commandments as they were propagated through the prophecy. It was not their concrete prescriptions or content that mattered so much as the fact that they 'promoted systematic unification, by relating the people's life as a whole and the life of each individual to the fulfillment of Yahwe's positive commandments' (1952: 255).

These two features add up to a world-view whereby the world is conceived as a 'meaningful totality' (Weber, 1968: 451). But unlike the mystics of Brahmanic Hinduism or Gnosticism, Judaic believers were not primarily trying to understand the meaning of their inward experience, but seeking to discern the god's mysterious and yet rationally understandable purpose. It is not a question of perfection or enlightenment of the soul in the face of a seemingly incomprehensible world, but an opposition between god's omnipotent will on the one hand and an imperfect world on the other.

This dualism produced several tensions. In one sense, Yahweh was considered to be the ultimate source of the meaning of religious life, his status as the provider of the meaning of the course of world-history having been established once and for all. Yet at the same time, he was regarded as continually reacting to particular ethical, political, legal, ritual and cosmological events and endowing them with a specific meaning. Again, in terms of his authority, Yahweh was both an ultimate and external source which could be appealed to – and at the same time, the overlord of the Israelite political confederation. A further characteristic of Yahweh was the changeability of his will, which meant that the believer could never be certain whether his demands had been satisfied. In these ways, a gap was created between divine omnipotence and the insignificance of human powers which put the believer under pressure to comprehend and meet the demands of a god who represented a 'meaningful totality'. This tension, as we shall see, forms the basis for the emergence of Western rationalism.[3]

How did this world-view come about? Partly responsible was the absence of a priesthood which could monopolize cultic and ritual practices. Priestly strata, in Weber's view, are typically predisposed to use their monopoly over various syncretistic cults to maintain privileged access to the sacred. This did not occur because of the particular historical circumstances in which the covenant was established. It was created at a time when the Israelite tribes constituted a loose political federation and the covenant represented a reciprocal agreement between Yahweh as protector and guarantor of this association on the one hand, and the loyalty of his chosen people on the other. The most important feature of this covenant was the *direct* responsibility of the Israelites to Yahweh. This completely binding relationship could only be sustained because it was reinforced by political and territorial factors. In the course of time, however, it was to grow more independent of these.

The covenant was construed as the sole basis on which demands could be made on Yahweh and whereby he could, in turn, impose ethical and legal obligations on his people. Here lies the reason for a further tension: namely, that the relationship between Yahweh and his people was at once fixed for all time – and yet the covenant constantly imposed new obligations on believers.

Importantly, with the covenant, all previous moral and social norms were, so to speak, suspended until they could be reendorsed by divine authority. Whereas elsewhere, a stable social order is typically reinforced by a network of magical and religious norms, the ancient Judaic world-view, rather than providing legitimation, created a new and unified basis for social obligations which, in turn, allowed other fundamental changes to take place. Even if concrete changes were not immediately evident, at least the way in which social norms were held to be valid had been radically transformed (Weber, 1952: 79).

If it had only been for the Israelite political confederation based on the covenant, the significance of Judaism would have been limited to guaranteeing territorial unity. As it was, this limitation was transcended by an increasing stress on Yahweh's universal nature and through the systematization of the notion of ethical salvation. Why did this shift take place? Partly because the pre-exilic prophets, harking back to an idealized version of the covenant during an earlier time of political and religious crisis, were able to intensify the attribute of Yahweh's all-powerfulness. With this, they were able to restore faith in the 'original' covenant and in his ability to provide a future kingdom of salvation. In the course of this idealization, the national or political basis of the original covenant was replaced by an emphasis on ethical obligation. Ethics could be stressed by reinterpreting the old covenant as an original state of purity in which the reciprocal obligations between Yahweh and his people had been duly fulfilled. From this vantage-point, the prophets could postulate a tension between an ideal relation to Yahweh, projected from the past and onto a possible future, as against the imperfect present ethical condition of believers.

Once more it can be seen that Judaism owed everything to its world-view: as Weber puts it, 'an ethic does not receive its peculiar nature through the special character of its commandments . . . but through the underlying central religious mentality' (1952: 317–18).

Given that this god was the source of all religious meaning, the believer had to undertake a complete reorientation of conduct in the light of this idea. And although all ethical commandments had been laid down in the Torah, still the fact that Yahweh's will was both intelligible and forever subject to change meant that in the mind of the believer, fulfilling his obligations took the form of a rational task. In Weber's terminology, the believer became a 'tool' rather than a 'vessel' of the sacred, an instrument of god's will rather than a repository of enlightened knowledge (1968: 544–6).

Another important feature of the covenant, as Weber repeatedly stresses, was the direct and collective responsibility of Yahweh's people to their god: direct in the sense that believers felt that their obligations were immediately imposed upon them by Yahweh's omnipotent will, and collective because the contractual relation was between Yahweh and his chosen people as a whole. Hence, ethical demands were not only imposed upon the individual believer, but each had to contribute towards the efforts of the community of believers.

Unlike the other world-religions which, as we have seen, each in its own way still incorporated elements of magic, Judaism completely broke with magic. There could be no magical compulsion within a dualistic system in which the deity determined the course of world-history and was at the same time completely set apart from an imperfect creaturely world (Weber, 1952: 298): 'The world was conceived as neither eternal nor unchangeable, but rather as having been created. Its present structures were a product of man's activities . . . and of God's reactions to them' (1952: 4). Again, the prophets here were tools of god, rather than being themselves endowed with divine powers. This led to the devaluation of sacrifice, ritual and cult. Even in later ancient Judaism, the rabbis were consulted because of their special knowledge of the written laws, and not because they could dispense sacramental grace or possessed mystical enlightenment. And since Yahweh's commandments applied to everyone, magic could not be used by the priests as a way of keeping the mass of believers under their control. The absence of concrete embodiments of the sacred also avoided sanctioning special access to the divine, or using religious legitimation for kingly rule.

To sum up: the important break in Weber's view was that the universalism of the Judaic world-view did not sanction an unchangeable order of norms, that the belief in ethical salvation did not allow for the efficacy of ritual and magic, and that the view of history as the product of god's will plus the correct conduct of the believers prevented the emergence of a multitude of functional gods. This world-view and the ethical conduct which was derived from it accounts for the uniqueness of Judaic religiosity. Hence Weber can say that 'magic did not have its usual dominance in Israel', and when he adds that despite this, magic 'never vanished completely from popular practice', this must be taken to mean that the more 'advanced' form of religion was unable fully to penetrate social life (1952: 219). Even with the transformation of Judaism from the pre-exilic prophecy into post-exilic rabbinicalism, a transformation that Weber otherwise regards as a regression towards routine and popular beliefs, still there was little recourse to magic. Ancient Judaism thus preceded Islam and Protestantism in being a religion which remained monotheistic even at the level of popular belief (Weber, 1968: 419). It was, Weber says, 'the instigator and partly the model for Mohammed's prophecy' and thus a 'turning point of the whole cultural development of the West and Middle East' (1952: 5). The break with (and elimination of) magic therefore allows Weber to locate the beginning of the process of 'disenchantment', which was to shape the entire development of Occidental rationalism, at this point (1930: 105).

Apart from the elimination of magic, *Ancient Judaism* (1952) occupies a central place in Weber's work because it provides the clearest example of the pattern of charisma and routinization, which lies at the heart of his conception of cultural change. Mommsen has commented that the struggle between charisma and routinization is a pervasive theme in his thought: 'In the end we must view charisma and rationalization as world-historical forces which, being in permanent conflict, are the essential origins of all social change as such' (Mommsen, 1983: 395). This is underlined when Weber says that 'charisma is indeed the specifically creative revolutionary force of history' (1968: 1117). We must therefore briefly examine how *Ancient Judaism* provides the paradigm for this struggle.[4]

It may be useful to recall before we do so that we discovered a confusion between two levels in Weber's idea of a struggle between charisma and routinization which is also clearly illustrated in the case of ancient Judaism. There is, on the one hand, the transition from individuals with extraordinary capacities to the more traditional and institutional forms of domination. But even more importance must be attached to a second level, to the transformation of a belief-system which, after the revolutionizing impact of a completely transcendent, universalist, and ethically demanding conception, developed at a later stage into a formalistic belief-system dominated by everyday piety and particularistic laws.

In order to describe these transformations in *Ancient Judaism*, three historical periods can be distinguished:[5] the first is the period of the confederacy. Schluchter summarizes Weber's view of this period as follows: it consists of a 'configuration of the warrior peasant and shepherd confederation, its center of gravity in the countryside, characterized by the competition between magicians, oracle priests, and prophets of war, as well as by the "unity" of religion and politics' (1989: 200). In this configuration, a novel and independent conception of religious meaning could evolve not only because of Israel's isolation from the other great cultural centres, but also in response to the constant political threat to which the political confederation was exposed. Thus the idea of an 'oathbound confederation', based on the mutual obligations between Yahweh and his people, could lend a new significance to the turbulent and precarious course of political events taking place in Israel (Weber, 1952: 75). It was only later, during the second period and with the moral fervour of the pre-exilic prophecy harking back to earlier times, that this idea became firmly rooted in social life.

During the period of the confederacy of tribes, however, the strength of the covenant was only assured because it coincided with the political needs of the Israelites. Yet despite this political importance, Weber stresses that for the charismatic bearers of this idea themselves, its significance was purely religious: 'The decisive characteristic' of charismatic endowment was 'that one must have personal intercourse with Yahwe' (1952: 107). At this stage, the role and prestige of the prophet had not yet become differentiated from that of the military leader and magician. It was this link between the sacred legitimation of the prophetic message and its political usefulness that consolidated Yahweh's religious and political authority.

The supposedly divine origin of natural catastrophes against the enemies of Israel also gained prestige for Yahweh, who was initially perceived as an anthropomorphic hero. This prestige, in turn, devolved upon his representatives: 'Confederate unity found expression in that a Yahwe certified war hero or war prophet regularly claimed authority also beyond the boundaries of his tribe. People came to him from afar to have him settle their legal disputes or to seek instruction in ritual or moral duties' (1952: 83–4).

This then is one level – the charisma of the prophets in the sense of their authority among believers – on which Weber describes the initial impact of Judaism. On the second level, however, Weber's focus is not on the extraordinary power attributed to individual prophets, but on the new conception of god's power. This force of charisma can be said to be inherent in the world-view itself. It was the covenant and its unique features which were responsible for the wide-ranging authority and influence of the deity in ancient Israelite belief. Not that the charisma of divine inspiraton or the notion of an oathbound confederation as such were unique here, but rather, as Weber points out, 'the peculiarity consists . . . in the extensive employment of the religious *berith* [covenant] as the actual (or construed) basis of the most varied legal and moral relations' (1952: 75). In this sense, as Bendix puts it, 'despite the absence of a unified and political organization, some degree of cohesion existed on the basis of common religious beliefs' (1960: 218). As we have seen, the notion of the joint and direct responsibility of believers to Yahweh devalued all other norms and could therefore reorient the conduct of believers and challenge the existing social order.

During the second, pre-exilic period of Judaism, the notion of an oathbound confederation protected by Yahweh reemerged in a different form. The covenant was reinterpreted in such a way as to provide a framework from which a system of dogma and ethics could issue. Schluchter summarizes this period as a 'configuration of kingship, its center of gravity in the city, characterized by competition between cultic priests, Torah priests, and Torah prophets and by the differentiation of religion and politics' (1989: 200). The competition between prophets and priests as to who should be Yahweh's true representatives provides the key to the further development of the Judaic belief-system. Both the far-reaching ideals of the prophets and the detailed knowledge of the laws of the Levitical priesthood contributed to strengthening Judaic belief, despite the fact that these two groups were to some extent rivals. An important factor which facilitated the efforts of both groups was that in a time of social upheaval, political crises and competition among cults, they could point back to the time of the confederacy and proclaim that it had been a period when pure faith and obedience had secured Yahweh's protection and beneficence. The prophets did not, however, simply add content to this idealized reconstruction of the covenant. While retaining the basic notion of joint responsibility between Yahweh as the protector of the confederacy as a political unit, they also transformed this into an ethical relationship between a governor of divine laws and his faithful and obedient servants. They gave the covenant a new meaning through a 'systematic unification' which entailed 'relating the people's life as a whole and the life of each individual to the fulfillment of Yahwe's positive commandments' (Weber, 1952: 255). Whereas the earlier period of the confederacy had been marked by a conflation of the religious and political functions of belief, the pre-exilic period brought the establishment of an ethical religion oriented solely towards salvation.

The new dimension which the prophets added to the idealized

reconstruction of the covenant was evident both in the attributes of god and the demands he made on believers. God was now a deity whose will was understandable and responsive to the ethical behaviour of his subjects. In this sense, he had become more predictable. At the same time, the collective fate of his people was made dependent on their loyalty to him and on obedience to his laws.

This transformation of the Judaic world-view had far-reaching consequences. Under the adverse circumstances of external political threats and of the establishment of a mostly disliked kingly court within, the prophets developed a theodicy of misfortune in which obedience to Yahweh's commands was the only way to secure a better future. The priestly rationalism of the Levitical teachers of the Torah reinforced this development. Despite the rivalry for authority between the prophets and the priestly stratum, the meaning that the former gave to the course of history actually gave added importance to the fulfilment of the legalist ethic of the latter.[6]

Secondly, and no less important, was the uniqueness of the carriers of pre-exilic religiosity: 'Here and here only plebeian strata became exponents of a rational religious ethic' (Weber, 1952: 224). The god of the confederacy had been particularly suited to the needs of a militarized peasantry, for whom he remained a god of war and of natural disasters – aside from being the contractual partner in the covenant. Now, the pre-exilic god increasingly had to suit the needs of demilitarized plebeian strata, and thus he became an overlord whose will could be understood and whose reactions were a response to the ethical behaviour of his people. This priestly teaching of the Levites who expounded Yahweh's positive commandments and systematized them in the Torah appealed to a stratum with a more urban way of life.

Weber ascribed great importance to this pre-exilic development,[7] to the systematic ethical teaching of the Levites as contained in the Torah, and to a plebeian stratum of lay intellectuals who were inclined to support such a universal and bookish ethic. As Schluchter points out, Weber attributed world-historical potential to this development: 'With this step a further ethical development seems prefigured: a universal religious ethic of conviction, producing worldly action and being free from magic, lies within the horizon of possibilities' (1981b: 47, my trans.; cf. 1989: 195). In other words, here we are only a small step away from the Protestant ethic of worldly asceticism, with all the possibilities for cultural change that this implies for Weber.

The reason why this further development did not take place lies in the later transformations of Judaism during the third period of exile and post-exile. For in this period, instead of intensifying Yahweh's demands and thereby producing the inward reorientation of believers, Judaism developed a framework of mediation between the divine and the believer. In short, Judaic religion became increasingly routinized. Weber would have agreed with the view (which is described as commonplace, but rejected by Isidore Epstein) that 'the prophets . . . were the exponents of an exalted religion and all they demanded was inward reality, character, and disposition, whereas the priests represented a lower view of religion with its insistence on ritual and ceremonial' (Epstein, 1959: 65). Weber thought that 'the stronger . . . the ritualistic nature of a religion . . . the more the worry about purely formal – for modern thought, ethically irrelevant – offenses color the religious relationship' (1952: 246). This idea, that a more ritualist or external religion produces less of an inward transformation, is one that we have already encountered, particularly in Weber's conception of the individual, and it certainly for him applies to late Judaism.

The ossification of ancient Judaism, from (in Eisenstadt's words) a 'prophetic ethic oriented toward universalism into rabbinical legalism' (1981: 138), already began during the period of exile. It was a period in which the lack of external threats and the absence of propaganda against an unholy and unjust administration, which had been so important to the prophetic message of deliverance by a wrathful god, resulted in an ethic that was more suited to everyday observance. During this 'peaceful existence enjoyed by Jews under their Persian ruler', Epstein points out, the teachers of the Torah 'accordingly sought to mitigate the apparent severity of the law, bringing it more into harmony with life, and with the fundamental human wants' (1959: 86). Along the same lines, Weber describes how priestly formalism came to gain the upper hand over the prestige of the prophets, a process that was completed in post-exilic times (1952: 380).

The priests increased their authority not only because of their specialized knowledge and intellectual schooling, but also through expertise in law and ritual. This monopoly, in turn, meant that it was in the interests of priests to supplant the universalism of the prophets by more closely defining the rules by which Yahweh governed, rules over which they had control. Thus 'there increasingly appeared now a purely ritualistic organization, a territorial organization at least in theory, with Jerusalem as the postulated capital' (1952: 337). This territorial segregation was partly influenced by the conception of Israel's chosenness, but it also rigidified in response to the threat of Hellenizing and other neighbouring influences.

Given that the priesthood maintained its control over believers by segregating them from non-believers through ritual means, the means to salvation also increasingly became narrowed to the formal observance of law and ritual. These more modest demands (because of their externality) went hand in hand with a change in the conceptions of Yahweh and of salvation. The tension between a severe and wrathful ruler and an imperfect world, which had earlier been the basis for the radical devaluation of the world, was replaced by a more harmonious relation between a wise and beneficent governor of the world and a belief in a peaceful world that 'is not evil but good' (1952: 400). Yahweh became an immanent redeemer who could be swayed by pious and humble obedience. As Epstein puts it, 'in contrast with the old covenant, the new Covenant was not to be grounded on the mighty acts which God did on behalf of Israel in the far-off days of the past, but in His deeds of salvation in their everyday life' (1959: 61). Weber notes that such a transformation marks the increasing influence of strata which were predisposed to this type of belief, bourgeois and petty-bourgeois strata which 'lived a peaceful and comfortable life in . . . modest circumstances' (1952: 369). In sum, routinization consisted of a shift in the conception of god, a change in the conduct demanded for salvation, the growth of priestly power, and an accommodation to the needs of believers. Together these amount to an everyday faith marked by merely formal and ritualist observance.

We are now in a position to summarize Weber's view of cultural change in ancient Judaism. One aspect of the development of Judaic belief, as we have seen, was the transferral of legitimacy from the individual prophets, who derived their charismatic endowment from being god's messengers – to an officially recognized priesthood which was bent on maintaining a monopoly on bookish skills and ritual services. Yet this explains only how the interests of one stratum (the priesthood) led to the establishment of a more routine or traditional form of religious authority. It is clear that the main emphasis of Weber's account is rather on the changing nature of Judaic belief itself and how its influence on social life changed accordingly.

In order to identify how the struggle between charisma and routinization took place on this second level, we can single out three elements. First, a world-view based on a single, completely transcendent, and omnipotent god. This world-view remained the underlying premise of religiosity throughout the development of Judaism and provided the framework for a divine order on which the validity of all religious claims and commands rested. Within this world-view, there are two shifts. At the time of the Confederacy,

Yahweh was the protector of an association of warriors and a god of natural catastrophe. He was partly a functional god who served political aims. During the pre-exilic period, he became both the universalist and wrathful god of the prophets and the understandable and predictable overlord of the priesthood. Still later, in exilic and post-exilic times, the notions of an immanent redeemer who provides individual salvation and of a wise governor of worldly affairs emerged (Weber, 1952: 129). Summarizing the whole course of this development, we can say that there was a shift from the ritual worship of an anthropolatric god, to an increasing emphasis on universalism and ethical obedience, and finally a move towards ritualism and legalism.

A second element was the systematization of belief and worship through the efforts of the priesthood. After a period of competition with the prophets during pre-exilic times, this stratum increasingly gained a monopoly over the means of worship. But while one aspect of this development was the shift of religious authority into traditional channels (as indicated by the first level of the routinization of charisma), equally important was the transformation of religious demands. In this respect, the continuing consolidation of priestly power meant that detailed ritual and ethical prescriptions came to the fore. But these were also more readily integrated into everyday life and, being more external or formal, made weaker demands on the inward life of believers.

Finally, the development towards routinization was occasioned by accommodating the needs of the believers. Although Judaism did not have to reintroduce magic or functional gods in order to cater to the mass of believers (for Weber, as we have seen, a unique and all-important achievement), there were nevertheless shifts in accordance with the main carriers of religion. The first was from a militarized peasantry to a demilitarized urban stratum, allowing for the success of the prophets' universalism and the priests' rigorous ethical demands. The later tendency towards ritualism and legalism was part of an unprecedented expansion of lay intellectualism among petty-bourgeois and bourgeois strata which produced hopes for an immanent redeemer and a belief in the possibility of attaining redemption through the fulfilment of formal obligations.

Ancient Judaism thus provides the most important illustration of the struggle between charisma and routinization (and of Weber's confusion of levels in his analysis of this struggle). In this context, it may also be noted that in this case, he pays much more attention to the historical *process* involved in cultural change, whereas in the other studies of the world-religions his accounts seem much more ahistorical. Yet the other two elements of Weber's conception of cultural change are also in evidence: the differentiation between the spheres of life is shown in the increasing separation of the religious from the political sphere during the earlier period. Later, we find the opposite process taking place, as religious barriers increasingly came to be imposed on the economic sphere through 'ritualistic segregation' from other communities and a 'dualism of the economic ethic' (1952: 336, 343). This created obstacles to the complete differentiation of religion from social life.

The inner logic of the ancient Judaic world-view has already been amply illustrated in terms of the transformation from the belief in a vengeful leader of the war-like confederation into a beneficent redeemer. Even greater significance, as we shall see, attaches to the further development of the Judaeo-Christian world-view.

Since Weber is most commonly associated with the Protestant ethic thesis, the importance of *Ancient Judaism* is often overlooked. Yet it was here, and not during the Reformation, that he located the roots of Western rationalism: of the prophets, he says that 'these giants cast their shadows through the millenia into the present' (1952: 334). What is more, this path-breaking significance must be attributed to the ancient Judaic world-view. Zeitlin underscores this view of its contribution to Western rationalism as follows:

> If the nation or an individual suffered and God failed to help, that was a sign that some commandment had been isolated. Which one? Irrational means of divination could not answer that question, only a knowledge of the laws and a soul-searching scrutiny of one's conduct. The idea of the covenant had thus led to a comparatively rational mode of raising and answering such questions. (1984: xi)

Weber thought that the origins of disenchantment, and thus the unique pattern of Western culture, could be found in this world-view. This then, too, is the sense which must be given to Weber's idea of 'rationalism'. Although he uses this term in different contexts, here it consists of the elimination of magic and the creation of a world-view which accounts for the meaning of the world in terms of a transcendent and universal whole. In his discussion of the 'significance' of ancient Judaism for modern capitalism, Weber comments that:

> in all times there has been but one means of breaking down the power of magic and establishing a rational conduct of life; this means is great rational prophecy . . . prophecies have released the world from magic [*Entzauberung*] and in doing so have created the basis for our modern science and technology, and for capitalism. (1927: 362; cf. 1981a: 308–9)

But although the pre-exilic prophecy created a universalist religion with an inward ethic disposed towards worldly action, its impact on the economic sphere remained traditionalist for two reasons. First, because Judaic religiosity did not endow economic pursuits with a positive significance. Instead, the economic sphere was an area of ethical indifference, which is 'the primordial economic ethic of all peoples everywhere' (Weber, 1968: 615). Secondly, the status of the Jewish people as a guest people prevented economic exchange. The fact that there were strong religious barriers to economic relations with non-Jews placed severe restrictions on economic development (1927: 358–60; 1968: 614–15). Nevertheless, the Judaic world-view not only provided a point of departure for the further development of Occidental rationalism, but also lay the foundation for the tension between an all-powerful and transcendent deity and an imperfect and changing world, which both early Christianity and Protestantism had to resolve.

Early and Medieval Christianity: a Regression in the Course of Western Rationalism

Apart from Islam, early and medieval Christianity are the major gaps in Weber's comparative studies of the world-religions.[8] As with Islam, Weber's remarks on the rise of Christendom can be pieced together in order to show, albeit in an inconclusive manner, what he might have said had he completed his task of an all-encompassing study of the world-religions. The reconstruction of this uncompleted part of his work is particularly important since it sheds light on his view of the growth of Western rationalism: was this a unilineal development in the sense of a progression from ancient Judaism to Protestantism by way of early and medieval Christianity? On the basis of Weber's scattered remarks, it would rather seem that Weber thought that Latin Christianity marked a regression in this development.[9]

Weber thought that the most important feature of the Judaic and Protestant world-views was the unbridgeable gap between an all-powerful and inscrutable divine ruler and an imperfect and sinful humanity. Early Christianity, by contrast, bridged this gap through its doctrine that an 'unlimited' or 'unconditional trust' in an incarnate saviour could produce salvation (1968: 567). The conduct that resulted from this view of salvation was indifference to the world on the basis of reliance on god's will. Christianity demanded only an inward devotion to the saviour, rather than a radical reorientation of conduct.

Examining the emergence of this world-view historically, we find that early Christian belief maintained some continuity with Judaism, particularly in its conception of an eschatological hope for a future kingdom. Yet Jesus's prophecy and the teaching that

followed from it nevertheless produced a completely different
system of belief which shaped the entire development of Christianity up until the late medieval church and beyond.

What was this new doctrine? By contrast with Judaism and
Protestantism, which Weber classifies as ethical salvation religions,
early Christianity, despite the ethical nature of its prophecy, was
dominated by elements of salvation through faith, magic and ritual.
These means to salvation emerged from the conception of the
sacred. Weber points out that 'Jesus appeared during the period of
the most intensive messianic expectations' (1968: 631) and therefore
characterizes him as being 'primarily a magician' (1968: 630). In
other words, in keeping with his conception of magic, Weber sees
Jesus as embodying charismatic powers within his person. Hexter is
perhaps making a similar point when he says that the uniqueness of
Jesus among Occidental saviours is that he is believed to have
'happened in history' (1966: 98). But this means that it is not the
intellectual knowledge of god or obedience to his absolute commands which are decisive for salvation, but rather faith in his
charismatic powers. Jesus came into the world as an intermediary of
the Lord and his spirit (*pneuma*) manifested itself in the community.
On this basis the early Christians believed in his divine power to
save and piously devoted themselves to him (Weber, 1968: 567). It
is this anthropolatric and magical cult of personal reliance on the
saviour out of which early Christianity arose.

Both Weber and his colleague Troeltsch emphasized the purely
religious origin of this doctrine, especially against Kautsky who
sought to give an account of early Christianity in terms of the theory
of historical materialism. Kautsky saw early Christianity as a
political movement of the proletariat aimed primarily at social
reform (1925: xiii). Against this, Weber and Troeltsch held that
although wealth was a possible danger to salvation according to
Jesus, and although his message was addressed to lower-ranking
strata – particularly to the 'poor in spirit' (1968: 631) – his prophecy
still emerged on the basis of purely religious motives (1968: 499, see
also Troeltsch, 1931: 39).

Early Christian belief displayed the characteristics both of magic
and of a religion of salvation. The emphasis in the teachings of Jesus
and Paul was on faith and devotion rather than knowledge.
Whereas Judaism and Protestantism could influence everyday life
precisely because of the uncertainty about whether god's commands
were being fulfilled or one's election was assured, Latin Christianity
did not produce this kind of psychological pressure. Not anxiety,
but unconditional trust in the saviour's magical powers was the
testing ground for salvation. For Weber, this means that the

Christian faith did not prescribe an ascetic rejection of the world's pleasures so much as it promoted an indifference to the world.

The partly magical and partly ethical deity of the Christian world-view produced an unsystematic type of faith which was character-ized at once by emotion and by ethical obedience. Humility and submission before the divine power were necessary requirements for the demonstration of faith. But in demanding this type of religious conduct, Jesus did not condemn sensuous enjoyment or wealth and luxury as such. They were considered dangerous to salvation only in so far as they hindered devotion and faith. In practice, this left a lot of room for a compromise with worldly affairs. Jesus demanded only a surrender to faith, a turning away from knowledge in favour of the belief in god's ability to save. The religious premium in this case was placed positively on trust and belief in the divine power, but negatively it was mainly the rejection of this faith which was ethically reprehensible. Weber therefore concludes that with the 'increasing stress . . . placed upon salvation by faith, there was generally but little tendency for an active ethical rationalization of the pattern of life to take place within everyday religion' (1968: 569).

Weber places particular emphasis on the anti-intellectualist char-acter of faith. This contrasts strongly with Judaic rabbinical legalism and with the doctrines of Greek philosophy. Weber suggests that Jesus was initially trying to appeal to an urban artisanate with his teachings (1968: 512; cf. Hexter, 1966: 59) as a way of rejecting scholars, Gnostic intellectuals (with their 'aristocracies' of salva-tion) and the educated upper classes in favour of the oppressed and the 'poor in spirit' (1968: 631). In addition, the rejection of ritual, mystical or soteriological knowledge was essential to Jesus's dog-matic assertion of the efficacy of spirit. This rejection was reinforced by the idea that an intellectualist lack of faith as well as arrogance against spirit and its adherents were the 'two absolutely mortal sins' (1968: 632). In short, the emphasis on the sufficiency of faith was specifically intended to counter the urban intellectualism of his time.

The ethic which resulted from this faith was not an ethic of rigorous and methodical conduct, but of brotherly love and charity. Its principal tenets consisted of mutual help and love for one's neighbour, and yet it construed these not as ethical commands but rather as an emotional attachment to fellow believers. Only god would finally reward those who had been kind and forgiving to fellow-believers and avenge those who showed pride and arrogance. In the meantime, injustice had to be suffered with equanimity and one's enemies loved and forgiven. Extraordinary ethical achievement could gain nothing in ensuring salvation, just as pride in one's virtuous actions would only indicate that they had been falsely motivated. As Weber puts it, 'the entire content of the law and the prophets was condensed into the simple commandment to love God and one's fellow-man', and this emotional attachment dominated the development of popular Christian faith (1968: 633). Weber's general position on the influence of an emotional type of religiosity on everyday life, however, is summed up in Abramowski's comment that 'an increasing amount of emotionality for Weber always means a lessening of the impulse toward the rationalization of worldly activity' (1966: 28).

Indeed, as Troeltsch points out, early Christianity did not give rise to social reform movements of any kind (1931: 39–41). The attitude of the early church to the state was to 'let man render unto Caesar that which is Caesar's' and in economics to 'let man pray to God for daily bread and remain unconcerned for the morrow' (Weber, 1968: 633). This ambivalent attitude to politics, stemming from the apostle Paul, in practice led to aquiescence to authority and a rejection of political activity as a sinful worldly preoccupation with power. Indifference to worldly affairs was demanded from the believer during the patient awaiting of the saviour's grace. The believer was 'required to abide in his position and in his calling . . . save where they demanded of him that he perpetrate a sinful deed' (1968: 634).

There is a similarity between this Christian ethic of indifference to the world (or of a rejection of the world in the sense that inner-worldly activity cannot help in bringing about salvation) and Buddhism which is at the same time a difference of both as against Judaism and Protestantism. Among the former, excessive concentration on inner-worldly activity is not only not meritorious, but a wicked preoccupation with powers that are merely human. Only an emotional and inward demonstration of faith can allow the believer to achieve spiritual security *from* the world, while it does not allow methodical conduct as a way to achieve mastery *over* it.

The important point to be made in this connection is that this world-view with its magical saviour who personally dispenses grace was the decisive influence on religious conduct. Indifference to the world, an emotional faith in spiritual power, and an attitude of humility and love towards fellow-believers and towards god were the hallmarks of this ethic. Such an ethic can only be understood as a result of the lack of a radical separation between the divine and the world.

The way in which this world-view found its initial expression in social life was through the message of the gospel and the missionizing activity of the disciples. Yet the attempt at making Christian values into a systematic doctrine were laden with contradictions. For although Jesus had claimed that his faith was to be universally accessible, there was in fact a separation between the rigorous ethic of the disciples and the simple faith and ethic of mutual help among the masses of believers. The former were supposed to renounce all possessions and undertake a 'complete emancipation from all ties of the world' (Weber, 1968: 632). Moreover, the fact that this small group had witnessed Jesus or directly derived their authority from him ensured their special status.

Early Christian doctrine was thus upheld by a small elite, prefiguring the later development of a specially empowered clergy and the rise of an institutional church. This later development transformed a small group of Jesus's disciples, who were seen as virtuosi with extraordinary qualifications, into an organized church with a clerical hierarchy. But this transformation could only take place after Christianity had become integrated into the Roman empire after the emperor Constantine's conversion. It is important to recognize that this move towards institutionalization was not only a product of the changing political situation in the Roman empire, but also the inevitable outcome (along the tracks of routinization) of the fact that spirit-endowed intermediaries were needed in this case. These intermediaries were necessary because 'every religion of belief' or of salvation from the outside 'assumes the existence of a personal god, as well as his intermediaries and prophets, in whose favour there must be a renunciation of self-righteousness and individual knowledge at some point or other' (Weber, 1968: 568). The contrast is with a religion where salvation comes from inside and is due to the believer's knowledge of god's will. In early Christianity, the charisma of the saviour had to be channelled through the apostles and it continued in the bishop's and the clergy's divine charisma of office. Another product of this institutionalization was that no rival religious claims could emerge because of a monopoly of religious qualifications, which also ruled out direct access to god among ordinary believers.

The existence of intermediaries increased the need for a centralized organization which would maintain orthodox belief. This took various forms: Christ's incarnate spirit was propagated through the apostolic succession and the ordination of bishops and priests. In addition, his miraculous powers were thought to be embodied in concrete form in the priestly performance of sacraments and rites and in the community of believers endowed with spirit. As Troeltsch points out, these vehicles of spirit were characterized by the fusion of divine and worldly elements:

The whole value of the institution as an organization . . . lies in the fact that it is so difficult to distinguish the Divine and human elements from each other, and that this combination of elements makes it very easy to invest a human order and centralization with the character of divine authority. (1931: 94)

Another feature of this clerical hierarchy, according to Turner, is that legitimate recognition in 'the history of Christian saintship . . . moves, as it were, in reverse order [to Islam] from spontaneous and local to determinate and central' (1974: 57). Despite the initial universal appeal to individual believers then, the Christian church in fact became a tightly organized community and hierarchy with membership qualifications and a leadership which was thought to possess extraordinary powers.

By the second century, with state and church drawing closer together, the educated upper classes also began joining the Christian faith. But it is important to remember that initially, Christianity had appealed mainly to lower-ranking urban strata and that the predispositions of these strata had played a decisive role. The message of Jesus had been addressed to the oppressed and the 'poor in spirit', and while wealth did not necessarily disqualify believers, still the 'continued attachment to Mammon constitutes one of the most difficult impediments to salvation' (Weber, 1968: 632). But whereas admission to the church was gained solely through humble acceptance of faith in the saviour, 'certain more tangible means are required to maintain the adherence of the mass of the faithful, who wish to participate personally in the gifts of grace made available by their god' (1968: 559). The emphasis came to be placed more on the sacraments and on ritual which, apart from increasing priestly powers, also established routine channels for taking part in the manifestation of spirit. Here then is another factor which made popular Christian belief develop in the direction of a faithful reliance on salvation by an external miraculous power, rather than towards a more consistent monotheism with an inward ethic.

The religious needs of lower urban strata, for Weber, tend towards an emotional faith reinforced by tangible signs of grace. Christianity accommodated itself to these needs, but it also increasingly addressed itself to what Weber calls a 'peaceful' middle class, and here 'faith as an instrument of salvation [can] take on the emotionally tinged character and assume the lineaments of love for the god or the saviour' (1968: 570). One direction which belief could take at this point was a passionate devotion to – and cultic worship of – the saints and the virgin Mary, where the divine qualities of these heroes were thought to be able to intercede on behalf of the believer.

Ritual and sacrament became an established part of orthodox belief and participation in these one of the essential requirements of church membership. Salvation could not be attained without baptism, communion and regular worship – which in practice also meant a strenghthening of the clergy. Its authority also grew with the systematization of dogma, and Weber points out that 'the Christian churches, as a consequence of the increasing intrusion of intellectualism and the growing opposition to it, produced an unexampled mass of official and binding rational dogmas, a theological faith' (1968: 564). Dogmatism elevated the status of the clergy, but for the mass of believers it simply meant that their salvation increasingly came to depend on the institutions of the church rather than their own efforts. At the same time, popular religion did not require extensive knowledge of dogma, but merely an explicit acknowledgement of the essential tenets of the faith. Not inward knowledge or certainty of divine grace, but an external or formal demonstration of faith in doctrinal authority was demanded.

Before we can trace the further consolidation of the institutional church and its hierarchical organization, it is important to mention a movement which did not develop in this direction. The Gnostics were a sect which rejected ritual and dogma as paths to salvation. Likewise, they did not recognize the power of clerical intermediaries or of the institutions of the church. Their means to salvation, as Pagels has documented, was an immediate and subjective experience of god (1982: 139). This attitude could equally well be said to follow from Jesus's original teaching as could the orthodox tradition (Pagels, 1982: 152). And if early Christian belief had placed more emphasis on the spiritual union with the saviour, this might have become the main direction of Christian development. As it happens, the orthodox interpretation prevailed and did not, for the reasons mentioned above, evolve towards an emphasis on mystical knowledge or on the manifestation of spirit to the individual believer.

For Weber, the significance of the Gnostic's attitude to salvation lay in its 'negative effect upon "action" ' (1968: 545). In concentrating solely on the mystical knowledge of god, the Gnostic at the same time denied the religious and ethical importance of worldly activity. The individual's salvation lay in ' "possession" ' of the divine (1968: 545), of being a vessel for illumination, rather than in being an ascetic instrument of god's will. This attitude also led to what Weber calls an 'aristocracy of salvation', a disciplined intellectual programme for gaining spiritual illumination which could only have restricted appeal. The masses of believers were either 'excluded from salvation or limited to a lesser-order salvation reserved for the non-intellectual pious' (1968: 565). Even for the illuminated elite with its mystical insight, however, striving for salvation could not produce rational or methodical conduct. The search for mystical enlightenment, Weber concludes, 'produces a characteristic quality of brokenness or humility' among the Gnostics because they can neither act on their incommunicable wisdom, nor embody their subjective knowledge in institutional or dogmatic form (1968: 563).

Although Pagels argues that this type of Christian belief can lead to an 'internal transformation' which is 'essential for spiritual development' (1982: 137), it is clear that Weber would not rate Gnosticism highly in terms of lending itself to inner-worldly activity. The impact of *gnosis*, of direct knowledge of the divine, on everyday life was negligible because salvation represented a flight from the world and took the form of contemplation. With such an exclusive emphasis on the subjective inner relation to god, there was no potential for influence on the other spheres of life. Weber does not indicate whether it is the Gnostic movement's promotion of passivity, its elitism, its inability to systematize dogma and establish an organized church, or the rivalry with orthodox belief which prevented its growth into a larger faith. But even Pagels, who sees in Gnosticism a significant contribution to Christianity (1982: 155), is nevertheless forced to conclude that 'Gnostic churches, which rejected that system for more subjective forms of religious affiliation, survived, as churches, for only a few hundred years', whereas 'we owe the survival of Christian tradition to the organization and theological structure that the [orthodox] church developed' (1982: 128, 147).

But although the Christian tradition was maintained by the orthodox church, its beliefs and ethical requirements also became weakened in the course of time. This transformation towards a routine and traditional type of lay religiosity prefigured the emergence of medieval Catholicism. While the church by and large subjected itself to existing political powers, yet by 'adopting for its own purposes the model of Roman political and military organization, and gaining, in the fourth century, imperial support, orthodox Christianity grew increasingly stable and enduring' (Pagels, 1982: 153). But inasmuch as Christianity concentrated divine authority in the hands of a centralized hierarchy, systematized a body of dogma and emphasized the official administration of sacraments and rites, the attitude of the believer was also bound to change. Increasingly, the divine power of salvation was thought to emanate through the grace of the institution. The test of conduct became less important than entrusting oneself to a church credited with being able to dispense salvation. For the institution, on the other hand, 'the personal religious qualification of the individual in need of salvation is altogether a matter of indifference' (Weber, 1968: 560). Everyone could attain salvation so long as the formal requirements of the church were met. In short, with routinization, the demands of Christianity came to contrast even more strongly with the inward ethic of Judaism and Protestantism.

Medieval Christendom represents an extension of some of these developments, particularly as it produced further tangible manifestations of spirit which could provide salvation for the masses of believers. But alongside the religion of the masses, there also emerged a strict ethic of asceticism for the religious elite. In this way, the ideal of Jesus's disciples lived on in the ethic of the priesthood, a body which claimed to be the real carrier of Christianity. It was only in monastic life that the world with its impious temptations could be fully rejected. The monk lived in strict accordance with the tenets of the faith and this qualification, in addition to the fact that priestly office was regarded as being endowed with extraordinary powers, made him into a 'virtuoso of faith' who could 'act differently from the layman in practical situations and bring about different results, far surpassing normal human capacity' (Weber, 1968: 567). In this way a wide gulf was created between the religious elite and the laity. But since lay religiosity had been weakened, it was left to the clergy to develop the ideals of the church further and it was mainly the conduct and organization of this group which had an impact on social life.

Troeltsch remarks that 'the rise of the clergy as a body of men entrusted with the leadership and government of the Church meant, that, owing to the need of the organization itself, the clergy as a class were always striving to perfect their own organization' (1931: 99). These efforts took the form of building up a hierarchical church structure and centralized administration. The unification of the church on an organizational level prevented the proliferation of cults and also served to establish a domain of religious life which was separate from the realm of practical, everyday affairs (Troeltsch, 1931: 100). Yet at the same time, the theocratic apparatus absorbed many aspects of secular life under its own authority. The church was able to appropriate political privileges, offices of state, educational authority, and even found itself having to enter the economic sphere. This interpenetration of the different spheres of life could only take place through the establishment of a hierocratic church, an institution capable of perpetuating itself and gaining authority *vis-à-vis* the non-religious spheres of life. Apart from the institutions of the church, however, the gulf between a priestly ethic and lay belief remained, with the result that the 'high' religion did not penetrate into everyday life.

During the Middle Ages, the impact of Christianity for Weber was mainly felt through its institutional and doctrinal authority and thus took the form of giving stability to social life.[10] Southern reinforces this view when he says that this 'may be defined as the period in Western European history when the church could reasonably claim to be the one true state, and when men . . . acted on the assumption that the church had an overriding political authority' (1970: 24). For the mass of believers, this did not entail a reorientation of conduct. In fact, 'the majority of people must mainly have been aware of the Christian religion as an intrusion of the supernatural into their lives in the form of miracles and ritual ceremonies' (Southern, 1970: 29).

How was the church able to maintain its monopoly on religious authority? First, through a clerical hierarchy which constituted the sole channel for the sacred. As an elite intellectual stratum, the clergy had an interest in maintaining this centralized administration and the system of patronage and benefices, which was ultimately controlled and unified by the papacy (later, the clergy would try to wrest power from the papacy and try to bring it within its own control in an alliance with a rising bourgeosie (Weber, 1968: 513)). Aside from economic exactions and privileges, the church could, secondly, confer legitimacy upon political authorities, which had initially been seen as lying within the realm of sinful worldly action. And finally, the church exercised control through a variety of religious practices. It administered a system of penances, confessionals, sacraments, ceremonies and the distribution of grace. The layman's path to salvation thus consisted of subjugation to the churches' institutional orders, its practices and officers. The individual was of little account and powerless before the almighty god.

Apart from securing obedience to divine authority, popular belief did little in the way of exerting a religious influence on everyday behaviour: 'During the medieval period, Occidental Christianity did not have a religious lay intellectualism of any appreciable extent, whether of a petty-bourgeois or of a pariah character' (Weber, 1968: 513). The Humanist education and culture which emerged from monastic life was generally 'antipathetic to the masses' (1968: 514). And most importantly, the demands that the church made on believers were merely formal or external ones. Weber's view of these demands is that since the simple requirement of obedience to the church is open to everyone, 'the level of personal ethical accomplishment must . . . be made compatible with average human qualifications, and this in practice means that it will be set quite low'

(1968: 560). Only an occasional demonstration of faith was required and confession could in any case ease the believer's burden of guilt. Instead of the methodical pursuit of an other-worldly goal, here the only constant religious attitude was the faithful reliance on salvation through the saviour's grace in its various institutional embodiments.

The same is true of the more narrowly economic consequences of popular religion. There was no psychological premium on one's secular vocation and from the viewpoint of faith, worldy affairs were at best a matter of ethical indifference. As Troeltsch points out, this was especially true of economic activity: 'In theological theory . . . trade was considered the most reactionary way of making a living, ethically lower on the scale than agriculture and manual labour' (1931: 128).

But whereas the everyday life of the laity was barely or only negatively affected by medieval religion, the monastic ideal of the priesthood produced an asceticism aimed at methodical self-control. Weber attached great significance to this ideal, commenting that this attitude 'predestined' the monk 'to serve as the principal tool of bureaucratic centralization and rationalization in the church' (1968: 1173). Furthermore, this single-minded pursuit of a religious vocation was to become an important model for the vocational ethic of Puritanism. Nevertheless, the highest religious premium was still placed on other-worldly – rather than inner-worldly – aims. That is, monastic asceticism led, in the end, to withdrawal from the world instead of mastery over it. For Weber, the most important progressive influence on social life during the Middle Ages was not the force of religious ideas, but the establishment of political rights within the autonomous city (1927: 334–5).

What is particularly important about Weber's view of the development from early Christianity to medieval Catholicism is the way it fits into his conception of the rise of Western rationalism. What is clear from our reconstruction is that this pattern can in no way be seen as leading from the beginnings of Judaism to modern secularization.[11] Rather, Judaism, Christianity, and Protestantism were separate parts of a pattern, each of them with its own internal dynamic of cultural change. Of these three dynamics, Latin Christendom had the weakest influence on social life. This is not because this form of religiosity remained static. In a sense, there was a clear line of development from the religious attitude of Jesus's disciples to the monastic ideal of the priesthood. The bestowal of divine powers on the disciples, their complete indifference to the world, their close adherence to dogma and their fraternal ethic were all gradually systematized into the world-rejecting asceticism of the monks. The resulting ethic included the complete rejection of worldly life, extensive training in theological doctrine, and the community of the monastery which together produced a life of methodical and constant self-control. In other words, the occasional and extraordinary powers of the disciples eventually found their expression in a way of life among the medieval priesthood.

This systematization did not, however, extend to the level of popular religion. Instead, the religiosity of the mass of believers took the form of occasional and external manifestations of faith. Again, this reliance on god and the church for salvation can be derived from early Christianity. The ideal established by Jesus's teachings was that salvation could only be achieved through faith in his power, but this meant that either the efficacy of god's power to save or the strength of the believer's convictions could be stressed. The Gnostics took the latter path to its logical conclusion since their path to salvation concentrated on the 'possession' of the divine. Orthodox dogma, on the other hand, developed the former path and created a system of channels through which divine grace could be bestowed on the believer. At the same time, the needs of various strata of believers had to be met, and an attitude of simple faith and devotion was increasingly made a sufficient condition for attaining god's grace.

Weber's view of cultural change within Latin Christendom can therefore be summarized as follows. The systematization of the early Christian world-view and its accommodation to the needs of believers resulted in a particularly formalist – and in this sense routinized – type of belief. There was a thoroughgoing interpenetration between the religious sphere and the political and economic spheres of life because of the church's increasing institutionalization, particularly during the Middle Ages. And finally, the inner logic of world-views dictated a development towards an increasing multitude of worldly embodiments invested with divine powers on the one hand, and an other-worldly asceticism among the religious vituosi on the other.

These features account for the distinctiveness of the impact of early and medieval Christianity. It was precisely because the divine and the human were not completely separated that cultural life promoted social stability in this case. Salvation was brought about through reliance on divine powers or through the miraculous intervention of the deity. The believer's conduct therefore consisted of subordination to the church and its especially empowered intermediaries. Judaism and Protestantism, by contrast, started with the premise of a radical divorce between the sacred and the world. Here the believer was forced systematically to reorient conduct so that it met the demands of a transcendent authority.

Religiosity was based on a world-view which radically devalued the world, whereas early and medieval Christianity took a variety of forms which bridged the gap between the divine and the world (cf. Dumont, 1983: 33–67). Only among the religious virtuosi was there a reorientation of conduct, yet it was aimed in a purely other-worldly direction. For these reasons, Latin Christendom, rather than representing progress in the course of the pattern initiated by ancient Judaism, must be seen as a regression in the course of Western rationalism.

The Protestant Ethic and the Spirit of Secularism

Weber's Protestant ethic thesis has been the subject of much controversy and is often dealt with in isolation from his other writings. It has been seen as a contribution to the debate about the origins of modern industrial society and a riposte to Marx's account of the transition from feudalism to capitalism. Yet for Weber, the Protestant ethic was part of an analysis of Occidental rationalism and of the 'disenchantment' of the world, processes which are of central importance within his analysis of cultural change. Two aspects of Occidental rationalism or of disenchantment which are not normally discussed in the context of the Protestant ethic need to be emphasized here. The first is the struggle between charisma and routinization whereby, in this case, the force of religious ideas in the end creates a routine way of life that encompasses the whole of social life. And the second is the elimination of magic from the world by means of a world-view based on a completely transcendent deity.

Although Weber mentions the second of these aspects in the *Protestant Ethic* (1930), he does not explicitly refer to the first and few indications are given that he wants to pursue this theme in his essay. Protestantism does not seem to gain its dynamic force from the charisma of religious leaders of the Reformation, nor does secularization seem at first sight to contribute to the establishment of more routine religious practices (although it did, in Weber's view, result in a more routine *secular* life). So does Weber ignore the schema of charisma and routinization, which is prominent throughout the rest of his examination of cultural life, in his most famous contribution to the social sciences? Is it perhaps the case that Protestantism does not fit neatly into Weber's conceptual schema?

I shall argue that although this schema is less explicit in this study than elsewhere, it is nevertheless equally important in his writings on the Protestant ethic. This is worth emphasizing because it illustrates how deeply Weber's concepts are embedded throughout his analyses of cultural change, and ultimately within his personal standpoint. As Mommsen has pointed out, Weber's use of the concept of 'charisma' was to a large extent based on a view of the modern world in which the individual's self-expression is constrained by impersonal and bureaucractic relations (1974a: ch. 5). The idea that 'charisma' potentially represents a countermeasure against this predicament does in fact find forceful expression in the *Protestant Ethic*, as do the other elements of his conception of cultural change.

The trouble with identifying the struggle between charisma and routinization in the Protestant ethic is the same that we have encountered elsewhere; namely, the confusion between two levels. The individual may be a convenient place to locate the origins of a belief-system, but this attribution of the origin and force of ideas to individuals is not always warranted by Weber's own description of the world-religions. As we have seen in the discussion of *Ancient Judaism*, for example, it was not so much the personal power and prestige of the Israelite prophets which initiated a revolutionizing effect, but rather the idea of a single and all-powerful creator-god itself. The same can be said for routinization: in *Ancient Judaism* this refers not only to the transfer of authority, but more importantly to the later, more everyday and stable form of religion. In short, Weber should – by his own account – have placed more emphasis on the role of ideas themselves, rather than on the role of the bearers of charismatic authority, in order to be true to his own description of the impact of cultural life and social change. The Protestant ethic merely provides another illustration of this disjunction between Weber's concepts and his substantive findings.

If we consider the *Protestant Ethic* in terms of the more general level of the capacity of world-views to generate social change, then we find, as in the other studies of religion, that the struggle between charisma and routinization is made up of three aspects: the initial conception of the divine which serves as the basis for its further development; the systematization of this belief into various forms of religious practice; and the accommodation of the belief-system to the needs of believers. The only difference between Weber's description of Protestantism and his other studies of religion (in terms of charisma and routinization) is that part of the systematization and accommodation of Protestantism, the second and third of these aspects, took the form of secularization. And although Protestantism contributed to secularization, the process of secularization has broader origins and consequences than those connected with Protestant religion. To see how secularization fits into Weber's analysis of cultural change as a whole, we shall need to recall the ultimate origins of disenchantment and, later on, take his view of science into account. Aside from this difference, however, charisma and routinization constitute an essential part of Weber's study of Protestantism.

Four themes in Weber's discussion of Protestantism will be important for our concerns: the Protestant world-view and its elimination of magic; the transformation of a religious belief into an economic ethic; the establishment of a routine type of religiosity in the sects; and secularization. As always, we must begin with the Protestant world-view, which put its mark on the whole subsequent development of Protestantism and the sects. What all the forms of Protestantism which Weber groups together in the *Protestant Ethic* have in common is that salvation is seen as dependent on the inscrutable will of a completely transcendent god. This core of the Protestant world-view finds its expression in the Calvinist idea of predestination, whereby the sole criterion by which one can be certain of gaining salvation lies in the impenetrable design of an all-powerful god. The Protestant god controls all events in the world and yet, since he is completely divorced from the world, neither divine interference nor human intermediaries are allowed to influence the quest for religious certainty. In short, the believer is at the mercy of a purely impersonal and unmanipulable force.[12]

Several aspects of this central postulate deserve comment. Weber wants to avoid giving the impression that he is construing the Protestant ethic in such a way that it is bound to lead to the result that he wants to attribute to it (that is, of bringing about the capitalist spirit). To do this, Weber emphasizes that Luther and Calvin were initially not at all interested in placing religious value on worldly aims. The motivation behind the notions of 'election' and the 'calling' was purely religious, and 'the salvation of the soul and that alone was the centre of [the] life and work' of the Protestant founders (1930: 89–90). In other words, initially at least, the central postulate of a transcendent and all-powerful god did not allow for involvement in the worldly spheres of politics or economics.

To the purely religious motivation of the Protestant world-view must be added another feature: the radical devaluation of the creaturely world. Not only does the Protestant notion of salvation focus exclusively on a religious end-in-itself, but it also positively proscribes any natural or creaturely means to this goal. On a personal level, this means that the individual's conscience is the only source by which religious worth before god can be assessed. Hence Weber speaks of the 'unprecedented inner loneliness of the single individual', the individual who cannot appeal to priests, sacraments, the church, or other forms of mediation between the divine and the world (1930: 104).[13] The individual stands alone before the incomprehensible and all-embracing will of god.

Also connected with the 'absolute transcendentality of God' is 'the entirely negative attitude of Puritanism to all the sensuous and emotional elements in culture and in religion, because they are of no use toward salvation and promote sentimental illusion and idolatrous superstition' (Weber, 1930: 105). This demand for subjugating the emotions to impersonal and constant motives was not only part of the individual's striving for salvation, but also represents the Protestant's attitude towards the natural and creaturely world. The external world was to be mastered and overcome by a methodical life-style. Again, that such a radical devaluation of the world could develop into what was in Weber's view a completely this-worldly orientation can be seen as an example of the unintended consequences of ideas. But this eventual consequence should not obscure the fact that the initial central postulate of Protestantism consisted in a completely – and in this sense consistently – other-worldly orientation.

These central features of the Protestant world-view can be highlighted by contrasting them with the notion of the sacred in medieval Catholicism. The Catholic god was not absolutely transcendent because the believer could rely on various embodiments of his power in the forms of the priesthood, the sacraments, and the church. But this also meant that a complete devaluation of the world was lacking inasmuch as the church and its officials bridged the gap between the transcendent deity and an imperfect world. Finally, the Catholic believer's conduct was shaped by the notion that ethical significance was attached to single acts, as opposed to the Protestant whose personality as a whole was subject to constant evaluation.

The complete separation between the sacred and worldly affairs and the internal consistency of the Protestant world-view constituted a radical break with medieval Christianity and these central features determined the subsequent development of Protestantism. This does not mean, however, that this world-view was given once and for all. There was an inner logic by which it was transformed from its originally 'weak' Lutheran form into the final and consistent Calvinist doctrine, a point from which no further development of the central tenets of this world-view – but only of its concrete manifestations – was possible (on this point, see also Dumont, 1983: 60). With Luther originates the idea that salvation was foreordained by the unknowable will of god and that there was a 'calling' to realize his will. Weber stresses not only that the idea of the calling was radically new, but also that it is only through this idea that later forms of Protestantism can be understood (1930: 80, 97). Luther's conception had not, however, been driven to its consistent conclusion, since his doctrine still allowed for a union with the divine. Despite god's transcendence, the Lutheran attitude was one of 'inward emotional piety' combined with a quietist indifference to the traditional social order (1930: 113). The world was not devalued because the believer was a 'vessel' of god, despite his absolute transcendence.

Only with Calvin were these Lutheran ideas carried to their ultimate conclusion, for here the notion of god's completely transcendent and impenetrable will 'is derived not, as with Luther, from religious *experience*, but from the logical necessity of his *thought*; therefore its importance increases with every increase in the logical consistency of that religious thought' (Weber, 1930: 102, emphasis in the German original). That is, Calvin's intensification of Protestant doctrine stemmed from his more radical separation of god from the world and from his notion that the creaturely world exists only for the sake of god. The individual now faced an unbridgeable gap between the striving for salvation in this world on the one hand and god's unalterable will on the other. Whereas Luther still attached religious significance to subjective piety, the Protestant believer after Calvin could only strive to achieve salvation through mastery over the self and the world.

It is at this point, for Weber, that the 'great historic process of *disenchantment*, which had begun with the old Hebrew prophets . . . and repudiated all magical means to salvation as superstition and sin, came here to its logical conclusion' (1981b: 123, my trans.; cf. 1930: 105).[14] From this consistent end-point in the inner logic of this world-view that had reached its climax in Calvinism, only two paths were open to Protestantism. One was for Protestant belief to concentrate exclusively on the conscience of the individual believer, with salvation solely dependent on the individual's fulfilment of impersonal and intangible demands. This path could only lead to secularization since the conduct that was required in this case could only be of a worldly nature. The second path was that various forms of mediation between the divine and the believer's fate could be created, giving more tangible support to the striving for salvation. This was the path towards a more routine form of religion in the shape of the systematization of doctrine, the greater role of tangible religious qualifications, of the priestly intermediaries and of the institutionalization of church and sect in the Protestant denominations. Let us note, however, that in terms of the inner logic of world-views, the process of disenchantment has to come to an end with the radical separation between a single, impersonal and transcendent force and the creaturely world – a point that we will need to return to in the discussion of science since this separation is also the fundamental premise of the modern scientific world-view.

Before we can trace these two paths, we must briefly examine the psychological consequences of – and the ethic produced by – the Protestant world-view. Weber thought that, initially at least, not only could one identify the above-mentioned central tenets underlying all forms of Protestantism, but also a common ethic. This distinctive ethic he describes as an 'ascetic conduct [which] meant a rational planning of one's whole life in accordance with God's will' (1930: 153). The way this ethic came about can be understood as the result of the following steps: the central tenets of 'election' and the 'calling', which were uncompromising and unalterable, led to the belief that it was not just the accumulation of meritorious acts, but an adjustment of the whole of one's personality which were required for salvation. This belief, in turn, meant that there was a constant uncertainty as to whether all ethical obligations were being fulfilled. The combination of permanent uncertainty and constant watchfulness, finally, produced a powerful psychological motivation.

The positive aim of this ethical standpoint was to establish the kingdom of god on earth. Equally important as this positive prescription, however, were the attitudes which this ethic proscribed or devalued. Foremost among these was the disdain for ostentatious wealth and luxurious living. All attempts at deifying the creaturely world were prohibited. Furthermore, god's radical transcendence ruled out a spiritual attachment to nature, and thus a 'negative attitude toward all sensuous culture [was] a very fundamental element of Puritanism' (Weber, 1930: 222). Indeed, the devaluation of the creaturely world positively fostered the subjugation of nature, 'for it was hoped from the empirical knowledge of the divine laws of nature to ascend to a grasp of the essence of the world [which] could never be attained by the method of metaphysical speculation' (1930: 249).

The Protestant ethic was revolutionary, in Weber's view, because it combined the pressure from this psychological premium with the simultaneous exclusion of all that could detract from it. It changed the believer from within, rather than demanding an adaptation to external or institutional norms. Weber's argument was partly directed against those who thought that it was the religious tolerance of the Enlightenment and a secularization of conduct that contributed to the spirit of capitalism. Instead, he claims that it was precisely the strict observance of religious demands that led to the emergence of rational and methodical conduct. Not ethical indifference, but a positive religious injunction to fulfil one's 'calling' broke through the barriers of economic traditionalism.

At this point we can return to tracing the first path taken by Protestantism, the path toward secularization. The effectiveness of the Protestant ethic lay in the fact that it focused on the innermost motivations of the individual. Yet this is also precisely the reason why Protestantism became secularized so easily. While concentrating on the means for achieving salvation, which were means of a purely worldly nature, the believer could lose sight of the transcendent religious premise of this orientation. The capitalist entrepreneur might initially have been motivated by the quest for salvation, but with the loosening of all external religious ties, success in a 'calling' could eventually be adopted as a purely secular goal. In this way, the influence of the Protestant ethic on everyday life paradoxically also contributes to the decline of the influence of Protestantism as a religous doctrine. This replacement of religious motives by the utilitarian calculus of economic success will have to be discussed further under the separate heading of the secularization of belief.

At this point we must trace the second path that Protestantism could take, namely the further development of those tangible forms whereby Protestantism mediated between the divine and the worldly. Along this second path there were two ways in which Protestantism became more adapted to everyday life: either the central tenets were weakened by allowing god's will to be embodied within institutional or doctrinal forms, or belief became accommodated to the needs of believers. It should be stressed that in what follows, we will be looking at ways in which Protestantism weakened or actually hindered the spirit of capitalism. This is not to say that the *secular* ethic that constitutes the main legacy of Protestantism could not continue to promote this spirit. None the less, in keeping with Weber's view of cultural change, he acknowledged that 'religious tendencies' could emerge from Protestantism which could 'at a later date . . . oppose certain progressive features of capitalist development' (1930: 191–2). It is to this routinization of charisma in Protestantism that we can now turn.

The accommodation of Protestantism to the needs of certain strata of believers can be discussed first because this development took place in all the various Protestant denominations. Weber suggests that during 'the time of the expansion of the Reformation', Calvinism and other forms of Protestantism were not 'bound up with any particular social class' (1930: 43). Nevertheless, the 'most genuine adherents of Puritanism were, for example, to be found 'among the classes which were rising from a lowly status' (1930: 174). Protestant belief for Weber was unique because it appealed to a broad stratum of society, namely the emerging bourgeoisie. No other salvation religion (except ancient Judaism) had such a wide-ranging influence untinged by magic.

Not all strata, however, were receptive to the Protestant ideals. The aristocracy reacted against them: 'The feudal and monarchical forces protected the pleasure seekers against the rising middle class and the anti-authoritarian ascetic conventicles' (Weber, 1930: 167). Apart from this, the stringent requirement that god's grace could not be ascertained by any visible signs was too severe for many believers. Hence weaker versions of Protestantism emerged which offered tangible criteria of one's election and in which obtaining god's grace was linked to the attainment of a certain social (as opposed to religious) status. In Weber's words, 'for the broad mass of ordinary men . . . the recognizability of the state of grace necessarily became of absolutely dominant importance' (1930: 110). This kind of 'cheating' from the perspective of the orthodox position naturally meant that other factors – such as church attendance or economic success – became increasingly important as signs of election.

To this we must add Weber's view that peasants were everywhere strongly inclined to remain tied to magical views, that magical views tended to remain in force wherever feudal powers continued to be dominant, and that the most fully developed expression of Christianity only took place in an urban environment (Weber, 1968: 468–72). In other words, certain strata remained tied to more traditional forms of religion despite the strong Protestant antipathy towards magic. While some of these points are not made explicitly in the *Protestant Ethic*, it is easy to see that they pertain as readily to Protestantism as they do to all other religions. Hence it is misleading to suggest that in Weber's view, Calvinism was uniquely and curiously exempt from the accommodation to the interests of certain strata (Parkin, 1982: 51, 53), although this aspect does receive comparatively little attention in the *Protestant Ethic*.

Weber does explicitly refer to routinization in the non-Calvinist denominations. By contrast with the effects of Calvinism itself, he says that 'the non-Calvinist ascetic movements, considered purely from the view point of the religious motivation of asceticism, form an attenuation of the inner consistency and power of Calvinism' (1930: 128). In German Pietism, for example, the impersonal or objective demands of Calvinist religiosity were transformed into a subjective union with god.[15] This change in emphasis is a reflection of changes in Pietistic doctrine. The reinterpretation of Calvinist ideas meant that more emphasis was placed on an emotional attachment or a mystical union with god as a means to salvation. This shift towards emotional religiosity, however, entailed a diminution of the capacity to promote a rational and methodical lifestyle. In its extreme form of 'religious ecstasy', the effect of Pietism was even 'the direct opposite of the strict and temperate discipline under which men were placed by the systematic life of holiness of the Puritan' (Weber, 1930: 130–1). Apart from doctrinal changes, Weber indicates that this transformation can also be attributed to the influence of certain strata for which this emotional type of piety had a particular appeal (1930: 134).

A similar increase of emotionality and subjectivism can also be found in Anglo-American Methodism, with slightly different results. Again, salvation was more of an 'immediate feeling of grace and perfection instead of the consciousness of grace which grew out of ascetic conduct in continual proof' in Calvinism (Weber, 1930: 141). By contrast with Pietism, however, there was more emphasis on a spiritual awakening, followed by a mixture of ascetic conduct and emotional faith. Although this did not necessarily outweigh asceticism, the fact that such an awakening took the place of the doctrine of predestination again, for Weber, suggests 'an emotional intensification' (1930: 142). Both Methodism and Pietism can therefore be seen as 'milder forms of the consistent ascetic ethics of Puritanism' (1930: 252).

With the Baptist sects, there was at once a weakening of consistent Puritanism and at the same time a strengthening of the Protestant ethic on an entirely new basis. Again, there was the notion of an inner awakening of faith, but here an awakening was supplemented by the continual demonstration of faith through meeting up to certain qualifications for membership of the sect. In this way there would be a constant affirmation of god's revelation in the sect as a group. In one sense, such an inner awakening meant an intensification of the Protestant ethic because in addition to the inward uncertainty about salvation, the believer also had to meet the (outward) requirements of the sect (Weber, 1930: 151). This latter requirement must be added to the central tenets of 'election' and 'calling'.

Yet in another sense, these additional qualifications could detract from the purely inward orientation of the believer and thus weaken the Protestant ethic. This is because the rules applying to sect membership constitute a different type of religiosity. They demand the visible manifestation of certain religious qualifications, such as the recognition of a fellow member of the sect as a good citizen. Weber cites the merchant who conducts business according to the motto that ' "honesty is the best policy" ' (1930: 151). These forms of religious qualification at the same time represent social qualifications, and as such they lose their specifically (inward) religious motivation and take on a purely (external) secular significance. The believer is no longer a tool of god's will, but instead follows the precepts prescribed by social custom. These factors allow Weber to speak of a 'weakening of the Calvinist conception of the calling' among the Baptist sects (1930: 150).

The fact that Baptism made two separate demands on believers means that its impact on social life is also twofold. On the one hand, the requirement of sect membership led to an intensification of the notion of the 'calling' and hence to a strengthening of methodical conduct (1930: 151). But on the other hand, the focus on the individual's conscience was weakened by the addition of sect qualifications which were of a purely social nature.

Apart from sect qualifications which added a new dimension to Protestantism, its impact therefore follows Weber's typical pattern of routinization. Having established how routinization took place, we can now resume the discussion of how the Protestant ethic gave way to secularization. One of Weber's interpreters has aptly summarized this process as follows: 'As its primary concern with salvation ebbed, a secularized worldly asceticism became indistinguishable from the spirit of capitalism' (Brubaker, 1984: 26). We have already noted in passing that Protestantism underwent secularization because of the unique nature of its central theological tenets. Weber saw this as the ultimate consequence or culmination of the long-term process of disenchantment:

> That great historic process in the development of religions, the elimination of magic from the world which had begun with the old Hebrew prophets and, in conjunction with Hellenistic scientific thought, had repudiated all magical means to salvation as superstition and sin, came here to its logical conclusion. (1930: 105)

The process had begun when Judaism started displacing the foundations of what Weber thought of as the essence of magic, the embodiment of extraordinary powers within concrete persons and symbols. The logic of the Judaic world-view led directly to the idea of the transcendent and all-powerful god of Protestantism. The notion that extraordinary power resided in a single entity completely divorced from the world had crystallized here into its most consistent form. The Protestant god no longer interfered in the course of history, as the Judaic god had done, but rather remained aloof from all earthly events precisely by virtue of his absent control over them. But as the gulf between the divine and the creaturely had become unbridgeable, the believer was forced into a completely worldly method of achieving salvation.

What has all this to do with secularization? In Weber's terms, it was precisely this unbridgeable gap between the sacred and the worldly which led to secularization. The tension between a divine will and human subordination now took place exclusively in the conscience of the believer. And since all tangible manifestations of religion had (at least in theory) been eliminated, the purely inward ethic of the believer could only issue in secular achievements. There was, in David Martin's words, a 'corrosive logic' inherent within the Protestant theological position itself (1978b: 35).

In actuality, of course, this 'corrosion' did not always set in. On the contrary, many developments strengthened the role of religious forces. So, for example, the growth of a priestly stratum increased the Protestant churches' control over believers. Likewise, the dispensation of grace by the church as a divine institution enhanced its position. But although these and other developments took place, they could not mitigate the central tenet of Protestantism which focused exclusively on the direct relationship between the believer and god. Setting up intermediate agencies between the believer and the divine was rather a result of the compromise of this central tenet.

Instead of this compromise, the corrosive logic of Protestantism represents a different path. In the first place, its workings can be observed within the psychology of the individual believer. The more consistently the Protestant doctrines of predestination and election were taken to their logical extremes, the more likely it was that the believer developed purely secular motives. This pattern follows from the nature of Protestant doctrine itself in so far as it stipulates that the individual's conscience can only be satisfied by means of worldly deeds.

Weber does not describe this process in detail, partly because he fails to distinguish the several steps that are necessary to transform Calvinist theology into the secular ethic of capitalism (on this point, see Poggi, 1983: 56). He seems more interested in the practical conduct that could be derived from the Protestant ethic. We can nevertheless reconstruct several steps that lead from Protestant theology to its dissolution in secular conduct: first, there is the orientation of the believer towards a certain world-view. In Calvinism, this means meeting the demands of a completely transcendent deity. Secondly, there is the psychological state produced by this conception. The uncertainty about one's election resulted in anxiety as well as inner loneliness. But such a state of mind, thirdly, generates a certain type of conduct governed by an ethic of continual improvement which is intended to maximize the chances for salvation. And in the end, Weber thinks Protestantism merely provided the entrepreneur with a good conscience regarding restless economic activity (1930: 176).

There is another aspect of secularization which follows on from Weber's view that Puritan ideals were most genuinely adhered to 'among the classes that were rising from a lowly status' (1930: 174). Once these strata had achieved economic success, he points out, they would often succumb to what would earlier have been derided as the ' "temptations" of wealth' (1930: 174). He quotes John Wesley to the effect that wherever wealth has been accumulated, ' "although the form of religion remains, the spirit is swiftly vanishing away" ' (1930: 175). In this sense too, the initial period of religious zeal gave way to one in which the this-worldly attitude towards work in a calling manifested itself in secular signs of one's election.

During the later phase of Protestantism then, religion became an obstacle to the further extension of capitalist activity, instead of a factor contributing to its growth (Weber, 1930: 72). The 'iron cage' of capitalism, in turn, with its creation of increasingly impersonal social relations, eventually dissolved religious norms and the ties of the institutional Protestant church. Still, the impact of the Protestant ethic was felt throughout the various spheres of life and this transformation of religious belief into various secular forces can be seen as another aspect of secularization. Particularly in the writings apart from the *Protestant Ethic*, we find that he describes how the vacuum left behind by the demise of religious beliefs is filled by various secular replacements. So, for example, in his political writings where he ascribes to the literati of his day a world-view which is akin to the Protestant one – namely, a world-view in which all values are unified within an all-encompassing whole. Or again, there are his comments to the effect that the bourgeois belief in the idea of progress can be seen as a cultural remnant of the optimistic faith in religious salvation among rising Protestant strata.

Nevertheless, Weber did not trace all ways in which Protestantism left a secular legacy. We may therefore briefly consider some other, more detailed accounts (which are Weberian in spirit) of the various cultural changes which followed in the wake of Protestantism. David Martin, for example, describes how the contents of different political ideologies depend on the type of religion they replace. While Catholicism tends to create strongly right- or left-wing political movements with a high level of commitment and which dominate the political landscape, Protestantism tends to create pluralism and democracy (Martin, 1978a: 24–5). This suggests that Protestantism is a stronger agent of secularization and promotes individualism, whereas Catholicism has a socially entrenched ideology which can serve the interests of certain strata – the elite in the case of the right, and a minority excluded from power in the case of the left (Martin, 1978a: 41). Martin's pattern therefore confirms Weber's link between radical individualism and the Protestant ethic.

We have seen that as Protestantism becomes secularized, the institutional manifestations of Protestantism which remain can present an obstacle to the progress of capitalism. Herberg's account of Protestant sects in America strongly echoes Weber's view of routinization:

> every religious movement carries within itself its own inner contradiction. Its very success tends to rob it of its dynamic and to harden into set forms what was once fluid and open. Religious revivals, of their very nature, are passionate strivings of the spirit, brief and tempestuous. When the passion is spent, reaction sets in; after the revivalists come the organizers and institutionalizers, who understand their responsibility as that of conserving the gains of the movement. Denominational lines are consolidated and become all-important again. The immediacy of spirit becomes an institutionalized form; indeed, a kind of institutionalized revival is itself incorporated into the system. (1955: 122)

Two interrelated aspects of Weber's notion of the routinization are touched upon here: one is the notion that the individual's initially direct relation to god becomes settled within formal and institutional relations. Such a development is intrinsically inimical to capitalism because the creation of rigid religious ties is likely to extend into the political and economic spheres. Secondly, Herberg too sees external or merely formal adherence to religious norms replacing an earlier sense of inward religious obligation. This type of religiosity, however, is likely to lead away from the rational and methodical pursuit of profit.

The more ritualized and institutionalized residue of religion has also been commented on by Alasdair MacIntyre. In his account of secularization in England, he suggests that the universal claims of Protestantism did not survive industrialization (1967: 15, 25), and only what he calls the 'secondary virtues' remain (1967: 24). The latter are more tied to a specific social context, serve more concrete needs, and change behaviour not in terms of a fundamental reorientation of life (as in early Protestantism) but only modify the particular means of achieving given ends (1967: 24). In Weber's terms, such particularism is the hallmark of routinization.

This pattern of secularization and routinization, both in Weber's writings and in the extension of Weber's ideas in the writings of others, must be seen as an essential part of the Protestant ethic thesis. Whereas the emphasis is often on the initial doctrines which revolutionized the life-style of believers, the pattern of cultural change here closely resembles that which recurs throughout his writings. The abstract and universal Protestant world-view in this case either lost its validity and was abandoned altogether, or it remained only in the form of particular religious norms that were limited to a certain social context. The religion that remained was tied to a formal and institutionalized character, with norms being imposed on the believer from the outside. An important part of this pattern was that religion became entrenched within the other spheres of life. This was as true of the individual believer, whose religious motives were transformed into economic pursuits, as it was of the accommodation of belief to certain social needs, whether they were the practical and everyday needs of particular social strata, or the institutional requirements which dictated that religion should fit into an established social framework.

The transformations of the Protestant ethic thus led to a stage where religion reinforced the social order instead of revolutionizing it. We must therefore supplement Weber's well-known thesis that the role of ideas led to the creation of a radically new social order (a thesis which has often been discussed and has not been dwelt on here), with the idea that the setting in of routinization, here as elsewhere, also brought with it the ossification of social relations. A second aspect of the secularization of Protestantism, however, was that the progressive elimination of various religious elements from social life left a vacuum that could be filled by secular forces. This creation of a vacuum demonstrates the force of the inner logic of world-views. Finally, in terms of the relation between religion and the other spheres of social life, we have observed an increasing separation of the religious sphere from the other spheres of life. Again, the vacuum created in the sphere of religion made room for the impersonality of the modern market and of the bureaucratic state, both now unhampered by religious forces.

Far from representing an isolated study of the origins of capitalism then, the *Protestant Ethic* must in fact be seen as part of Weber's larger project of examining cultural change in a comparative perspective. Althought the Protestant ethic can also be seen as a contribution to the debate about the causes of modern capitalism as an economic system, it is more appropriate, given that Weber was interested in the emergence of a rational and at the same time routine and everyday world, to consider it as an analysis of the origins and distinctiveness of modern culture.[16] For Marx and Durkheim, the central feature of the modern world was the division of labour. For Weber, however, it was rationalism – consisting here both in the routinization and disenchantment of social life. These consequences, although they fundamentally reshaped economic and political life, have their most profound (cultural) significance in determining everyday conduct within the modern social order – in other words, within the arena of cultural life itself: 'One of the fundamental elements of the spirit of capitalism, and not only of that but of all modern culture: rational conduct on the basis of the idea of the calling, was born . . . from the spirit of Christian asceticism' (1930: 180). Having charted the origins and the distinctiveness of this order, we can now consider the trajectory of the cultural consequences within it.

Notes

1. The fact that Judaism was free of magic does not mean that all elements of magic were eliminated from popular religion, but rather that Judaism remained on the whole a non-magical religion (Weber, 1952: 219).
2. The translators of *Ancient Judaism* use the spelling 'Yahwe', whereas here the currently accepted 'Yahweh' is used.
3. Compare Gellner's suggestive account of the role of the Judaic world-view – and a similar assessment of its significance (1988: 82–3).
4. It may be noted in passing that the source of Weber's idea that ancient Judaism was marked by a struggle between charisma and routinization can be traced, among others, to the writings of Julius Wellhausen, to whom Weber makes reference (1952: 426). See also Liebeschütz (1964; 1967, chs 8, 10) where, for example, he discusses a dynamic in Wellhausen's analysis of ancient Judaism that is very similar to Weber's conception of charisma and routinization (Liebeschütz, 1967: 262).
5. In fact, as Schluchter points out, ancient Judaism can be divided into five periods: 'The period of the covenant, the period of the kingship in its different variants, the period of the Exile and the post-exilic period, which in turn can be divided into the times before and after the destruction of the Second Temple' (1989: 200). In terms of our attempt to convey Weber's view of cultural change in *Ancient Judaism*, however, it will suffice to follow the text in distinguishing between three main periods.
6. The distinction between the prophets who create a new, monotheistic conception of god on the one hand, and the priestly stratum, systematizing the ethical laws on the other has, incidentally, been challenged in a recent sociological account of ancient Judaism by Irving Zeitlin. He argues that the monotheistic idea originated in the priesthood too, and that it had more popular appeal than Weber is willing to allow for (Zeitlin, 1984: 259–60, 266, 282–3).
7. There are interesting parallels here with Jacobson's account, from the perspective of literary criticism, of the significance of this new world-view, which consists for him of the 'universal nature of the prophet's moral injunctions' (1982: 128).
8. The other important gap is Eastern Christianity. For a reconstruction of 'The Economic Ethics of Russian Orthodox Christianity', see Buss (1989).
9. The most extensive attempt to reconstruct Weber's ideas about early Christianity

is Schluchter (1989: 205–48). He argues that early Christianity represents both a regression and an advance in the development of Western rationalism. To this effect, he quotes the *Religion of China* (1951: 226) where Weber says that there are two criteria for the 'level of rationality' attained by religion: one is the degree to which a religion has rid itself of magic (disenchantment) and the second 'the degree to which [a religion] has systematically unified the relation between God and the world and therewith its own ethical relationship to the world', Schluchter argues that early Christianity represents a regression in so far as it did not reject magic to the same extent as Judaism (1989: 230). But he also claims that early Christianity represents an 'advance' in terms of the second criterion (1989: 230). Against Schluchter's second point, it will be argued here that early and medieval Christianity included such a variety of relations between god and the world – such as mysticism, anthropolatric hero-worship and the cult of saints – that this type of religion must be seen as a regression rather than an 'advance' in the course of the development of Western rationalism.

10. It is not surprising that Collins, who offers a Weberian analysis of medieval Christianity, comes to the opposite conclusion, namely that 'the rise of medieval Christendom was the main Weberian revolution, creating the institutional forms within which capitalism could emerge' (1986a: 76). This difference derives from the fact that Collins emphasizes organizational capacities and material conditions, whereas here Weber is interpreted as focusing on world-views and cultural change.

11. Such a developmental perspective on Western rationalism is implicit in the interpretations of Schluchter (see above, note 9) and Habermas (1984).

12. Strictly speaking then, the charismatic force of the Protestant world-view is derived from two sources: one is the idea of the radical transcendence of god, originating from the Israelite prophets, and the other the combination of the ideas of the calling and of predestination found in Luther and Calvin.

13. Keith Thomas also attaches great significance to the radically transcendent nature of Protestantism: 'In the long run it may be that the Protestant emphasis on the single sovereignty of God, as against the Catholic concept of a graded hierarchy of spiritual powers, helped to dissolve the world of spirits by referring all supernatural acts to a single source' (1971: 561).

14. The English version (Weber, 1930: 105) omits the term 'disenchantment' here.

15. The way in which Weber's understanding of Pietism was derived from his personal background and certain strands in German intellectual and religious life is reconstructed by Albrow (1990: 62–77; see also Weiss, 1975 and Andersson, 1977).

16. The fact that Weber is concerned above all with a comparative analysis of the 'specific and peculiar rationalism of Western culture' (1930: 26), or again with the 'universal-historical problem . . . of the modern European culture-world' which consists of 'cultural phenomena . . . within a developmental direction of *universal* significance' (1981b: 9, my trans.; cf. 1930: 13), is made clear above all in the 'Introduction' to the studies of the world-religions (1930: esp. 26–30). This aim is also attested to in a letter from Weber to his colleague Rickert, quoted in Marianne Weber's biography: 'In June or July [of 1905] you will receive an essay on cultural history that may be of interest to you: Protestant asceticism as the foundation of modern vocational civilization [*Berufskultur*] – a sort of "spiritualistic" construction of the modern economy' (1975: 356).

4

THE IRON CAGE OF MODERN RATIONALISM

Politics in a Disenchanted World

For Weber, the rise of modern capitalism goes hand in hand with the growth of impersonal relations of domination and the disenchantment of the world by science. His despairing outlook on modern social life is particularly evident in his writings on politics, which are contained both in his political sociology and his polemical newspaper commentaries on contemporary political events.[1] Weber himself wanted to keep these two separate. He warns, for example, against treating his political journalism as if it had social scientific validity (1980a: 306, 448). Yet, as those who have written about his political ideas have pointed out, maintaining a clear-cut distinction between the two is impossible (Giddens, 1972; Mommsen, 1974a). As we shall see, they are both parts of a larger pessimistic view of modern culture.

The best illustration of the continuity between his political ideas and the writings we have examined so far is the theme of charisma and routinization. We have already found on several occasions that this opposition is central to his studies of the world-religions, and there are strong parallels between religious and political change. In his typology of legitimate domination, the extreme poles of charismatic leadership and bureaucratic stagnation are similar to the poles of religious innovation and routine: 'Bureaucracy . . . is a permanent structure . . . oriented toward the satisfaction of calculable needs with ordinary, everyday means. All *extra*ordinary needs . . . have always been satisfied . . . on a *charismatic* basis' (1968: 1111, emphasis in original). Weber also spells out this opposition more explicitly in terms of the effect on the individual:

> Bureaucratic rationalization . . . revolutionizes with *technical means* . . . as does every economic reorganization, 'from without': It *first* changes the material and social orders, and *through* them the people, by changing the conditions of adaptation . . . by contrast, the power of charisma rests upon the belief in revelation and heroes . . . charismatic belief revolu-

tionizes men 'from within' and shapes material and social conditions according to its revolutionary will. (1968: 1116)

It is no wonder then that the need for political leadership and its freedom from bureaucratic constraint are a constant theme in Weber's political writings.

Ultimately, the opposition to increasing bureaucratization and calls for charismatic leadership represent an attempt to maintain the possibility for dynamic change in a world which Weber sees as becoming more and more culturally ossified. In order to find out why he nevertheless holds out little hope for such a revitalization of social life, we must first briefly sketch the background of the routinization of modern social life.

Although Weber argued that religious belief was a necessary factor for the emergence of the spirit of capitalism, he also thought that once this spirit had become firmly established, it provided its own dynamic of cultural change. Where previously the strict ethic of Protestantism had created a new mode of conduct, in modern times this ethic of compulsive work was dictated by non-religious forces:

> The Puritan wanted to work in a calling, we are forced to do so. For when asceticism was carried out by the monastic cells into everyday life, and began to dominate worldly morality, it did its part in creating the tremendous cosmos of the modern economic order. This order is now bound to the technical and economic conditions of machine production which today determines the lives of all the individuals who are born into this mechanism, [and] not only those directly concerned with economic acquisition, with irresistible force. (Weber, 1930: 181)

While it may seem then that Weber is primarily concerned with the routinization attendant upon the economic relations within modern capitalism,[2] in fact he is mainly intent upon discussing the routinization of the sphere of politics (itself, as we shall see, conceived in a cultural manner) and the sphere of intellectual life or culture proper, where religion is displaced by knowledge. Within the sphere of intellectual or cultural life, the growth of scientific knowledge continues the disenchantment of the world, a process whereby magical or irrational forces are eliminated.

Disenchantment has important ramifications in the sphere of politics, as Weber explains in the lecture on 'Science as a Vocation'. One of the main themes of this lecture concerns the consequences of the modern scientific belief in the rational calculability of the natural world. This belief means that other beliefs about the world – beliefs about the extraordinary qualities attributed to charismatic leaders, for example, or intellectual constructions of the 'meaning' of the world – are increasingly replaced by scientific knowledge. What Weber calls the disenchantment of the world must therefore contribute to calculability and rational control in the political sphere too.

Yet science alone does not produce the routinization of belief since the advancement of science *as such*, at least in the natural sciences, produces only empirical knowledge. Wherever science is applied to practical or technical problems in economics or politics, however, the routinization of belief and increasingly impersonal social relations inevitably follow. The economic sphere, for example, has become 'rationalized' for Weber by the 'extension of the productivity of labour . . . through the subordination of the process of production to scientific points of view' (1930: 75). This includes a thoroughgoing division of labour to meet the demands of efficiency within large-scale enterprises. The expansion of capitalism not only entails the separation of the worker from the means of production, but also requires more and more efficient means of administration and keeping pace with technological advances to enhance productivity. With respect to the impact of science on the economic sphere then, Weber thus arrived at conclusions similar to those of Marx and Durkheim. He foretold the inexorable advance of an increasingly impersonal and specialized economic order in which the individual was no more than a cog in a machine.

But Weber also goes much further than Marx and Durkheim do in extending this process across the different spheres of life. As in the sphere of knowledge, the rationalization of the economic sphere inevitably leads to increasing mastery over the world and to the domination of social life by the calculability of means and ends. Not only intellectual conceptions of the 'meaning' of the world, but also traditionalism as a way of life is displaced by this process. Hence Weber's bleak pronouncement at the end of *Protestant Ethic* where he describes modern social life as an iron cage:

> No one knows who will live in this cage in the future, or whether at the end of this tremendous development entirely new prophets will arise, or there will be a great rebirth of old ideas and ideals, or, if neither, mechanized petrification, embellished with a sort of convulsive self-importance. For of the last stage of this cultural development, it might well be truly said: 'Specialists without spirit, sensualists without heart, this nullity imagines that it has attained a level of civilization never before achieved'. (1930: 182)

With this routinization of culture, there would be an increasing adjustment to material interests and to the demands of a mundane, everyday existence. The lives of human beings would come to be dominated by their material needs and they would adapt themselves to the most routine ways of securing these needs.

Finally, in the political sphere, the increasingly instrumental nature of the means of administration and the advance of legal–rational domination create more routine political institutions. Bureaucratization, the establishment of organizations with a strict hierarchy of command and the specialization of tasks, encompasses both the organs of state as well as the organization of political parties. Power is therefore concentrated in the hands of those with technical expertise: 'Bureaucratic administration means fundamentally domination through knowledge. This is the feature of it which makes it specifically rational' (Weber, 1968: 225). Hence decisions are left to an elite stratum of professionally trained officials who, according to Weber, carry out their specialized functions in a strictly detached and rule-bound fashion. Apart from establishing formal rules and with them impersonal social relations, bureaucratization, with its search for the most efficient means to achieve *given* ends, constitutes an ' "adaptation" to the possible' (1949: 24). To this must be added that Weber thought that 'bureaucracy is among those social structures which are hardest to destroy . . . [it] is practically indestructible' (1968: 987).

The growth of bureaucratic authority is a wide-ranging phenomenon for Weber. For example, as a consequence of universal suffrage, political parties were turned into highly organized bureaucratic 'machines' in order to enlist and maintain the support of a mass following. Similarly, the administration of laws was subject to bureaucratization, not least because Weber thought that legal norms needed to satisfy the demand for logical coherence on the part of an elite of legal specialists. Thus the state's enforcement of legal norms was bound to expand into a complex system of formal rules which were at once predictable, neutral, and all-encompassing. The political sphere then, like all other areas of social life, becomes more and more characterized by impersonal forms of domination and instrumentalism. Again, this process occurred at the expense of traditional systems of meaning and restricted the scope of value-oriented attitudes.

Before we examine the views that Weber put forward in answer to this increasing routinization of modern social life, it should be emphasized that this process is such that its occurrence in one sphere of life reinforces the same process in the other spheres. The increasing division of labour in the economic sphere, for example, can also be applied to the sphere of politics such that administration is most effective if the bureaucratic official is completely separated from the means of production – or in this case, the coercive power of the state. Or again, scientific calculability obviously has revolutionizing consequences for improving the techniques of production, and in this way helps the spread of calculability in the economic sphere.

Weber could not ignore the fact that, in one sense, the combination of these processes constituted progress. During the rise of capitalism, these processes undoubtedly contributed to industrialization and modernization. But in terms of the future and of their effect on the individual, Weber chose to emphasize the other side of the coin, namely that they amount to a thoroughgoing routinization of social life. He speaks of the 'parcellization of the soul' and of the 'sole dominance of bureaucratic ideals of life' and asks how a 'remainder of humanity . . . can be preserved against' the inexorable advance of bureaucratic 'machinery' (1924b: 414). And again, this 'inexorable extension of bureaucratization' is not so much a political as a cultural dilemma: He writes of 'the struggle between the type of the "specialist" [*Fachmenschen Typus*] against the older "cultured humanity" [*Kulturmenschentum*] which affects all intimate questions of culture' (1980b: 578, my trans.; cf. 1968: 1002).[3]

Against the background of this iron cage of modern rationalism, the primary aim of Weber's political sociology – as well as the views expressed in his political writings – was to promote charismatic leadership within a 'plebiscitary leader-democracy' (Mommsen, 1974a: 113). The advocacy of strong leadership can partly be seen as a response to the political situation of Weber's day. For example, he often points out that forceful leadership was needed to fill the vacuum left behind by Bismarck's powerful and almost autocratic rule. During the First World War, this view took on an even greater urgency as Weber deplored Germany's aimlessness and the irresponsibility and lack of vision among its politicians.

Yet Weber's political views are even more strongly shaped by his conception of the struggle between charisma and routinization since, in the end, his political recommendations are subordinate to his larger analysis of an increasingly impersonal and disenchanted modern social life which needs to be counteracted by a dynamic national political culture. The focus on charismatic leadership can thus be seen as an attempt to give more scope to the role of ideas against the demands of a routine, everyday social life. Or, as Mommsen puts it, 'Weber was an advocate of democracy on the grounds that, under the social and political conditions of a modern bureaucratic society, it offered a maximum of dynamic leadership' (1974a: 87). This concern for the dynamic role of ideas is evident in several areas. It begins with Weber's view of an individual's leadership within a parliamentary democracy, proceeds to the level of parties and elections within national politics, and culminates in his analysis of the world-historical role of nations.

The powerful role which Weber assigns to the charismatic leader must be seen against the backdrop of his conception of the modern state and parties as bureaucratic 'machines'. 'Bureaucratization', he says, 'is the definite yardstick of the modernization of the state' (1980a: 320). With the advance of capitalism, both state and party are forced to become more like rationally organized enterprises with a strict division of labour and the concentration of the means of production (or, since Weber defined the state as the bearer of a monopoly of legitimate violence, the concentration of the means of violence). Thus Weber could say that 'from the sociological point of view, the modern state is an enterprise just like the factory – this is precisely what is historically unique to the modern state' (1980a: 321).

The increasing bureaucratization of state and party also entailed the centralization of authority and a hierarchy of offices. Again, a typical result was the loss of value-oriented behaviour and its replacement with purely formal or technical calculations of how to achieve given ends by the most efficient means. In Mannheim's words, this would 'turn all problems of politics into problems of administration' (1936: 105).

Weber stressed time and again that it could not be the official's role to act independently or to promote personal political commitments. Instead, the official's role is to carry out the demands of an organization as strictly and efficiently as possible on the basis of specialized knowledge:

> The peculiarity of modern culture, and specifically of its technical and economic basis, demands this 'calculability' of success . . . it develops this peculiarity the more perfectly . . . the more successfully it is able to 'dehumanize' itself, to eliminate love, hate and all purely personal – or generally all irrational – emotions, which are obstacles to calculability, from the pursuit of official business. In the place of the personal sympathy, favour, mercy and gratitude displayed by the lord of the older orders, modern culture demands, for the external apparatus which supports it, the impersonal and strictly 'objective' [*sachlich*] expert – the more so, the more complicated and specialized it becomes. (Weber, 1980b: 563, my trans.; cf. 1968: 975)

Since such complete subordination and impersonality are required by the very nature of bureaucratic organizations, Weber thought that only a strong leader could give aims or goals to this type of apparatus. The administration both of the state and of the modern mass party were to be subordinated to charismatic leadership in order to leave the widest possible scope for individual decision-making. The charismatic leader would thus be allowed to pursue goals which are uncompromising, far-reaching, and not subject to everyday or material circumstances.

These ideas are amplified in Weber's view of the relations between leaders and of their following. In the case both of the state apparatuses and parties, the following of charismatic leaders should be completely subordinated. This means that the people's choice of a leader represents their 'blind' subjection to one person's will or ideals. The deputies of the party should similarly subordinate themselves to those with leadership qualities and responsibility at the head of the party (1980a: 348). Weber's view of the masses during an election was that their role is 'to express their confidence and belief' in the authority of the leader (1980a: 393). Irrespective of the type of constitutional arrangement, Weber thought that 'democracy and demagogy went hand in hand' in the modern mass state (1980a: 393).

He did not, of course, favour an unrestrained demagogy. Within the party, the charismatic leader needs the approval of its members and with it their confidence that the leader can successfully gain a share of power for them. Success could be achieved either by winning a majority of the elected party delegates for parliament or by securing the leadership of the state in the case of a plebiscite. Weber favoured the method of plebiscitary elections because it would be the most unmediated and uncompromising way of gaining or withholding assent for the leader's programme. Nevertheless, parliament would present a check on charismatic leadership, because within this body the leaders of the party would have to prove themselves at responsible decision-making. Furthermore, parliament would place limits on the powers of the head of state by being able to veto particular measures or expressing a vote of no confidence. Thus, from a practical point of view, Weber saw parliament as a training ground for party leadership and for leadership of the state.

In spite of these restrictions, he recognized the danger that a person with great leadership abilities could become the head of state. Such a charismatic leader could exploit the emotionality of the masses in order to gain more power. The only insurance against such an eventuality, Weber thought, was a strong parliament and the formation of well-organized political interest groups – instead of an amorphous and therefore easily manipulable mass of voters.

This brings us to Weber's idea of a 'plebiscitary leader-democracy'. Within the legal and institutional framework of a democracy, Weber tried to facilitate the emergence of a leader who would most directly be able to translate the support of the masses into the authority to realize personal political ideals. That is, the main concessions that he was prepared to make to the modern theory of liberal-democracy was to let a majority of voters determine whether a leader was to be successful, as well as imposing some constitutional restrictions. Aside from this, he wanted to ensure that charismatic leadership would be able to create the dynamic of ideas that had characterized charismatic breakthroughs throughout history.

In the face of the expansion of bureaucratic domination throughout society, he thought that the assertion of the charismatic leader's ideals could possibly provide a counterweight against routinization. In the face of further gains of power by a caste-like elite of officials who only reached for the 'possible', Weber wanted to concentrate authority so that a striving for far-reaching goals could be promoted. And finally, beyond the adjustment of people to material interests and being tied to technical and economic progress, Weber favoured a nation that would aspire to establish certain cultural ideals and national prestige for the benefit of future generations. Such a cultural dynamic would at the same time work against the routinization of social relations generally by counteracting the ossification of the different spheres of life.

With these ideas we are led to Weber's view of the contribution of charismatic leadership to the establishment of cultural ideals that are embodied in the nation. As Beetham points out, for Weber, 'the nation was concerned with the realm of *Kultur*; the state with the realm of power' (1974: 128). Only the nation, however, backed by the might of strong state – and for Weber this meant one which dynamically pursued geopolitical eminence – would be able to take part in the world-historical competition for cultural prestige.[4] None the less, again, his ideas about the cultural importance of the nation apply beyond Germany too (as shown, for example, by his comments on the role of 'smaller' nations). They are a logical extension of his view of modern social life and the pattern of routinization.

Weber thought that the further expansion of capitalism would inevitably bring about the levelling of cultural and economic differences. But partly as a result of this development, other areas of conflict between social groups would come into the foreground, particularly the conflict between nations: 'With the democratization of culture', he says, 'national conflicts will necessarily become stronger' (1980a: 177).[5] Weber's idea was that this competition between nations would take place not only on the economic and political levels, but mainly in terms of the prestige or honour of a national culture (1980a: 13–14).[6] The attainment of prestige for future generations and the adoption of policies that lead to this goal would therefore inevitably become the uppermost national priority. As Beetham has argued:

> to Weber it was not power in itself that was important, but rather the quality of national life that was associated with a 'world political' role, and the ethical and cultural significance that he attached to exercising responsibility towards the future in the use of that power. (1974: 137)

By describing the increase in cultural prestige as the ultimate future aim of a nation, Weber is making the dynamic assertion of cultural ideals into the yardstick of political success. Indeed, his advocacy of charismatic leadership here finds its counterpart on the level of the nation. How much this view was shaped by the idea of the pattern of charisma and routinization is shown by the fact that Weber considered only nations with strong leadership capable of participating in this historical struggle for national prestige, while other nations – especially those dominated by 'an uncontrolled [bureaucratic] officialdom' – would do better to stay out of this struggle (1980a: 442). Or, in his provocative formulation, 'only master nations (*Herrenvölker*) have the calling to enter the spokes of world-history' (1980a: 442).

Weber's analysis of modern politics and its cultural significance can thus be summarized as follows. The routinization of the modern world – both in terms of the spread of bureaucratic domination and in terms of the adjustment of the masses to a routine form of social life – represents the background against which Weber's political standpoint is developed. The ossification of political domination cannot be divorced from stagnation in the spheres of economic and cultural life. To counteract these, Weber advocates charismatic leadership as a potentially dynamic political and cultural force. This advocacy extends up to the level of the competition between nation-states. But although he favoured political arrangements which facilitate stemming the tide of routinization, he nevertheless held out little hope for a charismatic breakthrough. For, as we shall see in his description of the impact of science, the inner logic of the modern scientific world-view dictates an increasing disenchantment of the world.

The criticisms that are commonly levelled against Weber's political thought can thus be seen in the context of his conception of cultural change within modern social life. The first is that he overemphasizes the role of charismatic leadership in the politics of Western democratic societies. This, as we have seen, is based on an overextended analogy with the prophetic charisma of the world-religions. Perhaps it is here that the ambiguity between the two levels of charisma and routinization, between the carriers of (in this case, political) authority and the effect of world-views, is most apparent. Although it may be appropriate to ascribe a far-reaching importance to religious leaders whose ideas shaped the world-views of civilizations, this impact can hardly be compared with what takes place in terms of the formation of a political will within representative democratic institutions of the modern state.[7] The fact that his thought leaves little scope for the democratic or liberal basis of legitimacy in modern politics can therefore be attributed to his 'culturalist' bias.[8]

The second criticism concerns his pessimistic outlook on modern social life. Although it could be argued that his view of the increasingly rule-bound and impersonal nature of modern social relations has on the whole since materialized, the pessimism about the loss of transcendent beliefs and traditional values that goes hand-in-hand with this outlook is perhaps, again, based on an all-too close analogy with the routinization of religious beliefs. Weber may have been correct to foresee the bureaucratization and disenchantment of the public sphere, yet the promotion of charismatic leadership does not provide a solution to this problem.[9] Weber's political ideas were informed by the central question 'how can one possibly save *any remnants* of "individualist" freedom in any sense' in a world in which the economic and political spheres are subject to the 'irresistible advance of bureaucratization' (1968: 1403) and which is disenchanted by the progress of scientific knowledge? Weber often expressed doubts about the possibility of a charismatic breakthrough, which suggests that he was more convinced by his pessimistic analysis of the predicament of modern politics than by his suggestions for a cure. The reason for this can be found in his analysis of the impact of the modern scientific world-view on social life.

Science and Modern Culture

Weber thinks that, in the modern world, science dominates cultural change. The advancement of scientific knowledge bears the single greatest responsibility for the onward march of rationalism and disenchantment, the roots of which have already been examined. The cultural significance of scientific progress also provides the context in which Weber formulates his methodological position and his view of the ethical implications of the sciences of culture.[10] His idea that the social scientist should adopt a value-free approach can, for example, be tied to his analysis of the growing specialization within the scientific disciplines. In 'Science as a Vocation' (Weber, 1948: 129–56), he argues that the scientist's role is limited to the advancement of objective knowledge. This position was directed against the pretensions of those scientists who tried to offer all-embracing and value-laden world-views in the guise of scientific truth. Such world-views, characteristic of magic and religion, would, he thought, increasingly come to be eliminated and replaced by an objective (and in this sense, rational) understanding of the world.

In order to establish the place of science in Weber's social thought, we must clarify several issues. First, there is the question of how the scientific world-view and natural science originated within the context of the growth of Western rationalism. Secondly, we must look at the role played by science in the modern social order in terms of its impact on the political, economic, and the cultural spheres of life. Thirdly, it is important to describe Weber's view of the new condition of humankind in a disenchanted modern world, particularly of the demands which face the individual. Only at this stage will it become possible to establish a link between Weber's methodological position (and at this point the methodology of the social sciences must be clearly distinguished from natural science) – his conceptions of the ideal type, of causality, and of 'cultural significance' (*Kulturbedeutung*) – and how they are informed by his view of the origins and role of science within modern social life.

Weber thought that modern natural science was 'essentially a product of the Renaissance', although its roots lie deeper in Judaeo-Christian and Greek civilization (1930: 13). While scientific endeavours also took place in other civilizations, it is only in the Occident that a science emerged 'which we recognize today as valid' (1930: 13). Two essential preconditions of this development were lacking elsewhere: the Greek idea of the 'rational "proof" ' and the technique of the 'rational experiment' in the Renaissance (1981b: 9, my trans.; cf. 1930: 13). Weber thought that the Platonic notion of an abstract '*concept*' which embodied the essence of a thing led to the idea of an '*eternal* truth' (1948: 141), thereby creating the scientific impetus to discover the truth behind worldly appearances. With the 'rational experiment' Weber seems also to have in mind the establishment of an empirical basis for scientific discovery in the sixteenth century (1948: 141). Modern science could thus only arise on the basis of a world-view in which a particular notion of truth had become enshrined.

Weber's scattered remarks on this topic can only hint at an explanation of the historical origins of science. What they show, however, is that he thought that the roots of our scientific world-view within Western civilization are closely tied to the patterns of rationalism and disenchantment. Scientific thought emerges with the development of an abstract, impersonal and law-like conception of the natural world. Moreover, it is the 'specific contribution' of Protestantism 'to have placed science in the service of technology and economics' (1927: 368).[11]

Yet aside from his ideas about the origins of science, Weber also comments on the unique development of the cultural significance of science in the Occident. Before the onset of our modern understanding of natural science, science had been seen as 'the path to the true *nature*' of things or by some Protestants as 'a way "to God" ' (1948: 142). It was believed that science, like religion, could help to uncover the meaning of the world. This attitude is completely abandoned in the contemporary world, in which any hope that science can reveal the meaning of the world, or provide guidelines for how we should live or act, is ruled out (1948: 143). Here, Weber is following Nietzsche's attack on the Enlightenment faith linking science to progress (1948: 143). Against this, he argues that an objective and value-free science can neither guarantee that its effects would be beneficial or good, nor lend the world meaning (1948: 143, 148).

Another important aspect of the development of science is the way in which the sphere of science became separated from the other spheres of life, particularly the sphere of religion. Before the onset of this separation, religion had typically had close ties to the sphere of 'intellectual life' (to which science, according to Weber, belongs). Weber's example is education, an area which was almost everywhere dominated by the priesthood. (The main exceptions, he thinks, are Mediterranean antiquity and Confucian China (1948: 352).) But this link between the world of learning and the world of religious meaning, which in previous times varied only in its intensity, becomes increasingly and irreversibly severed with the onset of modernity. Ultimately, Weber stipulates that religious belief must demand the 'sacrifice of the intellect' (1948: 352). And since the advancement of science pushes the boundaries of secular and causal knowledge ever further, there is a shrinkage of the domain in which a sacrifice of the intellect is possible. Not only then are the spheres of religion and science bound to become increasingly divorced, but the latter will inevitably assume dominance over the former and make different demands on the individual.

The origins of science therefore lie partly in the emergence of an intellectual sphere that becomes differentiated from the other spheres of life. In this sphere, science, which dominates modern cultural life, 'has come forward with the claim of representing the only possible form of a reasoned view of the world' (1948: 355).[12] Nevertheless, unlike other forms of culture such as religion, the increasing domination of the intellectual sphere by science means that it 'becomes less and less likely that "culture" and the striving for culture can have any inner-worldly meaning for the individual' (1948: 356).

At the same time, despite this increasing differentiation, the impact of science in the modern world progressively pervades the other spheres of social life. So, for example, the role of science within the economic sphere means that economic relations are increasingly subject to a scientific assessment of how to achieve a given end by the most efficient means. Before the onset of capitalism, economic relations were often governed by the ethical considerations promoted by the world-religions. The demand of brotherliness, of sharing goods with one's fellow-believers, or the idea of ethical compensation for economic misfortune by a reward in the beyond – these are now systematically replaced by economic individualism and the competition for worldly rewards. Science contributes to this development in so far as ethico-religious imperatives are increasingly displaced by the demand for an objective assessment of the relation between achievement and reward.

Science also furthers 'the extension of the productivity of labour . . . through the subordination of the process of production to scientific points of view' (Weber, 1930: 75). But such a development in the economic sphere must, in turn, feed the demand for further scientific advance: 'The growing complexity of the technical and economic base of social life . . . fuels an ever-growing demand for specialized technical knowledge' (Brubaker, 1984: 30–1). In short, Weber's view is that the application of scientific knowledge inevitably leads to the growing impersonality of the economic sphere.

The same applies to the political sphere. The ongoing bureaucratization of modern political life can be attributed to a large extent to the application of technical expertise to the task of administration: 'The more complicated and specialized modern culture becomes, the more its external supporting apparatus demands the personally detached and strictly objective *expert*' (Weber, 1968: 975). No doubt this development constitutes progress in one sense, but Weber is also aware of the dangers of extending science into the political sphere. He draws attention to the way in which 'technical progress' makes possible 'the political, social, educational, and propagandistic manipulation and domination of human beings' (1949: 35). Both Weber's political sociology and his political writings make it clear, however, that he expects the application of specialized knowledge to the apparatus of political domination to continue and the role of the bureaucrat to become ever more powerful.

Whereas Weber's comments about the impact of science on the economic and political spheres are scattered, his account of the influence of science within the sphere of intellectual life is more systematic. The sphere of intellectual life is the sphere which was previously occupied by religious and other belief-systems. These allowed human beings to construe the world as a meaningful totality. One example of such a totality was the Protestant world-view, with its conception of the deity as an absent controller of *all* worldly events. But the all-embracing nature of Protestantism led, paradoxically, to a thoroughgoing elimination of religious meaning from cultural life. The fact that a vacuum is created in the cultural sphere is a result, as we have seen, of the way in which Protestant doctrine focuses solely on the conscience of the individual before god. Since the Protestant world-view (in its pure form) does not allow for institutional or other ways of anchoring religious belief, the corrosive logic of this world-view during the course of secularization entails that only the purely *worldly* ethic of Protestantism remains as a residue of the former content of the religious sphere.

This vacuum is not, however, simply filled by a new scientific outlook. Instead, the idea of the world as a meaningful totality is gradually and systematically eroded by science. Weber's view is that, although the nature of Protestantism was to a large extent responsible for the secularization of the modern world, the human need for a coherent and meaningful world-view is not thereby also eliminated. In the modern world, various secular attempts to endow life with an overall meaning still persist. Yet these attempts are bound to come into conflict with science. This, as we shall see in a moment, is a paradoxical aspect of Weber's understanding of science: science is a world-view that replaces others, yet it undermines all attempts to construe the world as a meaningful totality. It replaces the previous content of the sphere of intellectual life, but fills it only with content of an impersonal kind which is subject only to the demand of objectivity.

In 'Science as a Vocation', Weber rejects the attempt at construing the world as a secular meaningful totality, the idea of the scientist who thinks that an overall meaning of the world can be arrived at through scientific truth. Because of the demand for objectivity, Weber argues, science can never establish the validity of a particular world-view. Moreover, the impact of science on the cultural sphere erodes not only this attempt, but all attempts at endowing the world with meaning. By offering an impersonal and objective explanation of worldly events, it systematically replaces other explanations which tried to account for these events by assigning them meaning within an overall world-view. Since science treats the world as a causal mechanism in which all parts are open to empirical investigation, it erodes all beliefs that are based on metaphysical or value-laden presuppositions.

This process, whereby attempts to construct a coherent and meaningful world-view are progressively eliminated, is an extension of the process of the disenchantment of the world, in this case spurred on by the inner logic of science. Weber thinks of the scientific world-view as a 'cosmos of truths' or a 'cosmos of natural causality' in which 'rational knowledge . . . has followed its own autonomous and innerworldly norms' (1948: 355).[13] This logic constitutes a continuation of subjugating the idea of truth to a systematic and all-encompassing whole which the inner logic of world-views had driven from ancient Judaism to its conclusion in Protestantism. And whereas one aspect of this process is the elimination of irrational explanations of the world, another is the routinization of modern life since, for Weber, the 'revolutionary force of "reason" works from *without*: by altering the situations of life and hence its problems, finally in this way changing men's attitude towards them' (1968: 245). We have already on several occasions encountered the pattern whereby the charisma of an initially powerful and revolutionizing idea is inevitably transformed, through its institutionalization and accommodation to everyday life, into a stable and routine way of life. In the case of science, Weber does not provide a systematic analysis of the 'charismatic' origins of the scientific world-view (although we have seen that he gives an indication of several among its sources, such as Western mono-theism, the Greek 'concept' and empirical scientific method). He does, nevertheless, give an account of science in the contemporary world which suggests that its revolutionizing impact increasingly gives way to the routinization of social life.

One aspect of this routinization is that there is less and less scope for far-reaching ideals. In Mommsen's words:

> routinization and rationalization pave the way for a new human species –
> namely the fully-adjusted men of a bureaucreatic age who no longer
> strive for goals beyond their intellectual horizon, which is in any case
> likely to be exclusively defined by their most immediate material needs.
> (1974a: 20)

If bureaucratization is partly to blame for this development, so too is science. Take, for example, the increasing demand for specialized knowledge. The technical experts that are needed for this onward march of scientific specialization are seen by Weber as 'specialists without spirit' (1930: 182) who, because of their limited concern with calculating the most efficient means to achieve a given end, are always constrained by immediate tasks. Hence they cannot allow more all-encompassing and far-reaching ideals to dictate the aims of their work.

A more general aspect of routinization is the growing belief that everyday life can be mastered by the calculation of means to given ends. Gone is the single-minded inward orientation towards transcendent values of the Protestant believer. In a secular world, Weber thinks, everyday problems are approached by seeking technically efficient solutions. Yet such an attitude, which accommodates itself to the immediacy and heterogeneity of existing circumstances, must rule out the possibility of single-mindedly pursuing more remote ideals. In Weber's words, it is only 'constancy' in relation to certain 'ultimate "values" ' which lifts the individual out of a 'dull and undifferentiated' everyday life (1982: 132, my trans.; cf. 1975: 192). But it is precisely this 'constancy' which cannot be maintained in the face of the routinization of the modern world.

Finally, routinization also takes place in institutions which are subject to scientific methods of administration. Some examples have already been mentioned, such as bureaucratic administration where, among other things, the degree of centralization is determined by scientific methods and which is typically oriented towards a clearly defined end. Again, subordinating such institutions to the calculus of means and ends demands an 'ethic of "adaptation" to the possible' (Weber, 1949: 24) since the individual has to adjust to the procedures dictated by the institution, rather than being able to pursue personal (and thus possibly far-reaching) ideals.

All these aspects of routinization can be summed up in terms of two contrasts. The first is between an objective world which is subject to the scientific calculation of the relation between means and ends, as against the orientation of the individual who pursues certain constant ends in a single-minded way. And the second is between an everyday world which is governed by immediate practical concerns as against a world which is reshaped by the force of far-reaching ideals. Or, in Weber's words, between the 'shallowness of our routinized daily existence' in which 'persons who are caught up in it do not become aware of . . . irreconcilably antagonistic values' as against that in which 'ultimately life as a whole . . . is a series of ultimate decisions through which the soul . . . chooses its own fate' (1949: 18). If Weber is correct in thinking that in the modern world, the impersonal, objective and everyday realm is becoming dominant, thereby curtailing the individual's scope for unfettered conduct, then it follows that value-oriented striving is bound to be replaced by a routine way of life.[14] As Weber points out at the end of 'Science as a Vocation', those orientations towards reshaping the world which had hitherto been a feature of some of the world-religions must inevitably retreat into a private sphere: 'Precisely the ultimate and most sublime values have retreated from public life either into the transcendental realm of mystic life or into the brotherliness of direct and personal human relations' (1948: 155). Weber acknowledges that science increases our mastery over the world, but it is his criticism of those who equate the growth of science with progress as well as his emphasis on routinization and disenchantment which set the tone for his view of science in the modern world.

The Demands of Science and the Ethic of Politics

How does this assessment of science relate to Weber's methodological standpoint in the sciences of culture? The place where this link is most readily apparent is in the discussion of the ethical stance of the scientist in 'Science as a Vocation'. In this essay Weber wants to dispel what he sees as a prevalent illusion among scientists about the aims and the potential impact of their research. In the first place, he argues, although science contributes to the growth of knowledge, it does not add to our understanding of how people should live or help us decide whether certain values are better than others. Such knowledge can never be arrived at by scientific means. Secondly, even the limited contribution that a single scientist can make towards the growth of knowledge is severely constrained by the narrowness of research in an age of increasing specialization. Even the best discoveries in a specialized field are bound to be superseded within a short time because of the rapid advancement of knowledge. Hence the scientist should not harbour any illusions about being able to change society by presenting an all-embracing 'truth' about the world.

But if this warning to the scientist is based on Weber's ambivalent view of the role of science, he also thinks that there is an aspect of personal heroism in the ethic of the scientist. In order to illustrate this point, it is necessary to contrast the ethic of the scientist with the ethic of the politician which is described in the lecture on 'Politics as a Vocation' (Weber, 1948: 77–128). The 'ethic of responsibility' which governs the sphere of modern politics demands that responsibility should be taken for the consequences of one's actions. But political goals must also be constantly assessed in the light of the likely success that can be achieved in a world in which values inevitably clash and there is a struggle between them, a world which is subject to the laws of realism – in short, a world of *Realpolitik*. The assertion of the personal aims of the politician is therefore doubly constrained: the ends must justify the means, and the means must be effective in a world of ceaseless political struggle.

The ethical position of the scientist, on the other hand, demands a single-minded pursuit of the goal of objective knowledge – without regard to personal ideals. The only demand to which the scientist is subject is one of 'intellectual integrity' (Weber, 1948: 146).[15] Unlike the politician, whose goal is to reshape the world according to personal ideals, the goal of the scientist is not a personal one, but a requirement that is *given* by the very nature of the scientific vocation: namely, a belief in the value of knowledge (although, Weber maintains, the validity of this belief itself can never be scientifically proven). Hence there is an inner pathos, similar to that which can be found in Weber's description of the Protestant ethic, in the ethical ideal of the scientist: it is a rigid and impersonal ideal, the final truth of which can only be asserted but never securely established. At the same time, this ideal demands that the individual should curtail all personal values in favour of imposing objective norms on the self.

It is curious that Weber does not explicitly formulate an ethic in 'Science as a Vocation' to parallel the ethic of responsibility in 'Politics as a Vocation'. This can be explained, however, by noting that politics requires the pursuit of a personal goal which is subject to consideration of the goals of others, whereas science is merely subject to impersonal criteria or demands. Weber argues that the curtailment of personal values and the single-minded pursuit of knowledge constitute the only legitimate ideal of science. Moreover, this ideal is evidently similar to the Protestant ethic. It can be seen as an ethic then, in so far as values are adhered to – not in the sense of everyday life, where values are always compromised or relativized in the light of other conflicting values – but as values which are upheld as a constant and uncompromising standard. This impersonal standard is externally imposed upon the individual by modern science. The personality of the scientist is characterized by an inner distance from the external circumstances that might conflict with the pursuit of knowledge.

This ideal can be linked to Weber's view of the role of science in social life since the demand made on the scientist results from the increasing specialization within the realm of intellectual life and from impersonal social relations which require the upholding of a vocational standard. Yet on the level of the individual, Weber wants to suggest that this personality ideal of the scientist, of living up to 'the demands of the day', can be a heroic posture in the face of circumstances which no longer permit adopting science as a substitute for faith (1948: 156).

Such a standpoint of resoluteness in the face of a pessimistic outlook on the modern world is also evident in Weber's idea of progress. His challenge to the view that the growth of knowledge will automatically lead to an increase in happiness has already been mentioned. In periods that were not yet tied to scientific progress, he says, the individual 'could attain an inner-worldly perfection as a result of the naive unambiguity of the substance of his life' (1948: 356). Such an attitude is no longer possible in an age dominated by scientific advance. Instead, scientific progress means that 'culture's every step forward seems condemned to lead to an ever more devastating senselessness' (1948: 357) since science erodes all traditional values that gave human beings a sense of the meaning of their lives.[16]

This critical stance towards the idea of progress is also the context in which to interpret Weber's assertion that there is 'only a hair-thin line which separates science from faith' (1982: 212, my trans.; cf. 1949: 110). Religious faith offers the believer a way of endowing the world with unassailable meaning. The belief in the value of science on the other hand, must be maintained despite – and perhaps heroically in spite of – the inability to prove the validity or meaningfulness of this belief. If there is nevertheless a similarity between the two in so far as both demand the affirmation of a certain value, there is also an irreducible difference: science constitutes objective knowledge. The more technical side of Weber's methodology of the social sciences (apart from his reflections on the ethic of the scientist and the meaning of the growth of knowledge) is concerned with showing precisely where this 'hair-thin' difference between belief and science lies.

Science without Foundations

In considering Weber's view of science up to this point, no separation has been made between the natural and the social sciences. In order to look at his philosophy of social science, however, it is necessary to limit the discussion purely to social science, leaving aside for the moment the question whether this involves an inseparable barrier between the human and natural sciences. Another issue that must be sidestepped here is the extent to which his position changed over the course of his writings.[17] Bearing these reservations in mind, it is possible to find a central idea about the relation between social science and values which pervades Weber's methodological writings. This idea focuses on the methodological standpoint that needs to be adopted – *given* the cultural significance of science in the modern world.

The relation between social science and values can be established by considering the following points. First, as far as the *individual* scientist is concerned, the aim must be to eliminate the intrusion of values upon scientific work as far as possible (for the reasons noted above). But, on the other hand, as regards the *past*, there has to be a selection of those events which possess a special significance in the light of the type of knowledge that is valued within the scientist's contemporary culture. The presupposition for the pursuit of knowledge within modern culture, Weber says, for human beings as *Kulturmenschen* or 'cultural beings', is 'not that a certain "culture" is considered valuable', but that 'we have the capacity and the will to adopt a stance toward the world and to endow it with meaning' (1982: 180, my trans.; cf. 1949: 81).[18] Hence, finally, the relation between social science and values must be sought in the *significance* that certain kinds of scientific knowledge have within contemporary culture (rather than in the value-standpoint of the individual scientist).

In the context of Weber's methodology then, Weber's conception of 'cultural significance' or *Kulturbedeutung* (1982: 180) which we have already encountered provides a starting-point for objective social scientific knowledge.[19] The social scientist, unlike the natural scientist who tries to discover laws in nature that are universally valid, must address problems that are significant in the light of those values which dominate cultural life: 'Empirical reality becomes "culture" to us because and insofar as we relate it to value ideas. It includes those segments and only those segments of reality which have become significant to us because of this value-relevance' (Weber, 1949: 76).[20] In other words, the social scientist must be able to place the phenomena of 'social cultural-life [*Kulturleben*] which surround us in their universal . . . context' (1982: 172, my trans.; cf. 1949: 74). An example is furnished by Weber's analysis of the rise of capitalism. Since modern capitalism had brought about changes in all areas of social life during Weber's time, as it continues to do today, it was a phenomenon of universal importance to contemporary cultural life. Hence in his studies Weber tried to single out those factors which had helped to bring about this all-pervasive system.

The criterion of success in this respect is whether the social scientist is able to hit the mark in terms of directing attention towards those values which are truly of great importance within a given cultural epoch. As one of Weber's interpreters has put it: 'It is demanded of the social scientist that he should guide the orientation of his researches by the most general interest. The ability to arrive at those values which dominate a "whole epoch" are the mark of a scientific genius' (Weiss, 1975: 32, partly quoting Weber, 1949: 82). The implication is that the more the scientist is able to eliminate personal or other partisan values, and aim instead at those values which are culturally predominant or significant, the greater will be the validity of the insights that are gained.

The values which predominate in a given epoch are, of course, subject to change.[21] Because of this, the values which direct the aims of research must also change: 'The light of the great cultural problems moves on. Then science too prepares to change its standpoint and its analytical apparatus and to view the stream of events from the height of thought' (Weber, 1949: 112). In other words, since cultural problems are bound to change, the whole question of what is 'culturally significant' must be fundamentally reassessed in each epoch.

This conception of cultural significance is closely linked with the personality-ideal described above. For the scientist to be able to achieve as great a devotion to objectivity as possible within a given cultural epoch, a degree of inner distance is essential, both from personal values and from one's immediate social and cultural surroundings. And the more wide-ranging the problem and its cultural significance, the more, Weber says, the need for inner distance since these problems rely to a greater extent on personal beliefs and less on empirical knowledge (1982: 153; cf. 1949: 56). This standpoint again points to the similarity between the attitude fostered by the Protestant ethic and a stance of what could be described as secular asceticism in Weber's methodological writings (see also Lassman and Velody, 1989: 182–3). But while Weber suggests such a stance for the scientist, the fact that he recognizes that 'the light of the great cultural problems moves on' (Weber, 1949: 112) underlines his position that although science can aspire towards objectivity, this objective validity can never attain the status of unassailable truth.

The idea that social-scientific interests must be determined in the light of contemporary culture might suggest that Weber's position is one of relativism. Yet this is not the case. In the first place, the values that characterize a certain epoch are likely to remain stable over a long period of time. But this means that the role played by the values of this cultural epoch will recede into the background:

> All research in the cultural sciences in an age of specialization, once it is oriented towards a given subject matter through particular settings of problems and has established its methodological principles, will consider

the analysis of the data as an end in itself. It will discontinue assessing the value of the individual facts in terms of their relationships to ultimate value-ideas. (Weber, 1949: 112)

Only when a cultural sea-change takes place can there be a wholesale shift in the problems and the conceptual tools of social science in accordance with their significance in the sphere of culture.

Secondly, Weber's conception of cultural significance avoids relativism since the actual research that is carried out (as opposed to the questions that are asked) is still open to empirical verification.[22] Such verification can, for example, take the form of establishing the causal role of certain events. Although a causal analysis may never be able to pinpoint the single necessary and sufficient cause of a historical event, it can still determine the candidates that are likely or unlikely to have played an important role. Weber thus leaves open the possibility of verifying social-scientific research by empirical means.

Again, Weber's approach in this respect should not be taken to imply that there is no difference between the social and the natural sciences. Weber rejects the idea that social science should try to establish universal laws like the natural sciences. Psychological or cultural events may indeed be governed by such laws, so that there is no reason for a fundamental distinction between the natural and social sciences on this basis (1949: 80). Yet there is also a difference in so far as the aim of social science is not to subsume all phenomena under the most abstract and general laws, but rather to examine concrete and specific events. Not what phenomena have in common with all others – but that phenomena have certain distinctive causes that are significant in the light of certain culturally dominant values – is important for the social sciences.

The fact that Weber's methodology argues for objectivity in the social sciences can also be linked to his view of science as a whole. Causal explanation can be seen as contributing to the disenchantment of the world, replacing previous views of the meaning of social relations with causal explanations. In terms of explaining particular social phenomena, however, there are potentially an infinite number of causal connections that can be made. Hence, although causal explanation can be used to verify the results of social-scientific analysis, there is a constraint upon its success in so far as the causes of a social phenomenon such as 'capitalism' can never be exhaustively established in the manner of natural science. There is therefore a limit to the degree to which the social sciences (as opposed to the natural sciences) can exercise an impact on social life. Furthermore, because of the limits of causal explanation, this method must be used side by side with others.

One such important tool of social-scientific explanation is the ideal type, which Weber describes as a 'utopia' or an 'analytical accentuation of certain elements of reality' (1949: 90; see also Burger, 1976). An ideal type one-sidely emphasizes only certain aspects of a phenomenon which is more complex in reality. When Weber distinguishes certain phenomena using ideal types, he often points out that while these phenomena may be separable in thought, in reality they seamlessly shade off into each other.

The ideal type cannot be understood in isolation from the rest of Weber's methodology.[23] It must be seen as part of Weber's aim of explaining social reality in the light of the cultural significance of phenomena. Indeed, Weber only justifies its role as a *means* towards such an explanation. He thinks that ideal types should be judged only by their success as a means of 'revealing concrete cultural phenomena in their interdependence, their causal conditions and their *significance*' (1949: 92, emphasis in original). As with the selection of material and causality, cultural significance provides the yardstick against which the ideal type must be measured.[24]

As an aside, it may be pointed out that although this methodological position, which can be found in the 'Objectivity' (1949: 50–112) essay, is maintained throughout the course of Weber's writings (Henrich, 1952), the question of the extent to which he applied this methodology in his own writings is a separate one. As Mommsen points out, in his substantive writings there is a shift from his early writings, where Weber is concerned with the cultural significance of specific social phenomena, to the later period of *Economy and Society* where cultural significance assumes a more general role and the concern with particular phenomena 'recedes behind the effort to create a system of ideal types' which can be applied universally and from different value standpoints (1974b: 222–3). Apart from this shift, there is, of course, the further question about whether Weber adhered to his own methodology in his sociological writings at all, or violated it completely (Fulbrook, 1978). But whether or not he applied his own technical tools, it is clear that his view of science as a world-view and of cultural significance are completely continuous with the analysis of cultural change throughout his writings.

Another shift, again in his substantive rather than in his methodological writings, occurs in Weber's conception of the 'understanding' (*Verstehen*) of the individual actor's motives. Early on, Weber thought that the motivation of the actor required an 'understanding' of its subjective meaning (Mommsen, 1974b: 218). In his later writings, especially *Economy and Society*, he categorized the different meanings of an actor's motives within the schema of four

types of social action (Mommsen, 1974b: 221). Although 'understanding' is involved in both cases, the former method emphasizes
the ('subjective') intentions of the social actor, whereas the latter is
based on the ('objective') categories of the social scientist. Both
methods, however, require objective or empirical verification. In
this way, the method of 'understanding' does not introduce an
intrinsic difference between the social and the natural sciences.

Another point that is worth making in relation to the 'understanding' of social action is that, as we have seen, in his substantive
studies, Weber rarely uses this methodological tool in relation to
individual social actors. Thinking of him as a methodological
individualist must therefore lead the reconstruction of his analysis of
cultural change astray. Where the notion of 'understanding' *does*
play a part is in the interpretation of the inner logic of world-views
and their influence on ways of life. Here, Weber can be said to use
'understanding' in the sense of a reconstruction of world-views on
the social scientist's part in order to account for shifts in their
meaning. 'Understanding' in this sense also helps him to grasp how
world-views change the orientations to the world of those who
adhere to them, and thus their way of life. But again, this does not
mean taking the actor's point of view. Indeed, there seems to be
nothing in Weber's substantive studies (as opposed to his methodological writings) that would require the adoption of such a viewpoint. In any case, 'understanding' becomes one of the tools for
creating ideal types and again, ideal types based on 'understanding'
are not exempt from social 'science' since there is no reason why the
interpretation of a world-view, for example, should not in principle
be supported by reference to empirical knowledge, even if this may
be more difficult in some cases rather than others.

Again, although there may have been a shift in Weber's methodological position, nevertheless with respect to the ideal type, too, his
methodology and his view of science in the modern world are
interconnected. For the 'utopian' nature of the ideal type suggests
that reality may be ordered in thought within an ideal schema.
Weber often stresses that empirical reality will always be more
complex than any social-scientific theory which tries to explain it.
Nevertheless, a system of ideal types can provide an idealized
reconstruction of the world in thought.

The 'utopian' nature of the ideal type can be derived from
Weber's view of the origin and aim of science: namely, from the
Platonic ideal of the 'concept' and from the ongoing attempt to
discover a knowable reality 'behind' what is empirically given (1948:
141–2). The ideal type is similar to the Platonic 'concept' in so far as
they are both abstractions from empirical reality. Yet the difference

is that the Platonic 'concept' was thought to lead to the *meaning* of the world, whereas for modern social science the ideal type is merely a *tool* with which to discover reality.

In the latter sense, the ideal type serves as an instrument for achieving mastery over the world by means of an increasingly thorough explanation of reality. On the one hand, the ideal type is therefore an ideal abstracted from reality, reflecting Weber's view of science as a search for the imposition of an all-embracing order on the world. On the other hand, it is merely a tool which helps to subjugate reality – just as all natural scientific knowledge does. Like science in general then, the nature of the ideal type is twofold – its ultimate *aim* is the truth that lies behind reality, yet in the modern age it is merely a *means* towards this end.

With this distinction between the aim and the tools of cognition in mind, we can finally return to the 'hair-thin line which separates science from faith' (Weber, 1982: 212, my trans.; cf. 1949: 110). As indicated above, Weber believed that the value of scientific knowledge could never itself be scientifically established. The fact that such knowledge has a certain value is merely a presupposition within a certain type of culture in which there are people who have an interest in the advancement of knowledge (*Kulturmenschen*) (1982: 180, 600; cf. 1948: 145; 1949: 81). In this sense, science (including social science), is merely the assertion of one faith among others: 'The belief in the value of scientific truth is the product of certain cultures and not given in nature' (1982: 213, my trans.; cf. 1949: 110). It is a science without foundations in so far as there are no values which underwrite its legitimacy. Apart from 'the rules of logic and method', Weber says, the only other presupposition of science is 'that what is yielded by scientific work is important in the sense that it is "worth being known" ', but 'this presupposition cannot be proved by scientific means. It can only be *interpreted* with reference to its ultimate meaning, which we must reject or accept according to our ultimate position towards life' (1948: 143; also 1949: 57).

Science goes beyond faith, however, in so far as it continuously attempts, by means of certain methodological tools, to explain social phenomena objectively. The notion of cultural significance provides the basis for this objectivity in the sense that the values inherent in 'cultural significance' are themselves subject to an objective assessment. Furthermore, objectivity is ensured through the openness to empirical verification. The aim of science can therefore only be asserted within a certain culture, while its tools may allow for scientific certainty.[25]

Weber is only willing to concede the intrinsic value of social science to humanity in one respect: it can help people to gain clarity about the best means to achieve ends that are given (1948: 151). In other words, if people have a choice between certain ends, science can help in assessing which of them is likely to meet with success. But again, the value of social science in this case is purely as a tool and the validity of the choice of any particular end or goal can never be established by science.

Weber's methodological position thus reinforces his ideas about the role of science in the modern world. An objective social science is bound to contribute to the ongoing disenchantment and routinization of the world. A certain part is played in this respect by the scientist's belief in the advancement of knowledge, the scientist who, by pursuing the inner logic of the scientific world-view, establishes an increasing mastery over the world. Yet this means that science is not only a tool for extending means–ends efficiency throughout the other spheres of life, but it also progressively eliminates other all-embracing views of the meaning of the world within the sphere of intellectual life.

The relation between Weber's view of modern science and his methodological position can therefore be summed up as follows. Despite the fact that Weber saw modern science as leading to an increasingly routinized world in which far-reaching goals would be progressively eliminated, he nevertheless wished to defend a personal ideal of living up to the impersonal demand of contributing to the advancement of objective knowledge. In response to this double-edged view, his methodological writings stressed both the necessity for a belief in the value of science (itself without a foundation in values) as well as the unsurpassable limits to the role and meaning of this knowledge.

Notes

1. For the purposes of the present argument, only a general account of Weber's view of the development and key features of modern politics will be given. It will not be necessary to include here what has become the most well-known part of his political sociology, the 'Types of Legitimate Domination' (1968: 212–307). For a discussion of the cultural basis of Weber's typology of domination, see Merquior (1980).

2. Weber thought that an even more thoroughgoing process of bureaucratization would characterize any future society organized on the basis of socialist principles (Beetham, 1974: 82–9).

3. Weber also speaks of the 'culture-dominating influence' of 'trained officialdom (*Fachmenschentum*)' (1981b: 11, my trans.; cf. 1930: 15–16).

4. With this topic, we must bear in mind the readership of Weber's journalistic essays and the dominance of the issue of nationalism in German politics during the latter half of the nineteenth century up until Weber's death in 1920. The

overriding continuity between his political journalism, from which most of the quotes are taken here, and his sociological investigations, can be seen by comparing his comments on nationalism in *Economy and Society* (1968: 922–6).

5. Compare also Weber's comment that 'all *culture* is and remains today tied to the nation, all the more so, the more "democratic" the external means of disseminating culture become in the way they spread and in their nature' (1980a: 128).

6. Weber speaks of a 'culture mission', particularly on the part of the 'intellectuals . . . who usurp leadership in a *Kulturgemeinschaft* [cultural community] . . . [and] have access to certain products that are considered "culture goods" . . . [and] are specifically predestined to propagate the "*national*" idea' (1968: 925–6).

7. Weber briefly considered the idea that natural rights, which he describes as the 'charismatic glorification of "Reason" . . . the last form that charisma adopted in its fateful historical course' (1968: 1209), could provide legitimacy for the modern political order. He did not, however, pursue this line of argument.

8. In his study of Weber's political sociology, Breuer also underlines its 'spiritualist bias' (1991: 21) and emphasizes that the political sociology must be understood as subordinate (a 'poor cousin') to his primary concern with the 'rational culture of the Occident' (1991: 31). See also Merquior (1980: 198).

9. For a discussion of the intellectual roots of the leadership ideal in German nineteenth-century culture, see Stern (1975: esp. ch. 11). An insightful assessment of the place of 'charisma' in contemporary social science can be found in Anderson's essay on the 'Further Adventures of Charisma' (1990: 78–93).

10. Despite this link, Weber's ideas about the methodology of the social sciences and his substantive sociological analyses are often considered in isolation from each other (see, for example, Runciman, 1972). As we shall see, however, this link is essential.

11. For an analysis of the relation between Protestantism and the rise of science which echoes Weber's account, see also Milton (1981) and Merton (1973: 228–53).

12. Weber adds that 'the intellect, like all culture values, has created an aristocracy based on the possession of rational culture . . . worldly man has regarded this possession of culture as the highest good' (1948: 355).

13. It should be noted that Weber's approach to the role of science in the modern world entails that the growth of knowledge and the *impact* of scientific knowledge on social life (for which some would use the separate term technology) are two sides of the same coin. This way of thinking can be linked to his way of distinguishing between magic and science and their respective forms of rationality.

14. A similar theme can be found in Simmel's writings, which Frisby summarizes as a 'dialectic of a growing material or objective culture and the increasing difficulty of realizing a genuine individuality in modern society' (1984: 40). One difference between them is that Simmel thought that there was a solution to this dilemma within what Weber thought of as the 'intellectual sphere'.

15. Weber goes on to spell out that this demand for objectivity rests on the distinction between questions of 'the internal structure of cultural values', which fall within the domain of this demand, as against 'questions of the *value* of culture and its individual contents and the question of how one should act in the cultural community and in political associations', which do not (1948: 146).

16. This applies equally, Weber goes on to suggest, to *all* callings – of science as well as of politics: 'The advancement of cultural values . . . seems to become a

senseless hustle in the service of worthless, moreover self-contradictory, and mutually antagonistic ends. The advancement of cultural values appears the more meaningless the more it is made a holy task, a "calling" ' (1948: 357).

17. Such a description would require a detailed analysis of the methodological writings. This is not necessary since the following presentation of his methodology is based on Weber's central statement on the issues in the essay on ' "Objectivity" in Social Science and Social Policy' (1949: 50–112). On the centrality of this essay, see Tenbruck (1959: 573–630, especially 614–20; and 1986).

18. This point is made again on the following page: 'All knowledge of cultural reality is . . . always knowledge from specific and particular points of view' (1982: 181, my trans.; cf. 1949: 81). But these points of view are not, for Weber, subjective as such, but presuppose that we, as cultural beings, value knowledge and that certain objects of knowledge have greater significance than others. This cultural significance, however, is bound to the cultural values which dominate a given historical epoch, and an attempt must be made to establish these as objectively as possible. The point that even these values are bound to change over the course of time or for different epochs (see below) sets Weber apart from Rickert, who believed in transhistorical or universal cultural values (on the relation between Rickert and Weber, but with an appraisal of Weber that is different from the one argued here, see Oakes, 1988). Here as elsewhere, Weber's standpoint is unmistakably Kantian.

19. It is sometimes thought that for Weber, the task of ascertaining 'cultural significance' falls to history, whereas sociology establishes general laws (for example, Beetham, 1974: 252). But even in the methodological part of *Economy and Society*, where Weber could be said to be at his most 'sociological', he says that sociology 'contributes to the historical–causal explanation of culturally significant phenomena' and goes on to point out that the difference lies merely in the use of different tools (1980b: 9, the translation is misleading; cf. 1968: 21). In his essay on ' "Objectivity" in Social Science and Social Policy' (1949: 50–112), he points out that social science can be subsumed within the category of those cultural sciences which treat phenomena in the light of their cultural significance (1949: 67).

20. It is precisely at this point, incidentally, that the importance of the concept of culture in Weber's methodology and in his conception of cultural change converge. In both cases, culture consists of the relation of human beings to empirical reality via the medium of values. In his conception of cultural change, this makes for the way in which world-views have the capacity to revolutionize social life, or how everyday life can be transformed by non-everyday conduct.

21. 'The cultural problems which move human beings remain fluid and form themselves ever anew and in different colours' (1982: 184, my trans.; cf. 1949: 84; see also 1949: 104).

22. Empirical verification is taken here to mean the methods of positivism generally, rather than any particular principle of verification or falsification.

23. Here too there is a link between the ideal type and its place within a cultural science – and cultural change within social reality. Weber points out that ' "ideas" which are influential' in the sense that they 'dominate human beings in an epoch' and as 'components of historical reality' can be grasped 'only by means of the ideal type' (1982: 197, my trans.; cf. 1949: 95–6).

24. Causality and the ideal type should not, however, strictly be counterposed, since

Weber points out that '*developmental* sequences too can be constructed into ideal types' (1949: 101). The distinction within 'cultural reality' between 'concrete causal relations' as 'real factors' as against 'heuristic means', is discussed on 1982: 237 (my trans.; cf. 1949: 135).

25. A more recent attempt to understand science as a 'cultural system' and at the same time spell out its consequences for social life can be found in Elkana (1981: 1–76).

5

THE SOCIOLOGY OF CULTURE: WEBER AND BEYOND

We have seen that Weber's writings, despite their fragmentary nature, are held together by a central concern: to offer an account of the role of culture in social life. And although he does not put forward a theory of cultural change in a systematic way, we have nevertheless been able to arrive at an analytically consistent understanding of it. At this stage, two questions arise: one is to what extent, on the basis of this consistency in his writings, we can also ascribe a theoretical unity to his position? In other words, does his method of analyzing how world-views translate into social reality add up to a distinctive and coherent way of looking at cultural change? This question will then prompt a further and final one; namely, how does Weber's sociology of culture compare with other theories – both classical and contemporary – which address the same issues? Does he offer an alternative to Marx, Durkheim and those who have since tried to advance our understanding of culture from a sociological perspective?

Weber's Theory of Cultural Change

In answer to the first question, it may be useful to summarize the main elements of his analysis of cultural change and to see how they fit together. We can begin, however, with his methodological position. Weber thought that the task of the cultural sciences was to understand and explain those aspects of social reality which possess cultural significance. This standpoint is based both on a conception of how objective cultural scientific knowledge is possible and of how meaningful conduct is an essential attribute of human beings. In other words, it rests on his ideas about objectivity and about what constitutes the social reality which is the object of the cultural sciences.

But this methodological position is not the only way in which culture provides a starting-point for Weber. Cultural change also emerges as the material on which he needs to focus in order to answer the main question that he is faced with – namely, what is the cultural significance of modern Western rationalism? This question necessitates his adoption of the comparative method, since it is impossible to answer without placing it in the context of a comparative 'universal history of culture' (1930: 23). His subject-matter and method are dictated by the conclusions he reached in the *Protestant Ethic*. The way that Weber establishes the distinctiveness of the modern world then, both in his analysis of Western rationalism and in his studies of the other world-religions, is to focus on culture.

The fact, incidentally, that most of the world-views that are dealt with in his writings fall within the sphere of religion, rather than within what he identifies as the sphere of intellectual life in the modern world, does not detract from the distinctive feature of his overall approach, which is to attribute an essential part in social change to the realm of ideas. In all of his major studies, his focus is dictated by his material, so that religion provides the most significant world-views within the cultural life of the pre-modern world, just as the scientific world-view is the most significant aspect of modern culture. In all of his major studies, he is concerned with how culture affects the other spheres of life. Thus, from both this methodological standpoint and his substantive focus, Weber is led to a concern with the fate of modern culture and its unique way of life (1930: 23–6).

Weber's methodological position thus gives a central aim to his writings. But how, specifically, does he conceive of the role of ideas in his studies? In order to assess the coherence of Weber's sociology of culture, let us first summarize the theoretical status of the particular elements which he uses to analyze the role of ideas. Once we have done this, we will be able to see how well these elements fit together and what type of overall theory emerges from their conjunction.

A large part, as we have seen, is played by the inner logic of world-views. One example of this is the rise of monotheism that emerged with the Judaeo-Christian world-view. By contrast with the world-views of the non-Western civilizations, which produced neither a systematic unification of the divine, nor a radical tension between the divine and the world,[1] the ancient Judaic prophets created a religious world-view in which the divine was endowed with all-encompassing powers and at the same time radically divorced from the world. This world-view was systematically unified in the sense that all worldly events could be interpreted as subject to the control of an all-powerful god. The stage was thereby set for the complete separation of the religious from the other spheres of life.

The inner logic of this world-view culminated in the Calvinist doctrine of predestination where the divine and the worldly became separated to the greatest possible extent. This complete separation of the realm of divine power was also a spur to the process of secularization since it meant that religion was no longer entrenched in the various other spheres of life. Secularization, in turn, created a vacuum in the religious sphere of life which could not be filled by other world-views. The inner logic of world-views has thus, in a self-destructive way (so to speak), contributed to the absence of all-embracing world-views in the modern world, and hence also to the fact that the various spheres of life contain irreconcilable views of the world. The world-view that has become dominant in modern social life is a scientific one, and yet the sciences – natural and social – can never provide a view of the world as a meaningful whole. This also means that a scientific world-view can never completely embrace the other spheres of life. In the light of the disenchantment of the modern world by science, it becomes the fate of modernity that an irreducible conflict between competing world-views increasingly comes into the foreground of social life.

This element of Weber's analysis of cultural change links the development of world-views to their internal consistency. His theory rests, in this case, on an interpretation of the meaning of a world-view – its coherence, ultimate presuppositions, and the type of meaningful picture of the world that emerges from it. This strategy of reconstructing the coherence of world-views on the level of their meaning allows him to attribute their transformation purely to an internal logic. But the contribution that the description of world-views makes to understanding cultural change goes further than merely accounting for the direction in which these images of the world develop. Weber thinks that the content of these world-views, in turn, determines the type of ethic or attitude towards the world which is adopted by the believer.

We will be able to get a clearer picture of the theoretical contribution of each element of Weber's sociology of culture to the whole by expanding upon the 'switchmen' metaphor. To recall, Weber's 'switchmen' metaphor states: 'Not ideas, but material and ideal interests directly govern men's conduct. Yet very frequently the "world images" that have been created by "ideas" have, like switchmen, determined the tracks along which action has been pushed by the dynamic of interest' (1948: 280). But in so far as this statement implies that it is (only) the interrelation between world-views and interests which accounts for the impact of ideas, it is misleading. As we have seen, world-views also have a certain logic or dynamic – or as Roth puts it, a 'directional logic' (1987: 87) – of their own, and in this sense have a direct impact on the conduct or way of life of their adherents. Contrary to the 'switchmen' metaphor then, Weber's conception of the role of ideas *does* allow that 'ideas . . . directly govern men's conduct' (1948: 280). The implication of this is that an interpretation of the meaning of world-views must be seen as an essential part of Weber's sociology, not only inasmuch as it accounts for the transformation of world-views, but also as a precondition for understanding the impact of beliefs on social life.

The struggle between charisma and routinization is more difficult to explicate in theoretical terms. It has been shown that this pattern operates on two levels. On the first level, which can be found in the concepts in Weber's sociology of domination, it represents the transferral of charismatic authority from an individual leader to a group of followers, in this way consolidating the initially revolutionary message into a routine teaching. Yet this transformation of authority is too narrow to account for the processes in Weber's substantive studies. The struggle between charisma and routinization must also be seen to operate on a second level, consisting of the typical changes in the impact of belief-systems; namely that they are initially a powerful force which gradually becomes routinized through systematization and accommodation to the predispositions of believers.

As we have seen, it is particularly this second level which is central to Weber's view of the role of ideas in social life. Although this struggle takes place in different forms in all systems of belief, the paradigm of this pattern is ancient Judaism. Here a belief-system which fundamentally transformed cultural life slowly gave way to its integration into routine, everyday existence. A different example of the process of routinization can be found in the modern world. As a result of the Protestant ethic, not only did a routine form of religiosity emerge, but more importantly, so did (as an indirect result) secular trends such as bureaucratization and disenchantment which also contributed to the routinization of social life.

This is the part of Weber's explanation of the impact of beliefs where his view that ideas are subject to an inescapable fate finds its expression. New systems of belief come into existence through charismatic breakthroughs and initiate new lines of social development. For this reason, Weber calls charisma the 'specifically creative revolutionary force in history' (1968: 1117). In the light of their origin, the impact of belief-systems can be seen to rest ultimately within the realm of ideas since Weber stresses that they cannot be reduced to other social forces, such as political authority or economic interests.

Again, it is important to note that this irreducible force has two aspects that Weber does not keep sufficiently distinct. One is that charisma is simply the mechanism by which he can account for the origin of belief-systems. But the other is that it is not this origin, but the original content of the world-views themselves, the way they endow the world with meaning and are able to reshape everyday conduct, that is central to his conception of cultural change.

The same applies to the two mechanisms which inevitably routinize this impact. One is the systematization of a belief-system and its extension to all aspects of everyday life, and the second the accommodation to the interests of various strata of carriers whose interests or predispositions, in turn, are shaped by their ways of life. Here too, it is not the mechanism whereby authority is transferred into routine channels which is decisive, but the integration of the world-view into everyday conduct and into traditional social relations. The struggle between charisma and routinization can therefore be seen as Weber's attempt to explain the relation between ideas and social reality in terms of the pattern whereby belief-systems exercise an influence upon – but eventually become integrated into – everyday life.

Again, the struggle between charisma and routinization sheds light on the 'switchmen' metaphor in so far as the pattern of a revolutionizing impact followed by an inescapable accommodation to everyday life describes the typical pattern of the interrelation between ideas and interests (quite apart from the autonomous influence of ideas which was discussed above). That is, whereas ideas initially alter social life, the interests which predominate in everyday life eventually reassert their dominance over human conduct.[2]

The third element that contributes to Weber's theory of cultural change is the increasing differentiation between various spheres of life. As we have seen, the pattern that emerges from Weber's substantive studies is that initially, during the stage of magic, the spheres of life overlap to a large extent. Increasing differentiation only becomes possible with the advent of the world-religions, particularly Judaeo-Christianity with its clear separation between the religious sphere and the economic and political spheres. And in the modern world, the spheres of life are differentiated to such an extent that they increasingly come into conflict with one another.

This element of Weber's conception strongly underlines his comparative perspective. The differentiation between the spheres of life is much more thoroughgoing in the Western world than elsewhere. Moreover, in the modern world, with its decline of the religious sphere and the attendant loss of all-embracing world-views, an increasingly intense conflict between the various spheres of life develops. This view of modernity is closely tied to Weber's pronouncements about the conflict between various ethical demands in the modern world.

The differentiation between the spheres of life is therefore not merely a heuristic device which allows Weber to distinguish between the major areas of social life. It also represents a reconstruction of how the relation between the spheres of life can impede or promote social change. The overlap between two or more spheres of life reinforces social stability, whereas conflict between the spheres of life increases the potential for social change. Apart from this, the harmony and conflict between the various spheres imposes certain ethical demands on the individual. The distinction between various spheres of life thus combines the idea that these spheres may stand in a relation of functional interdependence or of functional differentiation – with an account of the internal coherence of certain ethical demands from the viewpoint of the choices available to the individual.

All three elements thus play an indispensable part in Weber's conception of cultural change. Furthermore, they are all specifically oriented towards an understanding of the realm of ideas. With the concept of charisma, Weber can account for the ultimate origin of ideas. By allowing for an inner logic of world-views, he is able to reconstruct their development. And finally, his analysis of how ideas translate into social reality is completed by showing how they eventually become integrated in the ways of life of different social strata and into the other spheres of life. It only needs to be added that certain constraints and possibilities for the unfolding of cultural change exist within each of the three stages identified by Weber, particularly in the light of the different relations between the spheres of life at each stage. The question now is whether these different elements – the inner logic of world-views, charisma and routinization, and the differentiation between the spheres of life – fit together so as to yield a coherent account of cultural change?

In order to answer this question, we can begin by examining the degree of 'fit' between these three elements. There is a close link between the inner logic of world-views and the struggle between charisma and routinization. The inner logic of world-views refers to the development of belief-systems in terms of shifts in their meaning. The changing social conditions in which belief-systems develop do not enter into the account at this level. Routinization, on the other hand, relates the transformation of belief-systems by reference to social circumstances. This pattern explains how belief-systems become accommodated to the interests or predispositions of different social groups. These predispositions, in turn, are tied to the ways of life of the various strata and in this sense quite independent of the different world-views that may come to be imposed on believers. It is only in the interrelation between the two autonomous patterns of ideas and interests that the actual development of the belief-system can take place. On the one hand, the inner logic of world-views imposes certain constraints on the direction in which belief-systems may develop, while on the other, the interests of the various strata give shape to the way in which a world-view becomes established and adapted to everyday life.

If we return to the 'switchmen' metaphor, it can now be construed as follows: once a world-view has come into being through the efforts of a charismatic prophet, it provides a paradigm which imposes constraints upon the direction in which the belief-system can develop. Limits are set on the kind of interpretation that the priesthood or the believers may give to it. But this selective interpretation also takes place in accordance with the predispositions or interests of believers. While ideas act like 'switchmen', the tracks along which they develop – the interests of believers – have already been laid. The impact of ideas on social life can thus be measured by the degree to which a world-view either revolutionizes or reinforces the (given) predispositions of believers. And despite the great differences in the degree to which this revolutionization or reinforcement occurs, it is nevertheless characteristic of all belief-systems that they eventually become routinized within the tracks of the interests of certain strata. If, therefore, one wanted to carry the 'switchmen' metaphor through to its logical conclusion, one might say that the success of ideas or 'switchmen' in promoting social change ultimately depends on how strongly they change the direction of the tracks. Or, to put it differently by paraphrasing Marx, 'real, active world-views make history, but they cannot do so howsoever they please' – because, it might be added, they only unfold among the interests of believers.

By combining these insights with the pattern of the increasing differentiation between the spheres of life, Weber's conception of cultural change gains another dimension. In order, for example, to examine the impact of religious belief on economic life, both the independence of a religious world-view from economic life and the increasing integration of religious belief into everyday social (and particularly economic) life must be taken into consideration. Yet Weber's distinction between the spheres of life does not merely offer a framework into which the other two aspects of his conception of the role of ideas can fit. As we have seen, in terms of the stages of magic, religion and science, he is also making a claim about the possibilities for differentiation at each stage.

These three stages can now be summarized in terms of the combination of all three elements. At the stage of magic there is little scope for the differentiation between the sphere of belief and the political and economic spheres of life. But this also means that no universal belief-system can arise which is at once all-encompassing and at the same time independent of its political and economic functions. Furthermore, since charismatic powers remain tied to authority in political and economic matters, their impact is limited to reinforcing traditional forms of authority. In other words, because of a lack of differentiation at this stage, the inner logic of world-views and charisma are constrained to the extent that they are, as it were, 'born' routinized.

At the stage of religion, the increasing differentiation between the different spheres of life means that belief-systems can play an increasingly autonomous role. There are two basic directions in which this autonomous role develops. Beliefs may either urge the believer to reject the worldly (that is, political and economic) spheres of life in favour of seeking salvation in a passive state of possession of the divine – as in mysticism. Or, a belief-system may demand an active engagement in the worldly spheres of life. Furthermore, at the stage of religion it becomes important to what extent a belief-system fits in with – or becomes accommodated to – the predispositions of various strata of believers, which are mainly the product of their economic and political circumstances. Bearing these characteristics in mind, we arrive at a conclusion that is implicit throughout Weber's work; namely, that the greater the tension between the demands of religious belief and social reality, the greater will be the impact of a religion.

Finally, in the modern world, the irreconcilability of the demands made by the various spheres of life has resulted in tensions between conflicting world-views and has imposed constraints on the possibility of a charismatic breakthrough which could revolutionize the other – that is, the economic or political – spheres of life.

In the light of the way these various elements fit together, it is readily apparent that the usefulness of each element in terms of Weber's theory of social change cannot be assessed separately, but only to the extent that they contribute to the whole. What we are forced to conclude then is that although his conception of cultural change is coherent in the sense that his understanding of the impact of beliefs on social life does not suffer from internal inconsistencies, nevertheless his ideas can only be assessed in terms of the inter-relation of the various parts. It may be noted in passing that if internal consistency seems a minor achievement on Weber's part, this still compares favourably with the deep-seated ambiguities in

Marx's account of ideology or in Durkheim's explanation of the function of belief-systems.[3]

A further feature of the theoretical status of Weber's works that has emerged is that apart from the focus on a particular subject-matter, which is dictated by his conception of the aim of the cultural sciences, and the set of concepts he uses to give an account of how cultural change takes place, there is no all-encompassing structure in his writings. One way of underlining this feature of his social thought is by noting that his analysis is not an evolutionist one. Although the rise of the West constitutes a distinctive pattern, it cannot, in Weber's view, be considered a linear development since, among other things, early and medieval Christianity mark a regression in its course. In so far as the rise of the West has a pattern at all, it lies in the increasing differentiation between the spheres of life and in an inner logic of world-views. Yet even these two patterns, as we have seen, do not follow an inevitable or evolutionary course. There is no inexorable advance towards Western rationalism, except in the sense that in the modern world, the logic of the scientific world-view and the differentiation between different spheres of life both increasingly disenchant the world.

Putting this point in a different way, we can say that Weber does not impose an overall pattern upon historical development. Instead of an overall structure, we find only certain key elements that govern the interplay of social forces, and these, as we have seen, are his distinction between the spheres of life, his allowing for an autonomous logic of world-views, and the concepts which he typically attaches to the emergence and subsequent systematization of ideas. But Weber could claim that these elements, rather than constituting an all-embracing social theory, are merely the terms that are required by empirical reality itself on the one hand, or merely the heuristic devices which fit this reality on the other. In Weber's terminology, these concepts can be seen as 'ideal types' (where this label may also be said to apply to concepts which he does not explicitly designate as such, for example 'spheres of life').

Whether these ideal types exist within empirical reality or only in the mind of the sociologist is a central debate within the philosophy of the social sciences in general and in the interpretation of Weber's works in particular. Again, this is not the place to enter the intractable dispute about 'realism' versus 'nominalism' since the interpretation of both the substance and methodology of Weber's writings offered here does not rest on this issue. Our main concern has been, not with Weber's methodology as such, but with science as a world-view and its impact on social reality. And although this relationship bears on this methodological debate, it does not resolve it in one way or another. If we focus on the social scientific rather than the philosophical significance of Weber's view of science, however, it is clear that science as a world-view plays an unrivalled role within modern cultural life.

This brings us to a related point which has already been mentioned in passing, which is that Weber's central question dictates his adoption of a comparative perspective. Once he has identified the uniqueness of the Western rationalism as a problem, the aim of comparing it with the other world-civilizations follows. And although he does not want to exclude economic or political factors, his claims about the role of ideas contributing to the rise of the West and about the traditionalism of non-Western civilizations (in the sense of necessary but not sufficient conditions) rest only on this comparison (1930: 30). That is, the comparative framework provides a skeleton, so to speak, on which the claims about the role of ideas can be mounted.

But of what elements does the realm of ideas consist? A further feature of Weber's conception of the role of ideas that has emerged is that it is not an explanation in terms of social structures, but rather one which concentrates on the meanings of world-views for individuals and groups and their implications for modes of conduct and ways of life. This is evident from his usage of such terms as 'spirit', 'mentality' and 'ethic' in places where he summarizes his findings, and from the way in which these fit into his conception of cultural change. It is also clear from his account of how the conduct of believers and their relation to the world are shaped by world-views on the one hand, and by the inherent predispositions that result from a certain way of life on the other.

Culturalism and Idealism

Before we assess the strengths and weaknesses of Weber's approach, we need to ask, in the light of the theoretical unity of his writings, what claims Weber can be said to be putting forward. We should now be able to specify the exact nature of his claims about the role of ideas, which is otherwise obscured by the seemingly irreducible complexity of his explanation. The most important debate on which the present analysis sheds light is the degree to which Weber should be seen as an advocate of the thesis that ideal factors determine social change. It was mentioned in the introduction that two views are commonly put forward on this issue. Some contend that Weber is committed to the view that ideal factors produce social change, whereas others think his analysis is a multidimensional one.[4] The former think Weber's claim that the

Protestant ethic is a necessary factor for the development of capitalism can stand on its own. The latter believe that this claim must be seen in the context of several other factors that Weber mentions and that contribute to the rise of modern capitalism. Among these factors would be listed, for example, the widespread use of double-entry bookkeeping, the development of the medieval city and the growth of modern science. This view gains support from some remarks in Weber's later writings where he mentions the importance of all of these factors (for example, 1927: 276–8).

In the light of the foregoing analysis of Weber's conception of cultural change, this debate can be resolved as follows. Firstly, Weber is not interested in modern capitalism as such, but argues that this concern must be subsumed within an analysis of the '*universal* significance' of 'cultural phenomena' (1930: 13) which are encapsulated in the idea of a 'specific and peculiar rationalism of Western culture' (1930: 26). And the claims he puts forward are set within the context of the 'limited purpose' of focusing exclusively on the 'points of *comparison* to our Occidental *culture*-religions' (1981b: 24, my trans.; cf. 1930: 30). *Within this context* his claims regarding both Western and non-Western civilizations are that ideal factors are an essential variable. To support this interpretation, we may recall that the Protestant ethic represents a unique belief-system in terms of all three elements of Weber's conception (which we have identified throughout all of his studies). It represents the culmination of the tension between the religious world-view and the world, the most thorough challenge to established ways of life and interests, and the most complete differentiation between the religious and the other spheres of life. Conversely, in each case a contrast can be made with the religions of non-Western civilizations.

This point is also underlined by the fact that, as we have shown, the impact of the Protestant ethic rests on the degree to which religiosity plays a role that is completely separate from other social forces. If this way of understanding Weber is correct, then the Protestant ethic thesis must be construed in a narrow way as emphasizing ideal factors. It is the separateness of the impact of belief – and not its combination with other factors – that is decisive.[5] Another point which supports this interpretation is that although Weber states on several occasions that the Protestant ethic was a necessary factor for the rise of capitalism, he neither relativizes this claim when he mentions other factors, nor does he make the same type of statement about any other factor.

This debate is closely connected with another. It is sometimes argued that although Weber focuses mainly on ideal factors in his account of the rise of capitalism or of Occidental rationalism, in his studies of the other world-religions (and why they 'blocked' this development) he gives much more weight to 'material' factors (see, for example, Hall, 1986: 75). The lengthy analyses of economic conditions in Weber's studies of India and China are cited as evidence for this view.

But as we have seen in previous chapters, in the cases of the Confucian 'mentality' and the 'spirit' of the Indian caste system, Weber argues that these were *necessary* (but not sufficient) hindrances to the emergence of Occidental rationalism. It is not that he wants to put forward a weaker claim about the impact of ideal factors in the studies of India and China – but rather that in both cases, the belief-system is much more integrated within the political and economic spheres of life. But this only means that, by contrast with the Protestant ethic, closer attention needs to be paid to the interrelations between the religious and the political or economic spheres of life.

It is also not the case that the studies of India and China are more 'materialist' because the impact on the individual believer is more indirect than in the case of the Protestant religious doctrine. This merely suggests that in the case of the Protestant ethic, the descriptive focus must be on the mentality of the individual believer, whereas in the cases of India and China, the link between religious doctrine and the political and economic life must be central to understanding Weber's studies (in addition to the ethic of the leading strata). The role of the Confucian and Hindu world-views is equally important – though opposite in nature – to that of the Protestant world-view. It is Weber's conception of cultural change – the inner logic of their world-views, the struggle between charisma and routinization and the differentiation between the spheres of life – which accounts for the differences between the role of ideas in each of these cases.

A further issue which our systematization of Weber's writings allows us to address is how the various elements can add up to a pattern of the growth of Western rationalism. Again, this term seems unclear because Weber does not systematically elaborate it. Nevertheless, it obtains a clear meaning when it is pieced together from its constituent elements. The origins of the rise of rationalism can be found in the ancient Judaic conception of monotheism. From this monotheistic world-view there is a direct link, in accordance with an inner logic, to the Protestant doctrine of predestination. In the same place we also find the beginnings of a process of differentiation between the spheres of life with the separation of the Judaic god from his political function and his assumption of a more purely religious and ethical role. Both these patterns underwent setbacks during early and medieval Christendom. It is only with the culmination of the first pattern and the intensification of the second in Protestantism, combined with the impact of a radically new world-view – namely, one which demanded a complete reorientation of the life of the individual believer – that the growth of Western rationalism achieved its most significant breakthrough. The corrosive logic of this radically transcendent world-view coupled with the disenchantment of the world by science – disenchantment in the sense of an increasingly impersonal, objective and causal explanation of the world – continues this process in the contemporary world. It is in terms of this sequence and this combination of elements that the uniquely Western pattern of the role of ideas – the growth of rationalism – should be interpreted.

Finally, a point that has emerged from our interpretation of Weber's conception of cultural change is how closely it is tied to his view of the modern world. That is, Weber's analysis of how social change took place in the past can be seen as a reflection of his views on contemporary social life – and vice versa. His focus on the inner logic of world-views can be interpreted as a counterpart to his identification of an inevitable shrinkage of the sacred within the modern world. This shrinkage is a result both of the corrosive logic of the Protestant world-view and of the ongoing disenchantment of the world by science. Secondly, the struggle between charisma and routinization mirrors Weber's concern about the levelling of far-reaching aims in a bureaucratized and disenchanted world. And finally, the increasing differentiation between the spheres of life can be linked to his view of the parcellization of the soul and to the emergence of a conflict between various ethical demands and world-views. All of these aspects converge on one of the reasons why Weber's project is so centrally preoccupied with cultural change: he gives an account of the distinctiveness of modernity, of its emergence from the pre-modern world and its similarity to the world before the advent of the world-religions. In this sense, he can be seen to fulfil his methodological aim of understanding the cultural significance of Western rationalism.

At this stage we can return to a question which was raised in the introduction – namely, to what extent does the fact that Weber's social thought revolves around cultural change make him into a 'culturalist' or an 'idealist'? First, it should be stressed again that he does not try to establish a boundary between the cultural sciences which deal with intrinsically human attributes (such as the meaning of behaviour) and the natural sciences. Although the former may sometimes use methods that are different from those in the latter, Weber argues that this does not make for an a priori distinction between them (Weber, 1982: 12, n. 1; Oakes, 1988). This means that the subject-matter of the cultural sciences is not in principle closed off from empirical verification or investigation.

Moreover, Weber's focus on cultural change in his major studies does not imply a general claim about the primacy of ideas in history. As he points out, his own studies need to be supplemented by others which trace the causal connections the other way around, from, say, the material or economic base of social life to the realm of ideas or of culture (1930: 27). Other factors may have played an important role in the rise of Occidental rationalism. Weber, however, claims to have uncovered only one (necessary) factor in this development.

In answer to our question then, we can say that the central role of cultural change in Weber's sociology derives from an important problem which contemporary social science cannot avoid, which is to understand the cultural significance of Occidental rationalism. His preoccupation with cultural change is a product of the answer he gives to this question. This preoccupation, however, has an important consequence. Because his subject-matter consists to such a large extent of world-views, religious ethics, ways of life and their different ways of shaping human conduct, the issue of how the meaning of world-views translates into social consequences must be central to our understanding of his overall approach.

A separate issue that follows on from this is whether we should consider Weber a 'sociologist' at all, given that his writings are devoted, both in method and in substance, to what he calls the cultural sciences (which for him includes both the historical and social sciences)? In his writings, Weber did not explicitly set out to create or contribute to a separate discipline, as is clear from his definition of sociology at the beginning of *Economy and Society*. Although he points to a pragmatic distinction between the more generalizing concepts of sociology as against the individualizing ones of history, both, he says, nevertheless take as their subject-matter those 'phenomena' that are 'culturally significant' (1980b: 9, my trans.; cf. 1968: 20). On a personal level, even towards the end of his life Weber was able to comment: 'I now happen to be a sociologist according to my appointment papers' (letter quoted by Roth, 1976: 306). Since even today the boundaries of sociology – Weber calls it 'a highly ambiguous word' (1968: 4) – are not yet fixed, the question whether his investigations with their central preoccupation with cultural change should belong to this domain can only be judged by the continuing validity of his insights.

Weber contra Marx and Durkheim

The distinctiveness of Weber's science of culture emerges most forcefully through a comparison with other approaches in this area. Before we undertake such a comparison, it may be useful to reflect briefly upon the labels which can be attached to the project of understanding cultural change. In Weber's case, as we have seen, it is appropriate to speak of 'culture' and 'cultural change' both because Weber sees his undertaking as part of the 'cultural sciences' and because his subject-matter fits this description. There are, however, two other rubrics under which his studies might come, those of 'ideology' and the 'sociology of knowledge', and it is instructive to consider how these differ from each other.

For Weber, the 'cultural sciences' embrace all the disciplines dealing with human conduct and its meanings and consequences. And his particular concern within this category lies in examining the relation between world-views and social change. The study of ideology, too, whether in political science or sociology, seeks to explain the role of beliefs in society. The difference is that ideologies are typically those beliefs which provide legitimation for existing political and social arrangements. This, of course, is also a large part, though not all, of what Weber deals with in his examinations of cultural change. We may say then that Weber's writings could just as easily fall within the rubric of the explanation of ideology, were it not for the fact that he goes beyond the question of legitimation and also looks at ideas as sources of change.

Another feature of the study of ideology, as of the sociology of knowledge, is that the beliefs or knowledge under consideration are taken to be false. This is also the case in Weber's writings, and most strikingly illustrated in his characterization of magic. Weber holds, like theories of ideology and the sociology of knowledge, that there is a clear (although 'hair-thin') separation between beliefs and social scientific knowledge. But whereas the emphasis in the sociology of knowledge lies in explaining the conditions for the emergence of knowledge, Weber's main interest is the other way around, to examine the consequences of culture for social life. Put differently, whereas for the sociology of knowledge and Marxist theories, ideology is typically false in the sense that it distorts truth or knowledge, for Weber culture or belief are simply separate from science or knowledge. Thus again, Weber's subject-matter partly overlaps with, but is not exhausted by, the sociology of knowledge.

These differences in the way that the social sciences conceptualize the study of belief are brought into stronger focus when we compare Weber with Marx and Durkheim. One way of categorizing the

Marxist conception of ideology, and the tradition of the sociology of knowledge which has built upon it, is to say that it is mainly interested in explaining why people hold the beliefs that they do. In other words, beliefs are seen as the outcome of other social forces.[6] Although Weber often also engages in this type of question, again at key points in his studies he departs from it and looks at the reverse process – that is, how ideas have an impact on other areas of social life.

Durkheimian sociology is also concerned with how ideas may bring about certain effects (in this case the cohesion of the social system), but here the exclusive emphasis is on how beliefs contribute to this cohesion. Moreover, only if beliefs result in 'social facts' do they constitute a valid subject-matter for sociology. The world-views that are the object of Weber's studies, by contrast, result in an inner reorientation of the believer which can only be explained by reference to their meaning. A further contrast with Durkheim, as we have seen, is that Weber does not have a conception of a 'social system' or of society to which ideas could lend cohesion.

The major difference between Weber, Marx and Durkheim then is that the latter two are, in the end, concerned with beliefs as the consequences of social forces, whereas Weber is mainly interested in their origins and their changing role. This point can be highlighted by noting that neither Marx's nor Durkheim's theories are well-suited to deal with changes in belief-systems over the course of time or with the motives of those who adhere to a belief-system. Both are typical shortcomings of functionalist types of explanation in general. Weber's conception, on the other hand, inasmuch as it typically involves unintended consequences, can only make sense by reference to both these aspects. The motives of social actors are important, but the link with their eventual outcome is only an indirect – or, as it has also been put, an 'ironic' – one.[7]

The centrality of the question of cultural change means then that, in order to be fully appreciated, Weber's ideas must be taken out of the context of the 'classical' questions of sociological theory and located within the debate about how to understand culture and the patterns of cultural change. There is only one major point where Weber enters into direct debate with classical social theory, and that is the emergence and distinctiveness of the modern world. But even here, his method of establishing the cultural significance of modern rationalism and capitalism within a comparative framework sets him apart from Marx's evolutionism and Durkheim's opposition between primitive and modern society. Apart from this, Weber is not concerned with conflict or cohesion within social life as such, but with processes of cultural change and their relation to the other spheres of social life. If Weber's central concern can be identified in this way, then his insights cannot be seen as an attempt to explain social change generally, but must be compared with other accounts of the interplay between ideas and social life.

What has emerged forcefully on a theoretical level is that Weber's approach is fundamentally different from that of the other founders of social science. And regardless of whether his overall conception of cultural change is still thought to be a useful one, in one respect at least his ideas represent an advance beyond them, namely in so far as human beings (at least in certain instances) actively shape social life through their beliefs. That is to say, like more recent social theory, Weber allows for the efficacy of culture (or 'ideology'). Or, to put it in more contemporary terminology, he allows as much place in his conception of cultural change to agency as to structure, although this dualism itself predates the conceptual framework within which his own schema is couched.

Since Weber's project took shape before many of the current debates in the social sciences crystallized, his cultural science is difficult to locate in another sense too. His aim of identifying the ultimate origins of cultural change – within charisma, within world-views and their logic and within a separate sphere of cultural life – emerged at a time when the controversy about the scientific nature of sociology was still unsettled, but before the split between a meaning-oriented interpretive sociology as against an empirical or positivist social science had solidified. The fact that he attributes an important role to culture and cultural change, too, can thus be seen in a context that predates the division of classical social theory into idealism and reductionism. Weber did not claim that culture was the only force of social change, but he did seek to explain its cultural significance and role.[8]

Weber and Contemporary Social Science: the Prospects for Idealism

Despite the complexity of Weber's theory, there is thus a sense in which – at least within the framework of his limited concern with cultural significance – he offers a coherent account of the nature of Western rationalism within the context of an all-encompassing analysis of the impact of beliefs which includes 'primitive' and non-Western systems of belief. The scope of Weber's project is still unrivalled and despite the many criticisms of the details of his studies, his general arguments have remained the subject of debate, especially those concerning the distinctiveness of the West. If this can be attributed not merely to the accuracy of many of his empirical observations, but also to the framework in which he made them, then his conception of cultural change should be seen as an important contribution to social science.

Apart from this contribution, however, how does Weber's project compare with more recent approaches in this area? Since we have been able to identify the core of Weber's writings as consisting of a science of culture, we are now in a position to address this question. So far, we have been able to find a theoretical framework that underlies his major works, to establish the exact nature of the claims he is putting forward about the role of ideas in social life, and to distinguish Weber's science of culture from other approaches. At this stage we need to ask what the insights and shortcomings of Weber's project are.

We can begin by noting that one of the distinctive features of Weber's sociology is that he focuses on the autonomous impact of ideas. As the comparison with Marx and Durkheim has shown, Weber's is the only approach to the study of beliefs which deals directly with this issue since Marx's and Durkheim's sociologies conceive of ideas as the outcome of other social forces. If his emphasis on the distinctive contribution of culture on social life is not misplaced, then it must be possible to attribute this to the various elements he uses to analyze it.

Identifying the emergence of world-views with a single and ultimate source (charisma) means that he is able to provide an answer to the question of where the diverse nature, the content and the efficacy of belief-systems ultimately derives from. Such a solution to this problem is open to criticism. In the first place, he is not consistent on this issue in his writings, as we have seen in the ambiguity concerning the two levels on which he uses the concept of charisma. Furthermore, in some cases he implies that sources apart from charisma (in the sense of an individual) were ultimately responsible for the emergence of belief-systems, as in his view of science or where he speaks of the 'charisma of reason' (1948: 149; 1968: 401, 1140, 1209). But perhaps more important than whether he is right in emphasizing the role of charisma in the way that he does is the fact that he feels compelled to address the question of the origins of ideas at all. In doing this, he is identifying a problem that has remained unresolved within sociological theory.

Even if it turns out that the question of how different world-views come about will be resolved in a different way, the separable issue of how they are able to initiate new patterns of social development must be an essential part of our understanding of social reality. One of the means by which Weber allows for this is by showing how the content of different world-views shapes conduct and social relations in different ways. He does this through a reconstruction of an inner logic of world-views and charting their changing consequences for social life. Furthermore, he identifies an autonomous sphere of culture since, on his account, it is only if we specify the extent to which ideas constitute a separate social force standing over or against the rest of social life that we can also attribute the developments of world-views to shifts in their meanings and to counterpose the efficacy of the realm of culture to that of the other spheres of life. A similar point can be made about his conception of the individual and of how conduct can overcome or remains integrated within the strictures of everyday life. And again, although such a conception of cultural change is one that has its limitations (how, for example, can such an approach be reconciled with other theoretical traditions within the social sciences?), at the same time without allowing for these forms of autonomy of the realm of culture, the role of world-views would become enmeshed within the other areas of social life.

This last point can be made in a different way. The distinctiveness of Weber's approach is that cultural change is conceived of as a two-sided process. It consists of both a realm of ideas and of other realms within which ideas can become integrated; of shifts in the meaning of world-views as well as the interests and constraints within social life to which world-views are subject; it relies on a view of the individual whereby the individual sometimes transcends and is at other times submerged within the web of everyday life; and it rests on a conception of social science and of social reality which distinguishes between human values and the empirical reality in which they are embedded. In short, for Weber the subject-matter of a science of culture has a distinctive place within the social sciences as a whole, and if this sense of the importance of culture is not misconceived, then his approach must continue to offer a useful point of departure.[9]

A separate issue is whether Weber's overall question is still an appropriate one for contemporary social science. Does it advance our knowledge to establish the origins and nature of Western rationalism? Here we can only recapitulate Weber's argument that in order to understand the social world at all, it is necessary to begin with an overall and objective assessment of the cultural significance of the type of social order within which social scientific knowledge is being sought. Only such a distanced assessment of the social scientist's vantage-point will create the basis for objective knowledge. And if only this type of macro-sociological viewpoint provides the basis for objectivity, then a comparative investigation of the dynamics of the different world-civilizations is inescapable.[10]

Finally, it is necessary to ask whether Weber's project as a whole, including both his overall question and his emphasis on a distinctive realm of culture, continues to provide an essential contribution to our sociological understanding. One argument in favour of this is that we are faced with the fact that an explanation of cultural change within the different world-civilizations and a comparison between them on a scale approaching Weber's still eludes us. And such an explanation remains essential unless we are prepared to accept that the 'world-religions and ethics are fundamentally *similar* . . . in their promise of salvation for the individual' (Hall, 1986: 20), and thus, it is implied, their content is secondary.

This is true not only of Weber's comparative analysis of the world-religions, but also of his assessment of the significance of modern culture with its scientific world-view. If Weber is correct in identifying the elimination of other world-views and their replacement by a rational, impersonal view of the world which rests on the growth of objective knowledge about the social and natural worlds – in short, disenchantment – as a central feature of the modern world, then his idea that this feature has world-historical significance as well as fundamental implications for the methodology of the social sciences must also be taken seriously.[11]

When we turn from the content of Weber's analyses of cultural change and the question of the uniqueness of Occidental rationalism to the more general problem of explaining social change, the picture is somewhat different. Against a Weberian perspective, it has been argued, for example, that the division between 'idealism' and 'materialism' is an artificial one and that progress can only be achieved within a social science that overcomes this division (Mann, 1979). If such progress within sociological theory should prove to be attainable, then it is indeed open to doubt whether a social science whose central focus is cultural change is possible without at the same time bringing other social forces within its scope in a more direct manner.

This limitation of Weber's conception of the role of ideas can be briefly underlined by comparing his approach with more recent approaches to the same topic. Randall Collins, John Hall, Michael Mann and Ernest Gellner have all attempted to explain the rise of capitalism or of industrial society in the West by means of macro-sociological analyses that both acknowledge Weber's continuing relevance and criticize him (Collins, 1986a: 7–13; Hall, 1986: especially 19–21; Mann: 1986, especially 22–4; Gellner, 1988). Like Weber, all of them want to ascribe a major role in this development to the impact of beliefs – though by no means as large a role as Weber. More importantly, they all differ substantially from Weber with regard to the nature of this impact. All of them emphasize the functional role of beliefs, their capacity to strengthen the cohesion (cultural, political and economic) of existing groups and civilizations. Furthermore, they concentrate on the role of intellectual or priestly strata mainly in terms of their capacity for maintaining various kinds of religious institutions which, in turn, increase the strength of political and economic organization. In other words, while remaining more in debt to Weber than to Marx or Durkheim, their approach is more functional and institutional, and thus opposed to Weber's emphasis on the content of world-views, their internal logic and their consequences for the conduct of believers. In this sense, their analyses of cultural change are both more open to empirical testing and more grounded in rigorous structural-functional approaches to socio-historical change.

If these and other social theorists are correct and it is possible to explain the impact of religion (and of other beliefs) in terms of their social function and their organizational role, then Weber's theoretical conception of the role of ideas must be seen as having severe limitations. If, however, the content of different systems of belief and the resulting conduct and ways of life played a decisive role in social change – as Weber claimed for them – then his conception seems to offer the only systematic and all-encompassing attempt at understanding this aspect of social life. His conception accounts for the origin of world-views, the dynamic of their development, their relation to the interests of various social strata, and the influence of belief on the other spheres of social life. On this level, the validity of Weber's as against more recent approaches to cultural change can only be decided by further empirically informed debate. It is as well to admit, however, that although his studies still offer some important insights, his analyses are often difficult to test and his successors have often incorporated his ideas and surpassed them.

Apart from identifying the coherence of Weber's sociology of culture and assessing its continuing relevance, there is another way of looking at his world-historical and comparative analysis of cultural change. We have seen that Weber allows for the autonomy of the sphere of culture, its logic and impact on social life in a way that goes beyond the reductionism of Marx and Durkheim, but is more restricted than the conception of several recent thinkers (who have also avoided this reductionism). One reason why Weber's approach is incompatible with more recent structural-functional analyses is that his mode of enquiry is tied to the presupposition of taking the cultural significance of Occidental rationalism as a starting-point. Moreover, as we have seen, his particular way of making comparisons with non-Western culture rests on this presupposition. This means that his main findings cannot be subject to a presuppositionless identification of the 'causes' of social change as such, nor do they provide a comprehensive theory of social change in which his specification of the mechanisms of cultural change are merely a part. In short, perhaps Weber's writings cannot give us an explanation of social change in the sense of specifying the causal role of ideas in the testable and presuppositionless way that contemporary social science has come to expect.

What Weber *does* offer, however, is a descriptive account of the distinctiveness of different cultures of world-historical significance, their uniqueness and the way in which they have left their mark on social life. And in this sense, his writings still make an essential contribution to social science. Even if he does not explain the role of culture in social change as such, or within a comprehensive theory of social change that encompasses all factors which should be given their due (and which he himself, it seems, had hoped to provide), he does nevertheless contribute to our understanding of the distinctiveness of different cultural forms and the way they shaped some of the central aspects of social life.

For this more limited purpose, the overall framework and the mechanisms with which Weber gives an account of different cultural dynamics are well-suited. Again, although they do not fit easily into subsequent theories of social change, his conception of the origin of different world-views, their relation to other spheres of social life and their integration into ways of life allow Weber to specify the distinctiveness and significance of different cultural trajectories themselves. In other words, inasmuch as Weber's question of the cultural significance of Occidental rationalism is still of concern to us as such, his writings do provide a suggestive and comprehensive account of what the distinctive characteristics and dynamics of different world-views *are*, even if by comparison with contemporary social science he does not convincingly explain how they *work*. He gives us an understanding of the content of different world-views, and the mark they have left on social life which sets them apart, in a way that is culturally significant, from Occidental culture. In short, Weber's sociology of culture ought to be seen as a more limited project than he himself conceived it. He gives us an account of how different world-views translate into different ways of life, even if he does not – from a present-day perspective – explain how they translate into social reality as such.

Inasmuch as contemporary social science remains wedded to the question of how culture works, rather than sharing Weber's concern with cultural significance and the dynamics of culture within social life, it will continue to draw on but develop beyond his perspective.

One of the reasons why social scientists have moved beyond Weber's project is its ambitiousness, of what he thought his science of culture could achieve. His central question concerning the cultural significance of Occidental rationalism derives from such a large-scale perspective that it is difficult to imagine at which point a final answer could be arrived at.[12] We are faced then with the dilemma that asking this question is unavoidable and at the same time, from our vantage-point of living *within* Western capitalist society, it cannot itself be subject to critical scrutiny. To understand the cultural significance of the modern world – and of Weber's project – perhaps requires that 'the light of the great cultural problems moves on' (Weber, 1949: 112). The contours of such a movement may be becoming visible. The world of industrial capitalism that had unsettled social life so disturbingly in Weber's time is no longer the same as the global and post-industrial social world whose origins may provide the searchlight for our theories in the future. That, however, is a problem that goes beyond the confines of this study and that another generation of social scientists with Weber's world-historical scope will have to address.

Notes

1. In this sense, again, Islam may be an exception, but for reasons mentioned in the discussion of Weber's view of Islam, this exception possibly remains outside the scope of his schema.
2. We might ask whether, if we accept Weber's view of the charismatic origin of world-views, it necessarily follows that we must accept his pessimistic conclusion about their routinization? On this point, see Campbell (1987: 209–10).
3. On Marx, see, for example, Minogue (1985); on Durkheim, Lukes (1973: ch. 23).
4. For a recent summary of this debate, see Collins (1986b: chs 3, 5).
5. Again, to avoid misunderstanding, it is not that ideal factors are always and everywhere decisive, but *given* Weber's question of the cultural significance of Western rationalism, *and* that his answer must be a comparative one, world-views play an irreplaceable role. This is discussed further below.
6. Elster (1985) and Cohen (1978) have both argued that Marx's analysis of ideology can only be understood in these functionalist terms. Against this, compare Weber's comment in the German version of the *General Economic History* (Weber, 1927), taken from the 'conceptual Preface' which is omitted in the English text: '[I]t must be emphasized that economic history (much less the history of "class struggle") is not, as the materialist conception of history would have it, identical with the history of the whole of culture as such. The latter is not a product, nor just a function, of the latter; but rather economic history represents only a base, without the knowledge of which, however, a useful investigation of the great areas of culture [*Gebiete der Kultur*] is unthinkable' (1981a: 17). Yet economics, or economic conduct, can itself *sometimes* be construed as falling within the realm of the investigation of culture, as when, at

the end of the *Protestant Ethic*, he argues that it would also be necessary to examine 'how Protestant asceticism, in turn, was influenced in its emergence and distinctiveness by the totality of social cultural-conditions [*Kulturbedingungen*], especially the economic' (1981b: 190, my trans.; cf. 1930: 183).

7. For a good discussion of this 'irony' of social action, see Campbell (1987: 207–10).

8. A different way of making this point is to note, as Thompson has done, that 'among German philosophers and historians during the eighteenth and nineteenth centuries . . . the term "culture" was generally used to refer to a process of intellectual or spiritual development' (1990: 123) and contrasted with 'civilization' which 'was associated with politeness and the refinement of manners' (1990: 124). Weber clearly owes a lot to his intellectual heritage, but while he wants to assign a central role to culture in his account of social change, his conception is much broader than that of his predecessors, encompassing not only their 'high culture', but also, among other things, the religion of all strata as well as the modern scientific world-view and its consequences. At the same time, his conception of culture is more narrow than that of some subsequent social thinkers such as, for example, the anthropologist Marvin Harris who defines culture as 'the learned, socially aquired traditions and life-styles of the members of a society, including their patterned, repetitive ways of thinking, feeling and acting (i.e. behaving)' (1987: 6). This is broader than Weber's conception in so far as it does not seem to exclude what he would regard as the other spheres of life.

Put differently, Weber's science of culture is not yet compartmentalized, as are those specialisms within the social sciences which deal with a particular subject-matter, such as the sociology of the media or of religion. But again, despite the central importance of culture in his method and in his studies of social change, for Weber the science of culture is not coterminous with the science of social life as such, since he often points to other areas which fall outside his range or with which his investigations must be supplemented (see, for example, 1949: 63–73). In order to avoid both misappropriating Weber by placing him within the context of subsequent debates, or assessing his works as a self-contained package on its own terms, they must be seen as a set of arguments about a specific area (cultural change) and compared with other attempts to understand the role of culture in social life.

9. In a similar vein, Kane has recently made a useful distinction between the analytic and the concrete forms of cultural autonomy, arguing that 'analytic autonomy can be regarded as a hypothesis and concrete autonomy as its proof' (1991: 55). In other words, the social scientist can stipulate the autonomous force of culture conceptually – if it can then be shown to have played a decisive role in particular circumstances. From this perspective, it could be said that the theoretical elements of Weber's conception of cultural change represent his analytical constructs (which are, *mutatis mutandi*, similar to Kane's), whereas his historical-sociological studies are an attempt to provide proof of the efficacy of culture within social life – or concrete autonomy.

10. An alternative to such a comparative framework would be an evolutionist one such as that which has recently been pursued by Mann (1986). A somewhat different way of formulating a comparative perspective like Weber's has recently been offered by Crone (1989: 168–75), who suggests that pre-industrial societies

ought to be seen as successfully institutionalizing stability, whereas industrial society uniquely departs from this 'norm' by being inherently unstable.

11. For a different perspective on this methodological issue, which nevertheless acknowledges the central significance of the great transformation ushered in by science, see Elkana (1981: 41) and Gellner (1988: especially 70–90). See also Gellner's account of 'Rationality as a Way of Life' in his *Reason and Culture* (1992: ch. 7) which draws extensively on Weber's concept of disenchantment, but also tries to show its limitations.

12. A similar point has been made in relation to the question of the emergence of industrial society generally (Gellner, 1988: 170).

REFERENCES

A bibliography of Weber's writings can be found in Dirk Käsler's (1988) *Max Weber: An Introduction to his Life and Work* (Cambridge: Polity). The most complete bibliography of secondary works on Max Weber in all languages is Constans Seyfarth and Gert Schmidt (1982, 2nd edn) *Max Weber Bibliographie* (Stuttgart: Ferdinand Enke). The references below include only those works cited in the text.

Abramowski, Günter (1966) *Das Geschichtsbild Max Webers* (Stuttgart: Klett).

Albrow, Martin (1990) *Max Weber's Construction of Social Theory* (London: Macmillan).

Anderson, Benedict (1990) 'Further Adventures of Charisma' in his *Language and Power: Explaining Political Cultures in Indonesia* (Ithaca: Cornell University Press), pp. 78–93.

Andersson, Sten (1977) *Som Om: Skiss till ett porträtt av Max Weber* (Gothenburg: Korpen).

Andreski, Stanislav (1984) *Max Weber's Insights and Errors* (London: Routledge and Kegan Paul).

Archer, Margaret (1988) *Culture and Agency* (Cambridge: Cambridge University Press).

Beetham, David (1974) *Max Weber and the Theory of Modern Politics* (London: Allen and Unwin).

Bendix, Reinhard (1960) *Max Weber: An Intellectual Portrait* (New York: Doubleday).

Berger, Peter and Luckmann, Thomas (1967) *The Social Construction of Reality* (London: Allen Lane).

Bloch, Maurice (1989) *Ritual, History and Power* (London: Athlone).

Bloom, Allan (1987) *The Closing of the American Mind* (New York: Simon and Schuster).

Breuer, Stefan (1991) *Max Webers Herrschaftssoziologie* (Frankfurt: Campus).

Brubaker, Rogers (1984) *The Limits of Rationality: An Essay on the Social and Moral Thought of Max Weber* (London: Allen and Unwin).

Burger, Thomas (1976) *Max Weber's Theory of Concept Formation* (Durham: Duke University Press).

Buss, Andreas (1989) 'The Economic Ethics of Russian Orthodox Christianity', parts I and II, *International Sociology*, 4 (3): 235–72; 4 (4): 447–72.

Caldwell, Raymond (1983) 'Max Weber's Rationalization Theme: Its Coherence, Analysis and Significance' (PhD dissertation, London School of Economics).

Campbell, Colin (1987) *The Romantic Ethic and the Spirit of Consumerism* (Oxford: Blackwell).

Cohen, G.A. (1978) *Karl Marx's Theory of History: A Defence* (Oxford: Oxford University Press).

Collins, Randall (1986a) *Weberian Sociological Theory* (Cambridge: Cambridge University Press).

Collins, Randall (1986b) *Max Weber: A Skeleton Key* (Beverly Hills: Sage).

Crone, Patricia (1989) *Pre-industrial Societies* (Oxford: Blackwell).

Dumont, Louis (1970) *Homo Hierarchicus: The Caste System and its Implications* (Chicago: University of Chicago Press).

Dumont, Louis (1983) *Essais sur l'individualisme: une perspective anthropologique sur l'idéologie moderne* (Paris: Editions du Seuil).

Eden, Robert (1983) *Political Leadership and Nihilism: A Study of Weber and Nietzsche* (Tampa: University Presses of Florida).

Eisenstadt, Shmuel (1981) 'Max Webers antikes Judentum und der Charakter der jüdischen Zivilisation' in Wolfgang Schluchter (ed.), *Max Weber und das antike Judentum* (Frankfurt: Suhrkamp), pp. 134–84.

Eisenstadt, Shmuel (1982) 'The Axial Age: The Emergence of Transcendental Visions and the Rise of Clerics', *Archives Européennes de Sociologie*, 23: 294–314.

Elkana, Yehuda (1981) 'A Programmatic Attempt at an Anthropology of Knowledge' in Everett Mendelsohn and Yehuda Elkana (eds), *Sciences and Cultures* (*Sociology of the Sciences*, vol. V) (Dordrecht: D. Reidel), pp. 1–76.

Elster, Jon (1985) *Making Sense of Marx* (Cambridge: Cambridge University Press).

Elvin, Mark (1984) 'Why China Failed to Create an Endogenous Industrial Capitalism: A Critique of Max Weber's Explanation', *Theory and Society*, 13: 379–91.

Epstein, Isidore (1959) *Judaism: A Historical Presentation* (Harmondsworth: Penguin).

Evans-Pritchard, E.E. (1965) *Theories of Primitive Religion* (Oxford: Oxford University Press).

Factor, Regis and Turner, Stephen (1984) *Max Weber and the Dispute over Reason and Value* (London: Routledge and Kegan Paul).

Featherstone, Mike (ed.) (1990) *Global Culture* (Beverly Hills: Sage).

Francis, Emerich (1966) 'Kultur und Gesellschaft in der Soziologie Max Webers' in Karl Engisch et al. (eds), *Max Weber Gedächtnisschrift der Ludwig-Maximilians Universität München* (Berlin: Duncker und Humblot), pp. 89–114.

Frisby, David (1984) *Georg Simmel* (Chichester: Ellis Horwood).

Frisby, David and Sayer, Derek (1986) *Society* (Chichester: Ellis Horwood).

Fulbrook, Mary (1978) 'Max Weber's "Interpretative Sociology": A Comparison of Conception and Practice', *British Journal of Sociology*, 29 (1): 71–82.

Gellner, David (1982) 'Max Weber, Capitalism, and the Religion of India', *Sociology*, 16: 526–43.

Gellner, Ernest (1981) *Muslim Society* (Cambridge: Cambridge University Press).

Gellner, Ernest (1988) *Plough, Sword and Book* (London: Collins Harvill).

Gellner, Ernest (1992) *Reason and Culture* (Oxford: Blackwell).

Giddens, Anthony (1972) *Politics and Sociology in the Thought of Max Weber* (London: Macmillan).

Goody, Jack (1977) *The Domestication of the Savage Mind* (Cambridge: Cambridge University Press).

Habermas, Jürgen (1984) *The Theory of Communicative Action*, vol. I (London: Heinemann).

Hall, John (1986) *Powers and Liberties: The Causes and Consequences of the Rise of the West* (Harmondsworth: Penguin).

Harris, Marvin (1987) *Cultural Anthropology*, 2nd edn (New York: Harper and Row).

Hennis, Wilhelm (1988) *Max Weber: Essays in Reconstruction* (London: Unwin Hyman).

Henrich, Dieter (1952) *Die Einheit der Wissenschaftslehre Max Webers* (Tübingen: J.C.B. Mohr).

Herberg, Will (1955) *Protestant – Catholic – Jew* (New York: Doubleday).

Hexter, J.H. (1966) *The Judaeo-Christian Tradition* (New York: Harper and Row).

Hume, David (1976) *The Natural History of Religion* (Oxford: Oxford University Press). [Original publication 1757.]

Jacobson, Dan (1982) *The Story of the Stories: The Chosen People and its God* (New York: Harper and Row).

Kalberg, Stephen (1978) 'Max Weber's Concept of Rationalization', PhD dissertation, State University of New York at Stony Brook.

Kalberg, Stephen (1985a) 'Weber, Max (1864–1920)' in Adam Kuper and Jessica Kuper (eds), *The Social Science Encyclopaedia* (London: Routledge and Kegan Paul).

Kalberg, Stephen (1985b) 'The Role of Ideal Interests in Max Weber's Comparative Historical Sociology' in Robert Antonio and Ronald Glassman (eds), *A Weber–Marx Dialogue* (Lawrence: University Press of Kansas), pp. 46–61.

Kalberg, Stephen (1990) 'The Rationalization of Action in Max Weber's Sociology of Religion', *Sociological Theory*, 8 (1): 55–84.

Kane, Anne (1991) 'Cultural Analysis in Historical Sociology: The Analytic and Concrete Forms of the Autonomy of Culture', *Sociological Theory*, 9 (1): 53–69.

Kautsky, Karl (1925) *The Foundations of Christianity* (New York: International Publishers).

Küenzlen, Gottfried (1980) *Die Religionssoziologie Max Webers: eine Darstellung ihrer Entwicklung* (Berlin: Duncker und Humblot).

Kuper, Adam (1983) *Anthropology and Anthropologists* (London: Routledge and Kegan Paul).

Kuzmics, Helmut (1984) 'Elias' Theory of Civilization', *Telos*, 61: 83–99.

Lassman, Peter and Velody, Irving (1989) 'Max Weber on Science, Disenchantment and the Search for Meaning' in their (eds), *Max Weber's 'Science as a Vocation'* (London: Unwin Hyman), pp. 159–204.

Liebeschütz, Hans (1964) 'Max Weber's Historical Interpretation of Judaism', *Leo Baeck Yearbook*, 9, pp. 41–68.

Liebeschütz, Hans (1967) *Das Judentum im deutschen Geschichtsbild von Hegel bis Max Weber* (Tübingen: J.C.B. Mohr).

Löwith, Karl (1982) *Max Weber and Karl Marx* (London: Allen and Unwin).

Lukes, Steven (1973) *Emile Durkheim: His Life and Work* (London: Allen Lane).

MacIntyre, Alasdair (1967) *Secularization and Moral Change* (London: University Press).

MacIntyre, Alasdair (1970) 'Is Understanding Religion Compatible with Believing?' in Bryan Wilson (ed.), *Rationality* (Oxford: Blackwell).

Malinowski, Bronislaw (1974) *Magic, Science and Religion and Other Essays* (New York: Doubleday).

Mann, Michael (1979) 'Idealism and Materialism in Sociological Theory' in J.W. Feinberg (ed.), *Critical Sociology: European Perspectives* (New York: Irvington), pp. 97–119.

Mann, Michael (1986) *The Sources of Social Power*, vol. I (Cambridge: Cambridge University Press).

Mannheim, Karl (1936) *Ideology and Utopia* (London: Routledge and Kegan Paul).

Marshall, Gordon (1982) *In Search of the Spirit of Capitalism: An Essay on Max Weber's Protestant Ethic Thesis* (London: Hutchinson).

Martin, David (1978a) *A General Theory of Secularization* (Oxford: Blackwell).

Martin, David (1978b) 'Traditional Religion and the Traditional Transitions to the Tradition of the New' in his *Dilemmas of Contemporary Religion* (Oxford: Blackwell), pp. 21–37.

Marx, Karl (1977) *Selected Writings*, ed. David McLellan (Oxford: Oxford University Press).

Merquior, J.G. (1979) *The Veil and the Mask* (London: Routledge and Kegan Paul).

Merquior, J.G. (1980) *Rousseau and Weber* (London: Routledge and Kegan Paul).

Merton, Robert (1973) 'The Puritan Spur to Science' in his *Sociology of Science* (Chicago: University of Chicago Press). [Original publication 1938.]

Metzger, Thomas (1977) *Escape from Predicament: Neo-Confucianism and China's Evolving Political Culture* (New York: Columbia University Press).

Milton, John R. (1981) 'The Origin and Development of the Concept of "Laws of Nature" ', *Archives Européennes de Sociologie*, 22, (2): 173–95.

Minogue, Kenneth (1985) *Alien Powers: The Pure Theory of Ideology* (London: Weidenfeld and Nicolson).

Mommsen, Wolfgang (1974a) *The Age of Bureaucracy: Perspectives on the Political Sociology of Max Weber* (Oxford: Blackwell).

Mommsen, Wolfgang (1974b) *Max Weber: Gesellschaft, Politik und Geschichte* (Frankfurt: Suhrkamp).

Mommsen, Wolfgang (1983) 'Rationalisierung und Mythos bei Max Weber' in Karl-Heinz Bohrer (ed.), *Mythos und Moderne* (Frankfurt: Suhrkamp).

Mommsen, Wolfgang (1984) *Max Weber and German Politics, 1890–1920* (Chicago: University of Chicago Press).

Mommsen, Wolfgang and Osterhammel, Jürgen (eds) (1987) *Max Weber and his Contemporaries* (London: Allen and Unwin).

Oakes, Guy (1988) *Weber and Rickert: Concept Formation in the Cultural Sciences* (Cambridge, Mass.: MIT Press).

Pagels, Elaine (1982) *The Gnostic Gospels* (Harmondsworth: Penguin).

Parkin, Frank (1982) *Max Weber* (Chichester: Ellis Horwood).

Parsons, Talcott (1937) *The Structure of Social Action*, vol. 2 (New York: McGraw-Hill).

Poggi, Gianfranco (1983) *Calvinism and the Capitalist Spirit: Max Weber's Protestant Ethic* (London: Macmillan).

Roth, Guenther (1976) 'History and Sociology in the work of Max Weber', *British Journal of Sociology*, 27 (3): 306–18.

Roth, Guenther (1987) 'Rationalization in Max Weber's Developmental History' in Sam Whimster and Scott Lash (eds), *Max Weber, Rationality and Modernity* (London: Allen and Unwin), pp. 75–91.

Roth, Guenther and Schluchter, Wolfgang (1979) *Max Weber's Vision of History: Ethics and Methods* (Berkeley: University of California Press).

Runciman, W.G. (1972) *A Critique of Max Weber's Philosophy of Social Science* (Cambridge: Cambridge University Press).

Scaff, Lawrence (1989) *Fleeing the Iron Cage: Culture, Politics and Modernity* (Berkeley: University of California Press).

Schluchter, Wolfgang (1981a) *The Rise of Western Rationalism: Max Weber's Developmental History* (Berkeley: University of California Press).

Schluchter, Wolfgang (ed.) (1981b) *Max Webers Studie über Antike Judentum* (Frankfurt: Suhrkamp).

Schluchter, Wolfgang (ed.) (1983) *Max Webers Studie über Konfuzianismus und Taoismus* (Frankfurt: Suhrkamp).

Schluchter, Wolfgang (ed.) (1984) *Max Webers Studie über Hinduismus und Buddhismus* (Frankfurt: Suhrkamp).

Schluchter, Wolfgang (ed.) (1985) *Max Webers Sicht des antiken Christentums* (Frankfurt: Suhrkamp).

Schluchter, Wolfgang (ed.) (1987) *Max Webers Sicht des Islams* (Frankfurt: Suhrkamp).

Schluchter, Wolfgang (ed.) (1988) *Max Webers Sicht des okzidentalen Christentums* (Frankfurt: Suhrkamp).

Schluchter, Wolfgang (1989) *Rationalism, Religion, and Domination: A Weberian Perspective* (Berkeley: University of California Press).

Schroeder, Ralph (1991) ' "Personality" and "Inner Distance": The Conception of the Individual in Max Weber's Sociology', *History of the Human Sciences*, 4 (1): 61–78.

Schütz, Alfred (1932) *Der sinnhafte Aufbau der sozialen Welt* (Vienna: Julius Springer).

Southern, R.W. (1970) *Western Society and the Church in the Middle Ages* (Harmondsworth: Penguin).

Stammer, Otto (ed.) (1971) *Max Weber and Sociology Today* (Oxford: Oxford University Press).

Stern, J.P. (1975) *Hitler: The Führer and the People* (London: Fontana).

Strauss, Leo (1953) *Natural Right and History* (Chicago: University of Chicago Press).

Tenbruck, Friedrich (1959) 'Die Genesis der Methodologie Max Webers', *Kölner Zeitschrift für Soziologie und Sozialpsychologie*, 11: 573–630.

Tenbruck, Friedrich (1980) 'The Problem of Thematic Unity in the Works of Max Weber', *British Journal of Sociology*, 31 (3): 316–51.

Tenbruck, Friedrich (1986) 'Das Werk Max Webers: Methodologie und Sozialwissenschaften', *Kölner Zeitschrift für Soziologie und Sozialpsychologie*, 38: 13–31.

Thomas, J.J.R. (1985) 'Ideology and Elective Affinity', *Sociology*, 19 (1): 39–54.

Thomas, Keith (1971) *Religion and the Decline of Magic* (London: Weidenfeld and Nicolson).

Thompson, John (1990) *Ideology and Modern Culture* (Cambridge: Polity).

Troeltsch, Ernst (1931) *The Social Teachings of the Christian Churches*, 2 vols (London: Allen and Unwin).

Turner, Bryan (1974) *Weber and Islam: A Critical Study* (London: Routledge and Kegan Paul).

Turner, Bryan (1981) *For Weber: Essays on the Sociology of Fate* (London: Routledge and Kegan Paul).

Weber, Alfred (1920/21) 'Prinzipielles zur Kultursoziologie' *Archiv für Sozialwissenschaft und Sozialpolitik*, 47 (1): 1–49.

Weber, Marianne (1975) *Max Weber: A Biography* (New York: John Wiley).

Weber, Max (1920–1) *Gesammelte Aufsätze zur Religionssoziologie*, 3 vols (Tübingen: J.C.B. Mohr).

Weber, Max (1924a) *Gesammelte Aufsätze zur Sozial- und Wirtschaftsgeschichte* (Tübingen: J.C.B. Mohr).

Weber, Max (1924b) *Gesammelte Aufsätze zur Soziologie und Sozialpolitik* (Tübingen: J.C.B. Mohr).

Weber, Max (1927) *General Economic History* (New York: Greenberg).

Weber, Max (1930) *The Protestant Ethic and the Spirit of Capitalism* (London: Allen and Unwin).

Weber, Max (1948) *From Max Weber: Essays in Sociology*, ed. H.H. Gerth and C. Wright Mills (London: Routledge and Kegan Paul).

Weber, Max (1949) *The Methodology of the Social Sciences* (Glencoe, Ill.: Free Press).

Weber, Max (1951) *The Religion of China: Confucianism and Taoism* (Glencoe, Ill.: Free Press).

Weber, Max (1952) *Ancient Judaism* (Glencoe, Ill.: Free Press).

Weber, Max (1958) *The Religion of India: The Sociology of Hinduism and Buddhism* (Glencoe, Ill.: Free Press).

Weber, Max (1968) *Economy and Society* (New York: Bedminster).

Weber, Max (1975) *Roscher and Knies: The Logical Problems of Historical Economics* (New York: Free Press).

Weber, Max (1976) *The Agrarian Sociology of Ancient Civilizations* (London: New Left Books).

Weber, Max (1977) *Critique of Stammler* (New York: Free Press).

Weber, Max (1980a) *Gesammelte Politische Schriften*, 4th edn (Tübingen: J.C.B. Mohr).

Weber, Max (1980b) *Wirtschaft und Gesellschaft*, 5th edn (Tübingen: J.C.B. Mohr).

Weber, Max (1981a) *Wirtschaftsgeschichte*, 4th edn (Berlin: Duncker und Humblot).

Weber, Max (1981b) *Die Protestantische Ethik I*, 5th edn (Gütersloh: Gütersloher Verlagshaus).

Weber, Max (1982) *Gesammelte Aufsätze zur Wissenschaftslehre*, 5th edn (Tübingen: J.C.B. Mohr).

Weber, Max (1984) *Max Weber Gesamtausgabe: Zur Politik im Weltkrieg*, I/15 (Tübingen: J.C.B. Mohr).

Weiss, Johannes, (1975) *Max Webers Grundlegung der Soziologie: eine Einführung*, (Munich: UTB für Wissenschaft).

Whimster, Sam and Lash, Scott (1987) 'Introduction' in their (eds) *Max Weber, Rationality and Modernity* (London: Allen and Unwin), pp. 1–31.

Winckelmann, Johannes (1986) *Max Webers hinterlassenes Hauptwerk* (Tübingen: J.C.B. Mohr).

Zeitlin, Irving (1984) *Ancient Judaism* (Cambridge: Polity).

Zingerle, Arnold (1981) *Max Webers historische Soziologie* (Darmstadt: Wissenschaftliche Buchgesellschaft).

INDEX

Abramowski, G., 30, 87
Albrow, M., 8, 111
Ancient Judaism, 17–18, 72, 76, 82–3, 97
Anderson, B., 138
Andersson, S., 111
Andreski, S., 30
Archer, M., 2
aristocracy, 103
Aristotle, 5
asceticism, 62, 67, 94, 103–5

Baptists, 104–5
Beetham, D., 119–20, 137, 139
belief systems, *see* world-views
Bendix, R., 3, 5, 78
Berger, P., 31
Bloch, M., 42
Bloom, A., 28
Brahmans, 58–64
Breuer, S., 138
Brubaker, R., 30, 32, 105, 124
Buddhism, 12
    and Hinduism, 64–5
    world-view of, 49, 62
bureaucracy, 1, 22, 94
    and charisma, 117–20
    in China, 47, 48
    and domination, 115–16, 117–19, 120
    and the modern state, 116–18
    and politics, 112–16, 124
Burger, T., 134
Buss, A., 110

Caldwell, R., 30
Calvin, J., 18, 30, 98–9, 100, 102–4, 106, 111, 142
Calvinism, 98–100, 103–4, 106
Campbell, C., 30, 163, 164
capitalism, 4, 24, 124
    and Confucianism, 43, 48–9, 54
    and division of labour, 114–15
    and domination, 112–14, 119
    and Protestantism, 43, 101–2, 105, 106–9, 151
caste system, 56–65
Catholicism, 91–4, 99, 107–8
charisma
    and Confucianism, 46–7, 52, 53–4
    and cultural change, 144–6
    in early and medieval Christianity, 85
    and Hinduism, 61, 63
    in Judaism, 76, 77, 82
    leadership, and bureaucracy, 117–20
    and magic, 19, 36–8
    and politics, 112–14, 116–17, 120
    and Protestantism, 96–7
    and routinization, 9–10, 17–23, 144–6
    and world-views, 10, 17–20, 158–9
Christianity, early and medieval, 12, 84–96
    and charisma and routinization, 85, 88, 91–2, 95
    and Gnostics, 90–1
    and magic, 85–6, 87
    and priesthood, 88–90, 92
    and rationalism, 94
    and salvation, 84–5, 88, 90–2
    world-view of, 84–7
    see also Catholicism; Protestantism
Cohen, G.A., 163
Collins, R., 3, 29, 111, 160, 163
Confucianism, 12, 15, 24, 52–3
    ancestor cult in, 45–6
    and capitalism, 43, 48–9, 54
    and charisma and routinization, 46–7, 52, 53–4
    ethic of literati, 43–55
    and magic, 43–4, 53–4
    and Protestant ethic, 43, 50–2

and Taoism, 49
traditionalism in, 44, 46, 48
world-view of, 43–4, 46, 51–3, 152
Crone, P., 164
cultural change, 2–3, 6–7, 9–10
and charisma and routinization,
17–18, 20, 114
and Confuciansim, 50–1
and idealism, 153–4
and Islam, 69–70
and Judaism, 81–3
and magic, 33, 148
and politics, 4–5, 120–1, 146
and Protestantism, 97, 107, 125
and religion, 33–42, 147–8
and science, 121–8
sociology of, 141–65
and spheres of life, 10, 23, 145–6,
148
and values, 131–2
Weber's theory of, 141–50, 153–4
and world-views, 26–8, 142–3, 146–8
cultural sciences, 6–11, 133–4, 154,
155, 158
cultural significance, 122, 131–5, 137,
141–2
culturalism, 150–5
culture, concept of, 2, 6, 131–2

democracy, 107, 118–19
disenchantment
and politics, 112–21
of Protestantism, 100–1, 105
and science, 122–3, 153
and social sciences, 133
domination
and bureaucracy, 115–16, 117–19,
120
and capitalism, 112–14, 119
and politics, 114–15
sociology of, 17, 19
Dumont, L., 63, 96, 99
Durkheim, E., 9, 109, 114, 141, 149,
155–8, 161, 163

Eastern religions, 33–71
economics, 23, 24, 83
and caste system in India, 61–2, 63
in China, 48, 50
and Protestantism, 15–16, 98, 102
and science, 124

Economy and Society, 14, 134, 154
Eden, R., 28
Eisenstadt, S., 11, 80
elective affinities, 20
Elias, N., 29
elites, 22
Elkana, Y., 71, 140, 165
Elster, J., 163
Elvin, M., 54
Epstein, I., 82, 83
ethic of politics, and science, 128–30
Evans-Pritchard, E.E., 33

Factor, R., 3, 5
Featherstone, M., 2
Francis, E., 28
Frazer, J.G., 33
Frisby, D., 7, 138
Fulbrook, M., 134

Gellner, D., 65
Gellner, E., 42, 70, 71, 110, 160, 165
Giddens, A., 112
Gnostics, 90–1, 95
Goody, J., 38

Habermas, J., 4, 5, 111
Hall, J., 50, 62–3, 152, 160
Harris, M., 164
Hennis, W., 1, 4–5, 28, 32
Henrich, D., 134
Herberg, W., 108
Hexter, J.H., 85, 86
Hinduism, 12
and Brahmans, 58–65
and Buddhism, 64–5
and caste system, 56–65
inner logic of, 63
world-view of, 55–8, 152
Hume, D., 31

ideal type, 134–6, 149
idealism, 150–5, 157–63
ideology, 2, 7, 20–1, 155
individual, concept of, 5, 14–16
intellectual sphere, 22–4
and Brahmans, 58–9, 63
and magic, 33–4
and science, 123, 125
Islam, 12, 22, 53
and cultural change, 68–70

as warrior religion, 65–70
world-view of, 65, 66–7, 68

Jains, 62
Judaism, 12
and charisma and routinization, 18,
  76, 82
and Confucianism, 52
covenant with Yahweh, 73–5
cultural change in, 81–3
and Indian religions, 63
and Israelite confederacy, 73–4,
  77–8, 81–2
and magic, 34, 72, 75–6
in post-exile period, 80–1
in pre-exile period, 78–9
and Protestantism, 105
and rationalism, 72–84
world-view of, 72–5, 79, 81, 83

Kalberg, S., 9, 20, 28, 30
Kane, A., 164
Kant, I. 29, 139
Kautsky, K., 85
kinship/kin groups
caste system in India, 61
in Confucianism, 46–7
economic traditionalism of, 48
knowledge
pursuit of in modern society, 131,
  136
and science, demands of, 128–30
Küenzlen, G., 30
Kulturbedeutung (cultural significance),
  122, 131–3
Kulturmenschen (cultural beings), 116,
  131, 136
Kulturreligionen, 33, 40
Kuper, A., 28
Kuzmics, H., 29

Lapidus, J., 70
Lash, S., 3
Lassman, P., 132
Levtzion, N., 70
Liebeschütz, H., 110
Luckmann, T., 31
Lukes, S., 163
Luther, M., 18, 98, 99–100, 111

MacIntyre, A., 31, 108

magic, 11–14, 21, 25, 35–8
and Brahmans, 58, 60
and charisma, 19, 36–8
and Confucianism, 43–4, 53–4
in early and medieval Christianity,
  85–6, 87
and Hinduism, 61–2
intellectualist approach to, 33–4
and Judaism, 72, 75–6
and philosophical anthropology,
  14–15
and Protestantism, 98, 100, 103
and religion, 12–13, 33–42
and science, 33–4
Malinowski, B., 33
Mann, M., 160, 164
Mannheim, K., 31, 117
Martin, D., 106, 107–8
Marx, K., 1, 7, 9, 96, 109, 114, 141,
  147, 149, 155–8, 161, 163
Merquior, J.G., 28, 71, 137, 138
Merton, R., 138
Methodism, 104
methodology of the social sciences, 6,
  8, 26, 131, 132–5, 137, 141–2
Metzger, T., 55
Mill, J.S., 22
Milton, J.R., 138
Minogue, K., 163
modernity, 4, 16, 112–40, 146, 153
Mommsen, W., 4, 10, 76, 97, 112, 116,
  126, 134–5
monotheism, 76, 142, 152

Nietzsche, F.W., 28, 123

Oakes, G., 154
objectivity, 133–4, 141

Pagels, E., 90, 91
Parkin, F., 1, 21, 103
Parsons, T., 3, 5
patrimonialism, 47, 48–9, 69
peasantry, 21, 103
petty bourgeoisie, 21, 23, 103
philosophical anthropology, 14–16
Pietism, 103–4
Poggi, G., 106
political sociology, 17–19, 144
politics, 4–5, 23–5
and bureaucracy, 112–16, 124

and caste system in India, 59, 61–2
and disenchantment, 112–21
ethic of, 128–30
parties, 115, 117
and religion, 24, 83, 87, 107
and science, 23–4, 124, 128–30
positivism, 8–9
priesthood
   in early Christianity, 88–90, 92
   in Judaism, 73–4, 78–82
   see also Brahmans
prophets, 39, 77–9, 81–2
Protestant ethic, 1, 104–5
   and capitalism, 151
   and Confucianism, 43, 50–2
   and Islam, 67
   and philosophical anthropology, 15
   and secularism, 96–110
Protestant Ethic, 6, 15, 51, 96–8, 103,
   107, 109, 142
Protestantism
   Calvinist doctrine in, 98–100, 103–4,
      106
   and capitalism, 43, 101–2, 105,
      106–9, 151
   and charisma and routinization, 18,
      96–7, 102–3, 105, 108–9
   and Confucianism, 50–2
   and cultural change, 97, 107
   and economics, 98, 102
   'election', 98, 101, 104, 106–7
   and Indian religions, 63
   and magic, 34
   and natural world, 98–9, 101
   and salvation, 98–9, 100, 101–2, 104
   secularization of, 104–9
   world-view of, 25–7, 97–101, 125
Puritanism, 99, 101, 104, 105, 107

Radcliffe-Brown, A.R., 28
rationalism, Western, 94, 109–10
   analysis of, 157–63
   and cultural change, 142, 150
   and idealism, 152–4
   modern, 112–40
   origins of, 72–84
   see also science
rationality, 34–6, 39–42, 113–14
rationalization, 4, 9
religion, 11–14, 23–5

aims of, 35–6
and charisma and routinization,
   17–18, 19
and cultural change, 51–3, 147–8
irrationality of, 35–6, 39–41
and magic, 12–13, 33–42
and philosophical anthropology,
   15–16
and science, 16, 123, 143
sociology of, 17, 19, 34–5
Religion of China, 43, 50, 52
Religion of India, 64
Rickert, H., 111, 139
ritual, 80–1, 83, 86, 90
Roth, G., 30, 143, 154
routinization, 126–7
   and Brahmans, 64
   and charisma, 9–10, 17–23, 144–6
   and Confucianism, 52, 53–4
   and cultural change, 144–6
   in early Christianity, 88, 91–2, 95
   in Judaism, 76, 80–1, 82
   and magic, 42–3
   and politics, 112–14, 116, 120
   and Protestantism, 96–7, 102–3, 105,
      108–9
   and world-views, 17–20
Runciman, W.G., 138

Sayer, D., 7
Scaff, L., 5
Schluchter, W., 4, 5, 28, 30, 32, 48, 53,
   70, 71, 77, 78, 79, 110, 111
Schroeder, R., 14
Schütz, A., 1
science, 11–14
   demands of, 128–30
   and disenchantment, 122–3, 153
   and domination, 112–14
   and magic, 33–4
   and modern culture, 121–8
   origins and development of, 122–5
   and politics, 23–4, 124, 128–30
   and religion, 16, 123, 136, 143
   and role of scientists, 121–2
   world-view of, 13, 125–6
   see also social sciences
secularization, 105–9, 143
Simmel, G., 138

social change, 5, 49, 51–3, 68–70,
    150–3
social reality, nature of, 3, 6–11
social sciences, 1–6
    and rationalism, 157–63
    and science, 122
    and values, 4, 130–3
social strata, 20–2, 57–8, 59, 65–6, 89,
    107
sociology
    of cultural change, 141–65
    of religion, 17, 19, 34–5
Southern, R.W., 93
spheres of life, 10, 23–5, 145–6, 148,
    152–3
state, modern, 116–18
Stern, J.P., 138
Strauss, L., 28
Sufism, 67
'switchmen' metaphor, 143–5, 147

Taoism, 49, 53
Tenbruck, F., 4, 11, 30, 32, 139
Thomas, J.J.R., 20
Thomas, K., 11
Thompson, J., 28
traditionalism
    and caste system in India, 61–2
    in Confucianism, 44, 46, 48
Troeltsch, E., 85, 87, 88, 92, 94
Turner, B., 1, 65–7, 69, 70, 89
Turner, S., 3, 5

values
    and culture, 4–5, 6–8, 131–2

and social sciences, 4, 130–3
Velody, I., 132

Weber, A., 29
Weber, Marianne, 111
Weiss, J., 111, 132
Wellhausen, J., 110
Wesley, J., 107
Western rationalism, see rationalism
Whimster, S., 3
Winckelmann, J., 29
world-views, 6–9, 19, 22, 142
    of Buddhism, 49, 62
    of Confucianism, 43–4, 46, 51–3, 152
    and charisma and routinization, 10,
        17–20, 158–9
    and cultural change, 10–11, 144–6,
        148
    of early and medieval Christianity,
        84–7
    of Hinduism, 55–8, 152
    inner logic of, 26–8, 41, 83, 142–3,
        146
    of Islam, 65, 66–7, 68
    of Judaism, 72–5, 79, 81
    and magic, 33, 34
    of Protestantism, 25–7, 97–101, 125
    of science, 13, 125–6
    systematization of, 20, 82
writings, Weber's, 1–2, 5–6, 28–9
    and sociology, interpretation of, 3–4

Zeitlin, I., 83, 110
Zingerle, A., 3

ACN 3611